Hare Krishna, Hare Krishna

Hare Krishna, Hare Krishna

Five Distinguished Scholars on the Krishna Movement in the West

Harvey Cox • Larry D. Shinn • Thomas J. Hopkins
A. L. Basham • Shrivatsa Goswami

Edited by Steven J. Gelberg
With a Foreword by Robert S. Ellwood

Grove Press, Inc./New York

First Evergreen Edition published in 1983

Library of Congress Cataloging in Publication Data

Gelberg, Steven J.
Hare Krishna, Hare Krishna: Five distinguished scholars on the Krishna movement in the West.

(Grove Press Eastern philosophy and literature series)
1. International Society for Krishna Consciousness.
2. Krishna (Hindu deity)—Cult. I. Title. II. Series.
BL1220.G44 1983 294.5'512 82-21055
ISBN 0-394-62454-8

Manufactured in the United States of America

GROVE PRESS, INC., 196 West Houston Street, New York, N.Y. 10014

Grove Press Eastern Philosophy and Literature Series
Edited by Hannelore Rosset

83 84 85 7 6 5 4 3 2 1

To the sacred memory of

ŚRĪLA A. C. BHAKTIVEDANTA SWAMI PRABHUPĀDA

. . . ebe jaśa ghuṣuk tribhuvana

CONTENTS

FOREWORD

This book about a well-known but much less well-understood modern religious movement accomplishes several tasks very well. First, through the effective medium of informal interviews with distinguished academics, all but one of whom is also a highly-regarded specialist in Hinduism and all of whom have a deep acquaintance with the Hare Krishna movement, it enables us to see anew the nature of that movement's strong Indic roots and its place in the Western context, and makes this perspective accessible to the general reader.

Second, it enables us to see the controversies which have swirled around the Hare Krishnas, including those regarding "brainwashing" and "deprogramming," through the eyes of men who, while certainly not lacking in sympathy for immediate human problems, are also accustomed to taking large-scale and long-range views of religious processes in history.

Third, the very existence of these dialogues speaks for itself as indication that the Hare Krishna movement has engaged the Western—and Indian—mind, raising fundamental questions for all of us about ultimate human values and meanings—questions that will not go away.

The most overwhelming realization that comes through these pages is of the remarkable uniqueness of the Hare Krishna movement. It is really an anomaly in most categories in which it is commonly placed. Although of recent origin in its present institutional form, it differs from most new religious movements and so-called "cults" in having clearly definable and highly literary sources in an ancient spiritual tradition, albeit one alien to the Western lands in which it now flourishes. Indeed, the movement sees as one of its major obligations the distribution of that heritage's voluminous and sophisticated literature.

On the other hand, while the Caitanya Krishnaism of which it is heir has had a long habitation within the Hindu world, it does not represent all of Hinduism, and indeed vehemently rejects some things commonly associated with it, such as the hereditary caste system and the Advaita Vedānta sort of "mystical monism." For Hare Krishna is unique also in being the only successful transplant, not of Hindu yoga or Vedānta, but of the *bhakti* or devotionalism which is so life-giving to millions in India, but which until now must have seemed virtually untransplantable. Yet here it is, and—still another uniqueness—practically without the acculturating sea-changes which leave the practice of most other imported religions significantly different from that of the homeland.

Behind all these uniqueness lies a most unique man. Several interviewees in this book comment on what an unparalleled figure Swami Bhaktivedanta, founder of the International Society for Krishna Consciousness, really was. There have been successful founders of religious movements before, and successful missionaries. But one must look far indeed to find another man who, at an advanced age and without funds or institutional support, founded a spiritual movement in a strange land as successful as the Krishna movement has become, and withal is regarded by many as both a genuine saint and amazingly productive scholar.

The interviewees in this book do not endorse every policy or doctrine of ISKCON, nor do I. Like fervent religionists in all times and places, its believers have not always eschewed intemporate zeal or credulity. Devotees have made mistakes which have stained the movement's image; some of these issues are matters of ongoing debate within the movement itself. But, to paraphrase another disruptive religious figure, let he whose own sect has been without sin in such matters cast the first stone.

Evidence here and elsewhere tells us the Hare Krishna movement is here to stay, and is maturing institutionally, laying a foundation for full public acceptance. As it acquires a widespread lay membership in addition to a highly-committed inner core of monastics and full-time workers, as it moves to a "church" or denominational structure—the sociologist Max Weber's "routinization of charisma"—and as generations raised within the movement partly take the place of those whose entry in the halcyon early days often made for snarled relations with families and communities, the Hare Krishnas are bound to find an abiding place in the West's spiritual ecology. More importantly, the challenges left with all of us by their way of faith and life will abide.

What is the highest good? What is the most important thing a human being can do with his or her time? How important is diet to the spiritual life? Where is spiritual authority to be found? What are the most important books to read?

The Hare Krishnas witness in word and deed to their forceful answers to these age-old questions. They are a living presence in our world, and we will ponder aright such questions for ourselves only if we take into our reckoning that witness.

Robert S. Ellwood
Bishop James W. Bashford Professor of Oriental Studies
The University of Southern California

AUTHOR'S PREFACE

I often lecture at universities on various aspects of Hindu tradition and at various public forums in which issues concerning new and alternative religious movements and contemporary spirituality are explored. And although I have been through the experience many times, I never cease to be amazed by the curious way in which some people approach me after they've heard my presentation. The analogy that most easily comes to mind to describe the situation is the scene one occasionally views in science fiction movies wherein earthling cautiously confronts visitor from outer space after a series of dramatic non-verbal exchanges which have proven the extraterrestrial to be friendly. "I didn't realize the Hare Krishnas were so rational, so . . . er . . . *normal*!"

The fact is that the American practitioners of Krishna consciousness are viewed as a rather strange and bewildering phenomenon, a bizarre addition to the contemporary cultural landscape. The "Hare Krishnas" have entered deep into the American pop psyche. Brief, scene-coloring glimpses of Krishna people chanting and dancing in the streets or working the airports have surfaced in at least half a dozen recent feature films and in numerous television programs, depicting Krishna devotees usually as benign religious zealots and occasionally as cultic zombies. But what has entered the domain of public consciousness through pop culture and through the mass media is not, in fact, the Hare Krishna people, but a silly caricature which bears only the most remote resemblance to the real thing. Short of actually visiting a Krishna center or approaching a Krishna devotee in public, if one wishes to understand who the Krishna people really are and what they're about, one is hard-put to gather any factual knowledge through conventional channels of public information. In the place of factual knowledge, a certain body of myths and misconceptions—collectively, an emerging folk wisdom—have been brought into play, reminiscent of earlier stories of Jews' cannibalization of young Christian children and tales of clandestine Mormon orgies.

There are many such stories: the movement's founder was an Indian entrepreneur who came to America to found a new, profitable business enterprise hidden behind the facade of an otherworldly Hindu sect; vast sums of money are collected from an unwitting public and channeled to ecclesiastical potentates who live in splendor while their underlings live in squalor; the innocent young are lured off the streets and into waiting vans by trained brainwashers who perform an irresistible kind of on-the-spot hypnosis; children are whisked away from their families and communities never to be seen or heard from again; psychic disorientation is induced in members by low-protein vegetarian diets and sleep deprivation; members perform strange secret rites in their temples involving the ingestion of the urine of sacred cows; devotees are forced to worship and prostrate before weird-visaged idols from foreign lands; vast quantities of guns and other munitions (even tanks!) are being readied for assault against the outside, hostile world; an army of zombies is preparing to march on the capital and take over the government (so reports the assistant district attorney of a large U.S. city). The list of horrors and atrocities goes on.

Although we live in a society that cherishes the notion of free personal and religious expression, that society has a curious and rather effective method for eliminating or devitalizing dissenting expressions. That method consists of denigrating and challenging the credibility of those dissident voices—often by raising doubts about their sanity—to such an extent that these dissenting voices, and the alternative messages they intone, are all but drowned out in a sea of public castigation. A glance at religious history reveals that stories like those recounted above tend to surface whenever religious movements arise which challenge the religious, social, or political status quo and call into question long-cherished assumptions about the nature of reality and the meaning of human existence. These myths always reflect the particular ideological orientations, as well as the fears and insecurities, of the society which creates them. And once these myths begin to receive constant and consistent play through official or unofficial channels of public information, it becomes unfashionable to doubt them. The public has a surprising capacity for accepting these stories at face value, and for investing almost total, uncritical faith in the mass-communications establishment, to which they grant unlimited rights to define, describe, and interpret reality.

In any case, I was always a little startled by the wide divergence between my own (an active participant's) perception, and the public's perception of the Krishna consciousness movement. In the course of time, however, I came into contact with a third category of observers of the movement. This additional category consisted of academic scholars who had studied religion and religious movements from a broad historical point of view and who had become curious about, even fascinated by, the Krishna movement. Their interest was not, of course, that of committed believers, but of students of comparative religion who, through their own researches, had come to view the International Society for Krishna Consciousness (ISKCON) as a significant new religious and cultural movement. Through many informal discussions, they shared with me their thoughts and observations and gradually I found myself developing new insights and perspectives on the Krishna consciousness movement and its parent tradition in India—viewing it in an enlarged historical, cultural and theological context. At one point, I realized that a collection of systematic dialogues with some of ISKCON's academic observers might serve as a useful introduction to the movement—an introduction that might be more credible than one attempted by a committed member with an apologetical motive. This book is the product of that realization.

This volume presents a series of spontaneous and far-reaching interviews with five different scholars, some of international repute, each of whom offers his own distinctive analysis of the Hare Krishna movement and the ancient tradition it embodies, as well as the various historical, sociological, psychological, and theological issues that an in-depth study of the movement invokes.

The interview that appears first in this volume is with Harvard Divinity School's Harvey Cox, the well-known Protestant theologian and author who, speaking from a liberal Christian perspective, explores the cultural and theological significance of the Krishna movement's appearance in the West, and offers a discerning critique on the issue of religious "brainwashing." Larry D. Shinn, a historian of religion and specialist in Krishna devotional tradition, closely examines ISKCON's internal spiritual and organizational dynamics and its public interface: who joins and why (and how), the role of the guru, the significance of chanting and book distribution, the brainwashing/deprogramming controversy, ISKCON's development from sect to institution, and the future of the movement. Thomas J. Hopkins, a historian of religion specializing in *bhakti* (devotional) Hinduism, focuses his attention on the historical and cultural dynamic of the transmission of *bhakti* tradition from India to the United States and the role of Śrīla Prabhupāda, the movement's founder, in that unique historical process. A.L. Basham, one of the world's pre-eminent historians of India, locates the movement's roots in ancient Indian spirituality and identifies its unique position within the historical context of Indian philosophical and religious influences in the West. The final interview is with Shrivatsa Goswami, a Hindu theologian of the Caitanya Vaiṣṇava school who offers a fascinating survey of the philosophical, devotional, and mystical tradition out of which the Hare Krishna movement emerged, and reflects upon the movement's historical significance in light of that ancient tradition.

As interviewer, while providing some basic direction, I have taken a clearly subordinate role in the conversations, encouraging the interviewees to articulate their own perspectives freely and uninterrupted except where, as an active participant in the movement and tradition under discussion, I felt that refinement, elaboration or a different perspective would nourish the discussion. In editing the transcripts of these interviews, I have tried to preserve the informal conversational tone of the original discussions, and have avoided stylistic homogenization.

In closing, I want to express my deepest appreciation to those whose consistently articulate and often eloquent comments appear in this volume, for their unhesitating willingness to participate in this project.

Steven J. Gelberg

Philadelphia
August 13, 1982
Śrī Vyāsa-Pūjā

INTERVIEW WITH HARVEY COX

Dr. Harvey Cox is Victor S. Thomas Professor of Divinity and Chairman of the Department of Applied Theology at Harvard Divinity School. One of the most prominent and influential Protestant theologians of our time, he is the author of a number of books, including the best-selling *The Secular City* (N.Y.: Macmillan Co., 1966), *The Feast of Fools* (Cambridge: Harvard University Press, 1969), *The Seduction of the Spirit* (N.Y.: Simon & Schuster, 1973), and *Turning East: The Promise and Peril of the New Orientalism* (N.Y.: Harper Touchstone,1978).

Professor Cox's first encounter with the Hare Krishna movement occurred one day in 1972 when a small group of Krishna devotees who were touring his neighborhood in Cambridge, Massachusetts, inadvertently knocked on his door. What ensued was a lengthy dialogue-encounter, a "paradigmatic event," which sparked Dr. Cox's fascination not only with the Hare Krishna movement, but with the entire phenomenon of Americans turning to the East for spiritual inspiration and direction. That interest led to his writing *Turning East* several years later, and to his becoming an active and articulate participant in the scholarly study of new and alternative religious movements in America.

Since that first encounter with the Hare Krishna movement, Dr. Cox has maintained an active relationship with the movement—visiting many of its centers in the United States (occasionally staying the night as a participant/observer), attending the movement's annual Festival of the Chariots in New York City, introducing his Divinity School students to the 4:30 a.m. service at the Boston Hare Krishna Temple, studying the movement from primary and secondary sources, and visiting the movement's spiritual world headquarters in Vṛndāvana, India.

The following interview took place at Dr. Cox's office at Harvard Divinity School on December 22, 1980. Professor Cox interprets the significance of the Hare Krishna movement and its impact in the West mostly from a Christian, theological perspective.

"Turning East"

SJG: In your most recent book, *Turning East*, you offer some perceptive observations on Americans' fascination with Oriental spirituality and the significance of this phenomenon for the West. What brought about your interest in the "turn East"?

HC: I'm not sure if it was the first exposure that I had, but my curiosity was strongly aroused when a small group of Boston Krishna devotees appeared at my front door here in Cambridge and asked to show me some of their books. I invited them in and we had a long and interesting conversation. It was that incident that focused my interest, which led to writing this book.

Like most people in the United States, I had heard something about religious traditions from the East, but I hadn't really troubled myself to think or to learn much about them, which is astonishing when you consider the fact that I had a Ph.D. in religion. But I did my formal academic study at a time when developing competence in Eastern religious traditions was not necessarily a part of advanced religious studies. My formal training, up to that point, had been almost entirely in the area of western religions, both from a theological point of view and also from the points of view of history, sociology, and anthropology.

But this visit by the devotees was one of those, what we call "paradigmatic events," that is, an event which has more significance than that ordinarily attached to it. This is a term that's especially important in Christian theology. It signifies certain events that are somehow more revealing than other events of God's plan or purpose in the world. The idea of devotees of a tradition stemming from North India knocking on my door in Cambridge seemed to be a sign that something important is happening. I remember noticing that here was an instance not only of turning East, but of the East coming West. In the career of Prabhupāda, after all, we have a person going half-way around the world at a rather advanced age, at the suggestion of his teacher, to introduce a form of spiritual awareness into a culture where it had not been known before.

SJG: Since that particular encounter in Cambridge, how much further exposure have you had to the Krishna consciousness movement?

HC: I would say I've had a good deal of experience with the movement. I've come to know a number of devotees personally. I've visited several temples around the country and I've stayed overnight at some of them and participated in the morning devotions. I participated in the Festival of the Chariots several years ago in New York. I've read a good deal of the social, scientific, and historical commentary on the movement, and have read a fair bit of Prabhupāda's translation and commentary on the *Bhagavad-gītā* and the *Śrīmad-Bhāgavatam*. So I am somewhat familiar with the canonical sources of the movement. This particular aspect interests me a great deal. I've come to picture ISKCON primarily as a theological movement.

A Visit to The Source: Vṛndāvana

Perhaps my most memorable exposure, however, was to

go and visit Vṛndāvana in India. In 1977, there appeared in one of my classes here at Harvard a man who is the son of a Vaiṣṇava priest of the Rādhā-ramaṇa Temple of Vṛndāvana. He is, in fact, a direct descendant of a disciple of one of the original disciples of Śrī Caitanya. I found this man, Shrivatsa Goswami, to be a sophisticated and credible interpreter of the Caitanya-Vaiṣṇava tradition. Through becoming a friend of Shrivatsa and entertaining him and his family at our summer home, it became evident to me that I would like to visit Vṛndāvana which I then did in November, 1978. That experience gave me the kind of exposure to the roots of your movement that most people in America simply never get. I find it humorous when the Krishna consciousness movement is viewed as a new religious movement, or as a cult. One can understand why people in the West would see this as a new movement and, in fact, in some ways it is new to the West. But it is only the particular organizational form that is relatively new. I think it's important for people to understand the enormously old, in fact ancient, lineage of this movement. Whereas one might be a little surprised to find people chanting Hare Krishna in the United States, after only a few days in Vṛndāvana you understand that this is not something unusual, and certainly not something new.

SJG: As far as you could tell, do the local residents of Vṛndāvana take the western Krishna devotees seriously, or might they view them, perhaps, as foreign faddists? How do they feel about the presence of an American-financed and built temple in their midst?

HC: From what I can determine, there is generally a positive, friendly attitude toward the western devotees who are there. I was impressed with the large number of local Indian people who came to the *ārati* ceremony at ISKCON's temple, the Krishna-Balarāma Mandir. The temple was full of people who seemed to be entering quite enthusiastically into the devotional activity. I certainly don't think the western devotees are viewed in any sense as a strange cult. It's hard to imagine people in Vṛndāvana thinking of Krishna devotees as a strange cult.

There may be some residual suspicion, though, of the western devotees inasmuch as they are foreigners. Foreigners have not been good to Indians over the course of history, whether they've been Moghuls or British. Indians have not had good treatment from the hands of people coming in from the outside. So there may still remain some of that suspicion. But by and large, the feeling toward western devotees seemed to be quite positive and there's even some pride in the fact that this beautiful temple, ISKCON's temple, has been built there. I also noticed that when the local people saw me in the streets, they would greet me with the "Hare Krishna" greeting, rather than the greeting "Radhe Shyam" which they generally use for each other. I think they have begun to associate the "Hare Krishna" greeting with western-looking people.

SJG: In visiting Rādhā-ramaṇa Temple or other temples in Vṛndāvana, how did the mode of worship strike you?

HC: It didn't strike me particularly because I'd seen it before. It was similar to what I'd seen in Hare Krishna temples in America. I think I might have been more struck by it if I had never seen it before. I suppose what did strike me was how similar it was. I've heard Catholics say how comforting it is to walk into a Mass anywhere in the world and see the same gestures and hear the same words, especially during the old days of the Latin Mass. You can walk into any temple in Vṛndāvana, or in ISKCON, and pretty much the same thing is going on.

SJG: Did you find your visit to Vṛndāvana in any way a source of personal spiritual nourishment?

HC: I've found all of my contacts with people of other religious traditions to be a rich source of deepening and strengthening of my own spirituality. But I must say that I always remember my stay in Vṛndāvana as a very important modal moment in my own spiritual growth.

SJG: How so?

HC: Well, you experience Krishna in Vṛndāvana. That's what they say, and it's true. The spirit of Krishna devotion hangs so thick, so to speak, that you can almost breathe it in. You cannot help getting some feeling for it. What I really began to appreciate there was the multiple forms that love of God takes. I was deeply influenced by the Vaiṣṇava perception of the infinitely variable forms that God's love for us and our love for God take, and how wrong it is, how shortsighted it is, to limit that relationship to a particular form or phase of love. It's difficult to try to summarize these sorts of deep impressions, but that was the insight that I came away with. That insight has in some ways enlarged my feeling for the omnipresence of God in the world—that God is in some sense present in all things. Not that you have to be meditating on that all the time, but you can be aware at a certain level of the presence of God in all kinds of situations and activities. The continuum between immanence and transcendence in Indian culture is unbroken, whereas we in the West have more of a dualistic frame. This doesn't mean that you don't have intense cultic expressions of communion with God in particular forms of worship. You have it, for instance, in the Eucharist. But that helps to uncover the omnipresent Christ who is there in all things. That was another insight. These were not all just conceptual insights. I felt some kind of affective deepening while I was in Vṛndāvana.

I was also impressed by a certain quality of life in Vṛndāvana, especially in the Goswami family and in their relationship to us as guests. I was especially moved by their combination of devotion to Krishna and their openness to life, to everyone. Far from contradicting or hampering their openness, their utter seriousness about their Krishna devotion seemed in some ways to enhance it and make it more viable.

Krishna Consciousness And Christianity: Common Ground

SJG: Did your trip to Vṛndāvana increase your interest, as a theologian, in the theological and spiritual background of Krishna consciousness—Caitanya Vaiṣṇavism?

HC: Oh yes, of course. One of the outcomes of my experience in Vṛndāvana is my determination to do a lot more reading and scholarly study of this tradition and this movement. One of the things that struck me during my visit is that the form of Hindu philosophy which has dominated the teaching about Hinduism in American higher education is the Advaita Vedānta form, and we have received a somewhat distorted or limited view, I think, of the full complexity and richness of Hindu tradition. It's unfortunate that we haven't received, for whatever historical or other reasons, a clear picture of the various swings of Hindu devotional philosophy, and I think more should be done with this tradition. It's especially intriguing for Christian theologians, maybe even deceptively intriguing, because of the obvious structural analogies to a lot of Christianity in the devotional Hindu tradition.

I find Vaiṣṇavism, and ISKCON itself, a fascinating and challenging spiritual and theological movement. My interest in it probably stems, in part, from the fact that it touches certain aspects of my own spiritual tradition, my own spiritual trajectory, in a way that other movements do not. You can see the obvious similarities. Here you have the idea of a personal God who becomes incarnate in a particular figure revealing what God is about and eliciting a form of participation in the life of God. There are many categories in your tradition that are similar to the ones I'm used to in my own form of Christianity.

SJG: It appears that the Krishna consciousness movement, being propagated mostly in the Christian West, is presenting that aspect of Hindu tradition which has a good deal in common with Christianity. How might Christians react—and how are they reacting?

HC: I think there's a paradoxical answer to that. On the one hand, in some ways it's more threatening to Christians, just as discovering any religious tradition which is similar to yours in some ways elicits discomfort and suspicion. It's a little too close for comfort. As far as Vedāntic Hinduism is concerned, however, one can think about it, intellectualize about it, but the biting edge of the emotional content is not as strong, at least for most people.

On the other side, since there is some similarity, I think a Christian will have some natural sensitivity to Krishna devotion. I should underline that the kind of Christianity I'm talking about here is the kind that is concerned with the devotion of the heart, that is, pietistic Christianity, the kind that I grew up in. This kind of Christianity would, it seems, be more receptive to your form of Indian spirituality than some other types of Christianity I can think of. Liberal Protestantism, for example, in which there is a strong emphasis on the rationality and reasonableness of the faith—certain forms of Unitarianism, for example, and those aspects of Calvinism that are extremely suspicious of religious experience—would not be as receptive. There are a wide variety of different traditions within Christianity, and I'm talking about one particular tradition that seems to be more structurally analogous in some ways to one of the major strains within the Indian tradition. I think that is important for a reason that I've learned a lot about from my colleague George Rupp, the Dean of Harvard

Divinity School. He feels that we have to get away from the idea that in the inter-religious dialogue—that we surely need in the modern world—you'll have all the Hindus on this side of the table, and all the Christians on another side, and all the Jews over there and all the Muslims over there. If you actually study the history and the composition of any of these movements, you will probably find elements within one tradition that are more similar to certain elements within another tradition than they are to other elements within their own tradition.

SJG: Such as shared elements between, in this case, pietistic Christianity and *bhakti* tradition.

HC: Yes. Another example is that those forms of Christianity which view transformation of earthly existence as important are in some senses more like Shin Buddhism than they are like those forms of Christianity which completely transcendentalize the whole action and presence of God into a future life or a different world. It is like when you are playing with the same deck of cards but you change the value of the suits. You reshuffle in a way, and you see tensions emerge where you didn't expect to, and similarities where you had not originally noticed them.

SJG: That certainly is an important insight, but it seems that if you took this principle far enough you'd find it difficult, ultimately, to speak about Hinduism, or Christianity, or Buddhism as such. You'd have to speak only of various theological or psychological types within the various traditions; the pantheist, the monotheist, the monist, the pietist, the fundamentalist, the exclusivist . . .

HC: That's exactly the mood of the current structuralists, those interested in a structuralist analysis of religion—to minimize or de-emphasize the doctrinal *content* of any particular religious phenomenon but look at the purely structural aspects of it, and then make comparisons with other religious phenomena on a structural basis. I am a little suspicious of going too far with that because I think that the doctrinal content is important. The fact that you, as a Krishna devotee, might have a relationship to Krishna that is structurally similar to a Christian's relationship to Jesus Christ, for example, leaves out the fact that there are real differences between what Krishna means and what Christ means. You have to talk about that too, not invidiously or in any kind of derogatory way, but you have to recognize that the content of the teaching is important and is not simply secondary or derivative. Although structuralist approaches to religion can be useful, they can also be misleading if overdone.

SJG: Do they tend to be?

HC: Oh yes, they're overdone quite a bit, especially in the psychological use of structuralist categories. In the "faith development" field, for instance, which is an important emerging field now, the thesis is that just as all people experience cognitive development (à la Piaget, for example), or just as they may be subject to stages of moral development (as Lawrence Kohlberg argues), they also move through stages of faith development. Although the content of beliefs and practices from one religious tradition to another may be different, the particular developmental stage, in terms of faith, that a person is going through in one tradition is structurally similar to faith development in another tradition.

SJG: I recall that last year, when you visited New Vṛndāvana, our rural community in West Virginia, with that group of students from Harvard Divinity School and from local West Virginia colleges, you suggested some interesting comparisons between Krishna consciousness and various forms of pietistic Christianity that your group was observing in West Virginia.

What were some of the similarities you noticed?

HC: That summer course was a study of religion in Appalachia, a research seminar offered jointly by Harvard Divinity School and the West Virginia College for Graduate Studies. It was taught jointly by Dr. Mary Lee Daugherty, an anthropologist from West Virginia, and myself, and it involved our moving around the state visiting churches, religious revivals, country fairs and observing and participating in the religious lives and practices of people in West Virginia.

We noticed several surprising similarities between what you might call Appalachian folk religion and Krishna consciousness. One was the importance of religious feeling—strong feelings of attachment and devotion to God—and praising God through singing or chanting of the name of God and ecstatic dancing. Both traditions put a big emphasis on joy, the spiritual joy of praising God. Another similarity we found was that both traditions emphasize puritanical virtues and practice certain forms of asceticism such as no drinking, no smoking, no non-marital sex and no gambling. Also, neither puts very much emphasis on the transformation of the present world into a religiously ideal world, such as the Kingdom of God. Both seem to put more emphasis on a future life or another world. Another similarity is what would appear to a liberal religionist as a somewhat uncritical attitude towards scripture, that is, a reticence to make use of historical-critical approaches to the understanding of a scriptural text.

So, we didn't expect to find very much similarity, but in the end we found quite a lot. One of the things that interested me was that the West Virginia students who were with us, who I think were more apprehensive about visiting New Vṛndāvana than the outsiders (the Yankees, who thought this would be an interesting thing to do), felt quite at home there, especially because it was a farm-like setting and a place where rural virtues are emphasized. They all really enjoyed their visit there.

Has Krishna Consciousness Anything To Offer Christianity Theologically?

SJG: Do you see any elements within the theology of Krishna consciousness which might nourish Christianity theologically?

HC: Yes, I have a very particular answer to that, which is that the relationship between Krishna and Rādhā adds a dimension of human relationality which is not developed in Christian theology. That lack of development exists largely because the gospels that we have in the Biblical canon are ones that were placed there at the expense of some other gospels in which the more feminine quality of God was emphasized more and in which the relationship of Jesus to his female followers drew more attention.

SJG: You're speaking of some of the Apocrypha?

HC: Yes, the gnostic gospels especially. The bowdlerized New Testament has not prepared Christians for the spiritual aspect of the male-female relationship. Although there's a rich tradition of this in the Old Testament in the Song of Solomon, there's not very much of it in the New Testament. We have some of that imagery in some of the Carmelite mystics and other Catholic devotional writings, but still it's not very developed. Therefore, the whole realm of male-female relationality has been almost totally excluded from theological affirmation and discussion, and from appreciation as a realm in which God is present, or at least as a realm from which we draw metaphors for our relationship with God.

The Christian emphasis is strongly on, you might say, filial piety, love for God as the Father. Then there is a devotion to the child Jesus, especially at Christmas time, and in Catholic devotionalism there are appearances such as the Infant of Prague. But the relationship of a man to a woman, which is one of many human relationships, and which is certainly a central and important one, is not developed in Christian devotion. It simply isn't. It's only touched on here and there: Jesus and Mary Magdalen or Jesus and his mother—but that's still parental. In the Krishna tradition, though, the relationship between Rādhā and Krishna, in addition to being taken literally, is an important paradigm of God's love for human beings and their love for Him.

SJG: Not to counter what you're saying, but I think that while talking about the relationship between Rādhā and Krishna as a paradigm for the soul's love for God and vice-versa, it's important to avoid a common pitfall that some Vaiṣṇavas in India—certain Sahajiyā sects—have fallen into: the mistake of sexualizing the soul's relationship with God and/or attributing divine status to the ordinary male-female relationship. According to Gaudiya-Vaiṣṇava theology, the various *rasas* or spiritual sentiments with which souls experience and relate to God, including the male-female model (*mādhurya-rasa*), are applicable only to fully liberated souls who have fully transcended bodily identification and, with it, attraction to corporeal sexuality. These mystical *rasas* are not something that can be casually experienced by worldly people.

So to speak of the soul's loving God as a woman loves a man is not a mere creative metaphor for a generalized sense of theistic piety, but a description of a specific and very lofty spiritual state beyond *mokṣa*, liberation. Although certain aspects of the Rādhā-Krishna relationship may externally resemble romantic sensuality, they are understood theologically to be utterly pure, spiritual and eternal. Although Śrī Caitanya was himself a very strict and ascetical *sannyāsi*, he advocated Rādhā's devotion for Krishna as the most exalted and sublime form of theistic devotion. In some Sahajiyā sects, devotees ritually assume the roles of Rādhā and Krishna and engage in ordinary sexual exploits. These sorts of left-handed tantric tendencies have affected even certain lines coming from Śrī Caitanya. Mainline Vaiṣṇavas consider this sort of thing an abomination. So I think this subject should be seen in its proper theological perspective.

HC: Yes, what you've said is quite helpful. Another point which I briefly mentioned earlier concerns the lack of emphasis, in Biblical sources, on the feminine quality of God. In your tradition, you have the understanding of Śrī Caitanya as the dual-incarnation of Rādhā and Krishna. Krishna transforms into Rādhā, as it were, in order to experience, as Rādhā, His own love. I think that's a very important theological insight, especially in an age of women's liberation and feminine criticism of the Bible for being patriarchal and excluding women. Unfortunately, this criticism has substance. So, it could well be that this specific theological insight could surface and be an interesting and important element in a future Christian-Vaiṣṇava dialogue. I think it could be.

Should the Movement be "Interpreted"?

A point I'd like to make now is that the Krishna consciousness movement really needs to develop philosophically and theologically articulate interpreters who are sufficiently aware of the various levels of religious interchange which have gone on and are going on "between Jerusalem and Benares" (as my friend Peter Berger calls it), so that that conversation can proceed here in America as I experienced it in India with Shrivatsa Goswami and others. Maybe it's too much to ask of a movement which is so young and still in the business of organizing itself and facing a lot of hostility and opposition. So this is really not a criticism. Christianity didn't develop Thomas Aquinas until 1300 years into its history, but Augustine hit along four-hundred years later, and St. Paul only thirty years later. So one could hope that some kind of intellectually sophisticated and yet still spiritually authentic articulation of this tradition would begin to appear in the West.

SJG: Are you calling for a deeper immersion, on our part, in our own tradition, or for an increased familiarity with other philosophical and theological traditions, or both?

HC: I'm afraid I mean both, and I know that's a big assignment. I think I may be betraying a theological or philosophical bias, which is that any religious tradition has to be constantly reinterpreted. It has to be reinterpreted because forms of language, the meanings of words, forms of thought, and social realities, change. We live in human history which is not stable, and therefore the job of interpreting a tradition is one that the theologians and the preachers of any tradition must do.

Now, it would be interesting to talk about this, because there is some difference of opinion among Indian religious intellectuals on this point. One of the most interesting conversations I had in India was with a group of Indian scholars some of whom agreed with me about the need for this ongoing reinterpretive task and others resisted that rather stoutly. They thought that that was caving in to modern thought. But I come from a particular expression of the Christian tradition, which is the Reformed tradition. Its paradigmatic moment was the sixteenth century, the same century as Caitanya in a different part of the world. One impetus for that Reformation was the genius of Martin Luther, who taught that God enables the faithful creature to reinterpret the tradition so that it lives in every generation—not as an act of cleverness or intellectual power on the part of the preacher, but as a continuing act of grace. That's why there's great emphasis on the Word of God. That shouldn't be too unfamiliar to the Krishna devotees; the idea of the Word, the power of spiritual sound, scripture, is important in both these traditions. The idea is that the faithful, through reformation and reformulation of the message in terms that will engage a person or a culture at the point where that person or culture understands itself, can keep a tradition dynamic and relevant. That is a constant task.

Now, one of the things that most interests me in the history of religions is how a spiritual tradition originating in one culture moves into another, in such a way that the authentic message is not lost, but genuine cultural engagement takes place. Christianity had to do that in its very first generation. Consider the fact that Jesus taught in Aramaic and yet we have the gospels in Greek. Within only thirty years of the original teachings of Jesus, you have this enormous transition of the teaching into a completely new culture, and a different world-view, a different conceptual apparatus. And I think that—this is just a thesis now—that if Jesus had been a Greek and had spoken articulate Greek all along, we might never have heard of him; he would have been, perhaps, one more minor philosopher. If, on the other hand, he had lived in Palestine and had taught only in Aramaic, and if his teachings hadn't moved into Greek culture with it's philosophical sophistication, it is also questionable if he would have had a lasting impact. It was precisely the fact that he appeared at the fusion of these two cultural points that gave his teaching the combined power of the Jewish vision and the instrument of philosophical interpretation and dissemination that the Greek world afforded.

Now, we live at a moment in which a similar thing is happening with the tradition you represent. That tradition is beginning to be articulated in a different culture and this is a very exciting enterprise. What interested me was that some of this tradition's interpreters in Vṛndāvana realize that and see the dangers. I mean this is dangerous business, in a way. It's extremely dangerous. It's better to keep the tradition wrapped up and never take it out of the package, because then it's absolutely safe. Never interpret it. Just like Bible-pounding fundamentalists: they just quote the Bible and say the same words over and over again and think that's all you have to do to communicate religious truth.

SJG: I think that some in my tradition would have a little difficulty with the word you keep using—"interpretation"—because of one of its connotations: inventive, self-serving speculation. I don't think you'd find anyone within the Krishna consciousness movement who would argue against the principle of communicating our tradition with sensitivity to time and circumstance, with a deep grasp of context. The relative success of the movement owes largely, certainly, to Śrīla Prabhupāda's genius for cultural adaptation.

But there is an in-bred distrust, as you well know, within Indian tradition against interpretative speculation in the realm of spiritual knowledge, and that is due to its distinctive epistemology. If religious truth is more than merely a product of history and culture, if it indeed precedes and transcends history and culture—that is, if it is eternal and transcendental—then it should not be so easily subjected to tampering by changing intellectual, theological, and cultural fashions. If it is, then something of the original purity and force may be sacrificed.

I can think, right off, of two dangers of interpretation, in the sense in which I'm defining it. One is that theological interpretation can become a tool for self-centered intellectual pleasure, or worse, an egotistic quest for intellectual prestige without reference to the ultimate, religious, purpose of theology, which is to understand the nature of God and spiritual reality. Speculative interpretation, by its very nature, emphasizes the speculative and cognitive over the revelatory and experiential approach to God and to spirituality. The other danger, is that in the name of interpretation, the theological enterprise can become one of compromising the spirit of revealed scripture in order to rationalize or justify personal modes of behavior that violate scriptural teachings, in letter or in spirit. That happens in every tradition.

HC: I agree with what you say about the dangers of interpretation. But let me also say that there's an enormous danger also in not interpreting. And by "interpretation" I mean simply the act of explaining and adapting a tradition to a different historical or cultural context, while remaining loyal to the spirit of the tradition. You can't avoid the danger. You described one danger, but the other danger is not interpreting at all, and history is studded with the fossilized remains of religious movements which have decided not to try to do that.

The underlying theological point that I'm making here is that *we* don't do the interpretation, *God* does the interpretation. That's the point that I'm trying to make from the Reformation. God is faithful to His Word, and when the preacher or interpreter is faithful to the Word, and not to his own idea of what the Word should be, that act of interpretation is blessed and empowered by God. I realize this is a particular theological point, a point that, if not unique to, at least is very characteristic of the Protestant Reformation—the idea of the proclamation of the living Word of God, the Word of God as a sacrament. I agree with you completely about pretentions in interpretive theology. But if God is God, the message of the eternal God is not going to be messed-up—at least not forever—by human beings. It's the Word of God, after all, and one has to have a certain confidence that if God is interested in and committed to relating intimately to human beings (which is a conviction that our traditions share), then God is going to preserve the power of the Word.

"Rice-Hindus" and Hare Krishnas

SJG: I agree that it's crucially important that the Krishna consciousness movement, while remaining loyal to the Caitanya tradition both theologically and practically, not hesitate to communicate and relate creatively and dynamically to contemporary western culture.

I'd like to begin to explore with you some substantive issues concerning how the Krishna consciousness movement is actually relating with the West, the dynamics by which it is becoming a religious and social reality within western culture. First of all, as you point out in *Turning East*, there is much faddishness and much that is artificial and superficial about the American fascination with Eastern spirituality. What about the Krishna consciousness movement?

HC: I don't think one makes that judgement entirely on the basis of the movement. One makes it on the basis of individuals within the movement. I suppose there are extremely sincere and utterly devoted adherents to almost any religion, and then there are people who are frivolous about their religious commitment. I don't think that has as much to do with the movement as it does with the person who happens to be drawn into its orbit. In the oriental countries there's talk about "rice-Christians." Have you heard that expression? People come to the Christian mission to get their rice, and when the rice runs out, they're not Christians anymore; they revert back to Buddhism or Hinduism or whatever.

I think we have in the West the psychological equivalent of that, in the form of "rice-Buddhists" or "rice-Hindus." While the psychological goodies are being passed out, they keep coming. As long as their affiliation with a particular group is affording some sort of desirable experiences, or fulfilling their need to be different, or providing an outlet for their spiritual gluttony, they stay. But if the satisfaction of these particular needs doesn't seem to be working out after a while, they drift away.

I don't know what the statistics are, but I'm sure you have had many such people who come and go. I'm interpreting your question as having more to do with the matter of serious or not-so-serious motivations of people who come to the movement, not with the movement itself. Now of course one may come in for the rice and actually get hooked on the substance, whatever that substance may be. My guess is that the substance, and antiquity and depth of the Vaiṣṇava tradition is such, in comparison to most other movements, that the chances that somebody might actually get touched by something profound seem better. But I wouldn't want to go any further than that. I don't think any tradition, yours or mine, is completely immune to being misused or trivialized. There are no built-in guarantees that it won't be. We have to recognize that and deal with it.

Perhaps we should recognize it with a little more compassion for the people who use it this way than I voiced in my earlier statement. When you want rice, you want rice, and you go to where it's available. If you're starved, you're starved. I'm speaking of people who are seduced into this gluttonous attitude by American society. They're not essentially evil, gluttonous people. They've been maddened by a consumer culture. I believe it's literally madness that people are taught by hundreds of thousands of advertisers sponsored by a profit-oriented, merchandizing, consumer culture, to invest in commodities and consumer goodies that promise to provide human fulfillment which is a lie, just a plain lie. The result is that they approach Eastern spiritual movements or any spiritual movement as gluttonous and capricious consumers. So, they're really victims, and I think that we have to see them as victims.

Śrīla Prabhupāda and America's "Cultural Readiness" for Krishna Consciousness

SJG: In your foreword to the first volume of *Śrīla Prabhupāda-līlāmṛta,* the biography of the founder of the Krishna consciousness movement, you suggest that among religious teachers, Śrīla Prabhupāda was "one in a thousand, maybe one in a million." What did you mean by that statement?

HC: Well, there aren't many people you can think of who successfully implant a whole religious tradition in a completely alien culture. That's a rare achievement in the history of religion. In his case it's even all the more remarkable for his having done this at such an advanced age. When most people would have already retired, he began a whole new phase of his life by coming to the United States and initiating this movement. He began simply, with only a handful of disciples. Eventually he planted this movement deeply in the North American soil, throughout other parts of the European-dominated world, and beyond. Although I didn't know him personally, the fact that we now have in the West a vigorous, disciplined, and seemingly well-organized movement—not merely a philosophical movement or a yoga or meditation movement, but a genuinely religious movement—introducing the form of devotion to God that he taught, is a stunning accomplishment. So when I say "one in a million," I think that's in some ways an underestimate. Perhaps he was one in a hundred-million.

To me, his is a very moving story: an old man with no personal wealth or possessions sails across the ocean, lands in New York City, and accomplishes spiritual miracles. When I went to Vṛndāvana, I felt in a sense that I was a little closer to him. I visited the tiny room in the medieval temple where Prabhupāda lived for a number of years before coming to America. It was a rather unimposing place, to say the least. There's really something about visiting a significant place like that that helps you feel that you know the person. This experience increased my admiration for him.

SJG: To what would you attribute his success in establishing Krishna consciousness in the West?

HC: That's a big question. I could answer that on several different levels. Certainly his own personal devotion, character, and determination had a lot to do with it. The cultural readiness of American society to hear something like his message certainly was contributive. Obviously, there was some need here. He didn't come into a vacuum. He came into a place where there was a high degree of hunger. That's something which was not so much the case fifty years ago.

SJG: In what way was America culturally ready for his message?

HC: In American society, I believe we're now in the late phase, the most deteriorated, decadent phase, of consumer capitalism. When I say "consumer capitalism," I don't mean simply the form of our economic life; I mean our whole culture. It's not just a capitalist economic system. It's a capitalistic culture, with personal lifestyles, values, morality, and meaning perceptions all in some measure shaped by this underlying ethos. And all this means that the value of the person is greatly underrated. Although we talk about the value of the individual a lot, we really mean, in a sense, the value of the individual *for me*, or *for us*. I think the term "value of the individual" is misleading in a way because we generally use the word "value" in such an economic way.

People's primal energies are fixated on commodities that are supposed to bring satisfaction of inner hungers. Through the suggestive and hypnotic power of the advertising industry, a direct connection is made from very basic and underlying needs and fears to material commodities which are touted as things which satisfy those needs; but of course they do not. Furthermore, the life pattern is pretty well set out through educational, occupational, and career structures which define for people the meaning of success in material terms, and in a way that people think that they're making choices. But they're actually being coerced and manipulated into a structure which really does not ultimately pay-off in terms of genuine spiritual satisfaction.

SJG: What's the end result of that?

HC: I think the result of that is manifold. The result, in the first instance, is the creation of a lot of unsatisfied hungers and unresolved fears which turn into anger and violence. I think a lot of the violence in our society is a result of this. Here I am, I've worked so hard and spent all this money to buy all these things and I still have no peace within myself. Maybe I should get some more things. I don't succeed as well as I'm told I ought to succeed and I'm upbraided for this by my employer. Ultimately, I become angry at the whole society that is the cause of my unfulfillment, and there's a tendency to take that frustration out on other people. So I think the whole web of violence in our society is related to this in ways that are not explored thoroughly enough by psychologists. Psychologists are more interested in why people get attracted to bizarre cults. A lot of psychologists and psychiatrists, of course, work for the companies which are exploring our inner motivations and designing advertising to match them.

Now, all of this elicits a certain kind of resistance in people, especially young people who have not been fully trapped into this whole system yet—especially those people who have begun to emerge from their homes and families (and so are no longer completely defined by the familial circle), but haven't as yet been pulled completely into career patterns, mortgages, and so on. It's at that age and in that condition that a lot of people are attracted to alternate life-meaning systems. The critics of the cults would say, well, these are the poor, lonely, vulnerable kids who are picked off the streets and brainwashed into the cults. The other way you can look at it is to say that here are people who have not yet been socialized into the existing distorted values of society and are open to other life-patterns.

Now, from my point of view, what Christianity should be doing in this country is providing an alternative to this capitalist-consumer ethos, in terms of personal values and ultimate meaning. There are a few Christians who are doing it, but the vast majority of people who call themselves Christians are, in fact, completely caught up in this un-Christian value system. So there is a chance for other visions of life to present themselves and to find some echo in people, especially young people who see that the path their parents and teachers and professors have taken hasn't produced what it promised to produce. So they try something else which they find more personally satisfying, at least for a while, if not for a whole lifetime.

Politically or socially speaking, I see this acceptance of radical lifestyle alternatives partly as an unconscious protest against the same kind of oppression that everybody else feels; but rather than actively question the oppressive structure, they look for alternatives to it. Given the possibilities before us in our time, especially with the current turn of events politically, it's probably as wise as any tactic you can think of. I don't think we're going to have a revolution which will produce a post-capitalist culture in America very soon. I hope we do some time, and when we do, I think there will still be inadequacies and dangers in whatever comes out of that. But that's another question.

Freedom and Authority: A Theological Critique

SJG: What you're saying at least partially answers the sociologists' question, "Why have young people, especially those emerging from a counter-cultural context—people who were actively protesting authority in different forms and apparently authority itself—why have they taken to authoritarian religious movements?" Your point is that their's wasn't a rejection of authority per se, but of authorities they viewed as corrupt, or authorities that didn't satisfy basic psychological or spiritual needs.

HC: Yes. I'm very interested in this whole issue of authority—where people look for it, how they find it, whether they need it—and I'm convinced that our received wisdom concerning what constitutes freedom and what authority and obedience are, is mistaken. That whole collection of concepts is basically wrong. We have a negative concept of freedom which is that "nobody tells me what to do: I do whatever I want to do, whatever comes to mind at the moment." The meaning of this is that I become, in effect, a victim of my own moods and whims. I think you will discover in most religions—and I'll speak especially of Christianity since I know it better—that there is a concept of authority which is absolutely paradoxical to the modern secular mind, a concept that I think is fundamentally true. It's expressed in a phrase that we have in *The Book of Common Prayer:* "Almighty God, whose service is perfect freedom." Now, to the modern psychological mentality, that's a contradiction in terms. How can you be serving somebody and be free? But the idea is that this is the *only* way you can be free—by serving.

But then the question is, "Who is the worthy object of that service? Whose service will produce perfect freedom?" The problem is that in recent years, we've had some terribly twisted objects of obedience: the state, the party, or whatever—concepts and structures that are not worthy of service and which ought to be questioned. Questioning them was a service that people rendered in the 1960's: "No, no, I won't go." Now, the problem in saying, "No I won't go," was that although they were saying "No" to corrupt and incredible authority, many people didn't realize that the structure of the human psyche is such that relation to a source of being and meaning is necessary in order to be a free person.

You learn that in little ways in life. You can learn that in marriage, for instance. People used to talk about marriage as a ball-and-chain, and so on. But people who are married and who find themselves fulfilled and deepened in their marriage know very well that that's not true, that they are freer in a profound sense when they are married to someone who is not merely a vehicle for their own growth or development, but an object of love and service. In that selflessness, one experiences a kind of freedom or release from limiting self-centeredness and egotism. One can experience this with children, with friends, with students, or any other potential object of devotion and service.

All of us have friends and acquaintances who, although they claim to be free, are actually driven, captive people, because they have no structure. They're not serving anyone or anything, and so they are literally the servants of their daily moods, of their desires, of the latest trends, or this or that idea. They are swept along by whatever comes along. So, I think a theological critique of existing psychological ideas of freedom, authority, and obedience would be a very important one. I would like to do that sometime. The widespread theory is that you can instill autonomy in a person by never subjecting him to any form of discipline or authority; by granting a person unlimited choices all along and never subjecting him to much direction or authority, somehow this autonomy will develop. That's a very precarious theory and not in keeping with what most parents know about raising children.

SJG: How does the need for credible authority manifest itself in the Hare Krishna movement, and what is it about that authority that some people find attractive?

HC: Many have a hunger for a mentor, a teacher, a guru, a *roshi,* and we don't have anywhere in the western educational system the equivalent of that intense relationship between pupil and teacher that exists in the Orient. It's a relationship in which there's a very intense interaction going on, of wrestling and struggling. I get a little of that with my graduate students, but still it's decimated by the fact that they work with other professors as well. We don't encourage in the western educational system that kind of long, devoted work with one particular person. It's taken to be a kind of peonage now, and somehow not appropriate. But I think some people look for that. I remember when the Casteneda books were around a few years ago, I read one of them. *The Teachings of Don Juan* and others of his books were part of the underground curriculum here at Harvard. Although they were viewed by many people as being popular simply because of all the trippy drug scenes in them, I think the other element which was attractive was that this young man found a type of relationship to a teacher that he's never had in his graduate study in anthropology. Don Juan, the Yaqui medicine man, took him on as his helper and apprentice, and there was this tough, combative relationship that went on between them, and he learned and grew a lot from the experience. Some people are looking for something like that, and they find it in some movements. Some people got that directly with Prabhupāda, especially in the earlier years of the Hare Krishna movement. It's important, I think, for those in the movement who are now gurus to provide some of that direct, dynamic interchange with their disciples.

"Zombi-itis": Fear of The Hare Krishna People

SJG: Why do you suppose that many Americans seem to fear a movement like Krishna consciousness? Why the often negative public reaction to the movement?

HC: I think the main thing is plain unfamiliarity, the apparent strangeness of the movement. I think on that count Krishna consciousness is now less controversial than it was at one time when people first saw groups of devotees chanting in groups on the streets. Now, it's a widely enough spread phenomenon that it's not all that unfamiliar to people.

You do, however, find an underlying fear in many people that they could easily be lured in, and therefore they're afraid of it. All the hysterical talk about people getting brainwashed and converted against their will has as it's underlying psychological dynamic the fear that "That could happen to me too; I'm not really in full control of my own mind." I think the reason that fear is there is that there is an underlying wish that I didn't have to be in control of my own mind. We fear the thing we hope for. This is the old concept of ambivalence, and I think this relates to our previous discussion about authority. People are attracted to authority against their own better judgement, and they're surprised, occasionally, at how often and how marked the need is. Now people will deny this, of course. Someone reading this will probably think, "Oh, it never occurs to me." I think the only way to explain that underlying constant fear is to point out that it springs from an insufficiently well-grounded authority structure in one's own life, and I would say that that has to do with not being related to God in a way which requires one's full devotion and which produces authentic freedom.

So the Krishna consciousness movement is another of what my colleague Krister Stendahl calls the "hot religions" (as opposed to the "cool" religions), where there is a high degree of devotional involvement. This devotion frightens people because it makes them aware of something in themselves. Otherwise, they wouldn't be frightened. Why should they be frightened? Just walk away, ignore it, go home. Why should they have to stop when they see people chanting and shake their heads? There's something that bothers them, and one has to ask what that is.

SJG: So, you're saying that they fear coming under the influence of some unknown external power, that they lack confidence in their own psychological autonomy?

HC: "I'm not really all that free," they're saying. "I *say* I'm free, but I could also become a marionette, a puppet, a zombie." This is not such an uncommon theme in literature and in science-fiction movies, that is, people's minds or bodies being taken over by alien, malevolent forces, people being turned into "pod people," "the living dead," "zombies," "robots." I think the fear that I am not really in control of myself—that I should be in control, but I'm not—is deep-set in the modern psyche, very deep set.

SJG: So what is it about the Krishna consciousness movement that makes some people think that its members are being controlled by some mysterious malevolent power?

HC: Well, they're told that. They're told that constantly by the press and, in addition, they see people doing things which appear irrational to them—shaving their heads, wearing unusual costumes, dancing and playing instruments, and so on. What else could have happened to these people except that they must have been possessed? That's the only category they have to deal with what they see.

SJG: Why should people be so resistant to the idea that people have made a choice to do these things out of free will? Why do people tend to opt more for the "brainwashing" paradigm?

HC: I think it's because there aren't many examples around of people who choose a path of religious asceticism, and devotion. There are so few examples of this that they don't have within their own repertoire of personal experiences any models for that. The people who understand the Hare Krishna movement better than many others are people who have a relative who's become a Benedictine monk or a nun. They know somebody who has chosen to do something which appears to the world to be crazy: giving up television, giving up family life, leaving professional careers and going off to live in a monastery. But that's legitimated in the Catholic system. I've talked with people about the Hare Krishna movement in this way and they can easily make the connection.

There are so few examples, in most people's lives, of anybody who does anything other than simply drift along with the existing current and the existing options of more or less similar lifestyles—a little bit more or a little bit less accumulation, a little bit more or a little bit less sexual promiscuity, and never much discipline or intellectual rigor. They just drift along. The heroic choice is a rare one. Few people make heroic choices.

"Brainwashing" and The Politics of Conformity

SJG: Could you take a closer look at this notion of "brainwashing?" Does it have psychiatric validity? How do you see it functioning culturally?

HC: Well, perhaps I can offer some random comments. First of all, the term "brainwashing" has no respectable standing in scientific or psychiatric circles, and is used almost entirely to describe a process by which somebody has arrived at convictions that I do not agree with. If a person has changed in the last few years, or months, or weeks, and we like the change, we say that this person has "improved." We say they've learned something, or they've grown, or they've seen the light, or they've had some remarkably effective therapy. If we don't happen to like the outcome, we say they must have been "brainwashed." I think it's Thomas Szasz who said that a brain cannot be washed any more than a cutting remark can draw blood. The term is obviously a metaphor, and it's so flexible in the possibilities for its application that I would again want to plead for care in not using it indiscriminately. I think it's such an ambiguous and loaded term that it shouldn't be used at all.

Of course, we live in a society in which the effort to control other people's ideas, preferences, and values is an overwhelming feature. In fact, our society probably spends more money and expends more energy and technology to control other people's minds than any in history. We have a multi-billion dollar industry which is designed specifically to stimulate needs, preferences and tastes and to persuade: the advertising industry. And besides commodity-advertising, we also have the general socialization process that goes on in society, enacted through its various institutions—the family, the educational system, the religious establishment, and so on. The act of persuasion, and its fruits, is noticed only when people, through one or another process of persuasion, socialization, or conversion—especially alternative systems—find themselves, or are seen as to be, in a situation that other people don't like for one reason or another. Then the term "brainwashing" is used.

I personally am made very uncomfortable by coercive forms, even mildly coercive forms, of persuasion. I don't like them at all. I object to it when it's used by advertisers, by military recruiters, by salesmen, by evangelists, by anyone. I have a strong distaste for it. However, I see absolutely no way that one can preserve freedom of inquiry and freedom of open interchange in society without preserving the rights of people to try to sell me or persuade me about things. And I think that's a valuable enough freedom to maintain that I'm willing to pay the price for maintaining it.

The term "brainwashing" first was used, I believe, shortly after the Korean War to describe the process that the Chinese put some American prisoners of war through in order to persuade them to change their ideological loyalties. You have to remember, however, that this process was performed on people who were physically confined and had no freedom of movement and no exposure whatsoever to the outside world. In my mind, then, coercive persuasion has to include at least some element of physical isolation and of forced imprisonment. If in any movement—religious, political, or otherwise—people were being physically prevented from getting out, I would be the first to lead the charge and rescue them and demand their rights to leave. However, short of a critical situation of actual imprisonment, you cannot take matters into your own hands and force a person to leave a movement which they sincerely feel they joined voluntarily. I do object, both aesthetically and ethically, to any form of browbeating or the use of some psychological knowledge to manipulate other people. I object to that. But I would object more strongly to putting the power into the hands of a government, a court, or the police, to prevent this from happening. The cost would be too high. I think it's simply the cost that we pay to live in a free society, and I'm willing to pay that cost.

Psychiatry and The Politics Of Sanity

SJG: There's an old tradition within psychology, especially since Freud, which tends to equate religious, mystical, or conversionary experience with mental illness. Do you think that perhaps this sort of anti-religious bias is coming into play here? Isn't there a tendency to view any expression of spirituality that goes beyond socially accepted religious norms as a sign of psychopathology or, more coloquially, as "brainwashing"?

HC: Yes, as a symptom of brainwashing, or as a symptom of psychotic, schizophrenic, paranoic, or some other deranged or unhealthy form of behavior. I think that's true. To some extent, this is a result of a severe limiting of the range of possible forms of behavior to that which is publicly acceptable, over even what we were previously allowed in our own society. You have to remember that if you had been there at the early Methodist frontier revivals here in America, where the grandparents of some of our present psychiatrists were saved, you would have seen some very ecstatic behavior.

Right in Martha's Vineyard, where I have my summer home, there are pictures of people at the campground jumping up and down and singing. This sort of ecstatic religious behavior is, of course, associated with religious devotion from time immemorial in virtually every culture. We happen to be living in a culture which is very restricted, unimaginative, and narrow in this regard.

A lot of this, I think, has to do with the real underlying goal of America, which is production, efficiency, and accumulation. You can't allow much eccentricity and ecstasy if everyone has to be geared into the productive process all the time. One of the criticisms that sometimes people make of the Hare Krishna devotees is that they're wasting their time. "They're just out there chanting. Why aren't they working? Why aren't they doing something *productive*?" There's some suspicion even of people who live in monasteries—that they're just sitting around, kneeling around, praying. They're not doing anything that's really *useful*. Now, there's something curious about this. It doesn't really matter what you're doing productively. You could be manufacturing hand-grenades or bottling liquor; but if you're working somehow or other, that's commendable. I think it's a curious idea that it's better to be working at destructive things than it is to be singing or dancing or praying.

So, what we have here is a set of cultural assumptions which are not self-evident. They are a particular set of assumptions which are drawn upon often by people who pretend to be very scientific and therapeutic, in order to enforce a particular view of reality or a particular standard of behavior on other people. And all this applies in the face of our insistence that we are a free and open society.

SJG: Sometimes the repetitive chanting of the Hare Krishna mantra, or for that matter any type of devotional practice, is viewed as a kind of "self-hypnosis." What parallels do we find for this kind of contemplative discipline in religious traditions other than Krishna consciousness?

HC: Almost every religious tradition I know of has formulae, prayers, chants or hymns, in which the repetition of sound, the repetition of names, sometimes with musical intonations, is used for a devotional purpose. Now, again, if you're operating from a different paradigm, you can call that "self-hypnosis." It's a little bit like the term "brainwashing"—nobody quite knows what "self-hypnosis" is. But it's evident to me that human beings are capable of a wide variety of different forms of consciousness and awareness and, again, we have certain forms which are declared to be okay and others suspect, depending on what the underlying goals of the dominant culture are. But I think that these criticisms of chanting or repetition of prayers as somehow mentally destructive are frankly some of the most uninformed and ignorant of the criticisms that I've run across. These sorts of criticisms cannot possibly be made by people who know anything about the history of religions, unless they want to come right out and say that they're against all religion, or all devotional practices, all prayer—which I think many of them are. At least they ought to be honest and not conceal their personal bias under allegedly scientific language.

SJG: Consider, for example, Dr. John Clark's testimony before the Vermont Senate, which at one time was investigating the "cult" phenomenon. While delineating the psychological dangers of cults, he offers several interesting examples of pathological aberrations found therein: The belief, held by some cults, that one is not the physical body but the soul, he diagnoses as "ego-loss." Living in any sort of a religious community is "loss of autonomy"; acceptance of religious authority, such as a guru or scripture, is "loss of critical thinking," and so forth. Since these particular criteria of psychological pathology can be applied to virtually any religion, I suspect they betray a real bias against any sort of spiritual lifestyle, especially a more intensive one.

HC: Using the term "ego-loss" as a therapeutic value judgement is unwittingly accepting the western understanding of ego. If you accuse Buddhists of encouraging ego-loss, they would say "That's right, that's what our whole tradition of five-hundred million strong is about. Ego is a mistake; ego is an illusion, and we happen to be trapped by this illusion." What disturbs me is the uninformed provinciality of such comments, which are then escalated into what appear to be scientific or medical judgements. And they're not. They're simply opinions based on a particular culture's understanding of what ego or self is, what autonomy is, what rational thought is.

Deprogramming, Conservatorship, and Religious Liberty

SJG: What about the use of what is popularly called "deprogramming," whereby parents hire a so-called "deprogrammer" to kidnap their grown son or daughter from a religious movement, bring that person to some isolated place and subject them to days or even weeks of intensive psychological and in some cases physical coercion aimed at convincing the person to repudiate and abandon his new faith? What does this say about religious liberty in America? Are there historical parallels for this kind of thing?

HC: I think the coercive forcing of people into treatment, psychiatric or otherwise, or coercive persuasion to do anything—to join a religious movement, to leave a religious movement, to join a political movement, to leave one—is reprehensible, destructive to human personality, and in every way evil. I'm especially shocked at the way some professionals allow themselves to be used and even enter into this kind of thing. I'm strongly opposed to it. It has, of course, its parallels in the history of religions. We've had our Star Chamber and the Inquisition and so on. So it's not new. The motive and the language now is more psychiatric than theological, but the process is similar.

SJG: Because kidnapping is risky and prosecutable, some parents, with the help of sympathetic lawyers, psychiatrists, and judges, have been able to obtain court-ordered conservatorships—guardianships—over their adult children, after which they have their son or daughter legally removed from the religious movement and subjected to a deprogrammer.

HC: I think that the use of conservatorship laws to pull people out of religious affiliations is a gross misuse of those laws. They were designed, in almost every instance, to protect older people who are losing their judgement, from being exploited. There may be an occasional instance in which a younger person needs to be placed under a conservatorship. However, I would insist that in every instance, before a conservatorship is granted, the person who is to be placed under the conservatorship should have the right to appear in court and contest such action. Granting a conservatorship when the person in question is not even permitted to testify on his own behalf is entirely unjust. In any case, judges ought to be extremely wary about granting one person such rights over another.

SJG: Do the use of deprogramming and of conservatorship laws extend to new converts to mainstream religions?

HC: They have already been used against members of so-called established groups. Some deprogrammers have gladly deprogrammed people in the Episcopal and Catholic churches, depending on the preferences of those who wanted them deprogrammed. As far as I can see, deprogrammers are simply hired-guns. They will deprogram anybody you pay them to deprogram. I suppose they may have some preferences of their own, but for the most part they're just practitioners of the deprogramming technique who are available, for a price, to use these techniques—isolation, browbeating, and so on—to get people into a mental state that somebody else wants them in.

Devotees And Families: A Christian Perspective

SJG: Although members of ISKCON are encouraged to maintain regular contact with family members (most do), their participation in the movement is sometimes viewed by family members as a threat because, as is the case with other religious orders, members tend to place their religious commitment over family commitments.

HC: This is a point that must have been very difficult for the early followers of Jesus because he insisted, in every instance, that they put loyalty to him above loyalty to their families, and he put it in very strident terms: "Unless you leave behind your wife, your family, and come and follow me, you can't be my disciple." And there's the famous story of the man whom Jesus told to follow him, and the man said, "I really can't, because my father has just died and I have to prepare the funeral." And Jesus said, "Don't do it. Let the dead bury the dead. It's time to drop that and come and follow me."

Now, somehow or other, over the years we've made Jesus into a kind of blessing of the patriarchal, bourgeois family. There's not one single text anywhere in the teachings of Jesus that supports this. Jesus is a person who's calling people to something that is more important than family. I don't think that literally means that you shouldn't love your family, your parents, and your natural siblings. It's a matter of ordering your loyalties, your priorities. I would even say that if you invest in your family the kind of loyalty and devotion that is only appropriate for God, you're not doing your family any favor. You're going to destroy the supportive human qualities that are there if you invest too much. By placing God at the center of one's devotion, one's highest loyalty, it releases you from the need to make other people into God.

So I would hope that families who see their children go into a movement like the Hare Krishna movement would first of all not panic, not become excessively worried, but stay in touch as much as possible. They should patiently try to understand their children's commitment to Krishna consciousness and assure them that they're still loved. Parents should recognize that there's a stage at which children, especially in the American culture, sometimes have to do something symbolically quite dramatic to take a step out of the nest, and that can be a difficult time. I'm a parent. I have teenage children. I'm not speaking of something that I'm not familiar with. I think a little perspective and a little patience will help.

Krishna Consciousness And Religious Revitalization

SJG: What ultimate effect, theologically or religiously speaking, might a movement like the Krishna consciousness movement have on western society?

HC: Let me just content myself to making one remark concerning the relationship between a religious tradition and a culture. When a religious movement moves into a foreign culture, frequently the intensity of the devotion of that movement becomes more noticeable and more attractive—in part because the people who are going to make the long journey to another part of the world to present their tradition are people generally of a higher degree of commitment to it than people who are living back in the homeland, and also the new recruits to that movement will display, as new recruits do, a lot of enthusiasm. Another reason why the intensity of the devotion of a movement entering a new culture will be more noticeable and attractive is that the movement is played off against a different cultural background. When a religious tradition has been around for a long time, especially three, four, ten, twenty, thirty generations, it tends to a large extent to have made significant compromises with the dominant culture. Even though from time to time they may have internal renewal or revitalization movements, still, there's a certain kind of cultural accommodation which dilutes the power of the tradition.

Now, all this is one reason—looking at it from a cultural standpoint—why your movement is attractive to many in the West. But this dynamic has happened in the other direction also, from West to East. Christianity has become very attractive to people in Oriental countries at different times in history. There have, for instance, been many Hindu converts to Christianity in India, and this has been made possible, in part, because the Hindu tradition has also, to some extent, been compromised and accommodated. There were mass conversions to Christianity in Japan in the latter part of the nineteenth century. The Jesuits who traveled to China in the sixteenth century were viewed by the Chinese as some kind of fantastic incarnations of wisdom and piety and they immediately became mandarins and advisors to the Emperor. There were even strong possibilities that many Chinese would have become Christians except that the Pope at the time thought that the Jesuits were making too many compromises with Chinese culture—not with material things, but with wearing mandarin robes and integrating the Christian theology with Chinese philosophy, and so on—and so he called them home and didn't allow them to pursue that course. So, there is always that tendency for a religious tradition, newly arrived from afar, to appear attractive to people in the resident culture.

The resident religious tradition anywhere can react in one

of two ways when this sort of challenge comes. It can be defensive and propagandize against the newcomers, persecute them, throw them out. Or it can view the new tradition as in some way a source of stimulation, challenge, correction, renewal, or grace. The Brāhmo Samāj movement in India in the nineteenth century was obviously, in part, a response to Christianity and a reform movement within Hinduism. I think it's virtually impossible to understand the enormous power and piety of Mohandas Gandhi without seeing him as a man who, while remaining in the Hindu tradition, was responding to certain aspects of Christianity.

There are many other examples of this sort of thing throughout the world and throughout history. I see this interaction as enormously fruitful. Other people seem to be frightened or hesitant about it. I think it's promising, and if viewed in that way it can benefit both parties and eventually lead to something much, much better than was there before. So, I think a movement like the Krishna consciousness movement can potentially have a tremendously stimulating effect on the religious life of the West. I welcome the global interaction of religions very much, and I have full confidence that God has a purpose in this, that this is something that's happening under providential guidance. I have no particular stake ultimately in the names or peculiar practices of any religious tradition including mine. I have no interest in defending my tradition against other traditions or in criticizing other traditions, because I have enough confidence that God's truth will eventually triumph, because God is God. So I'm one who welcomes this stimulation, and I think it's an exciting time to be thinking and writing in the field of religion.

INTERVIEW WITH LARRY D. SHINN

Dr. Larry D. Shinn received his doctorate in the history of religions from Princeton University and is currently Danforth Professor of Religion at Oberlin College (Oberlin, Ohio) where he has taught since 1970. He is trained in South Asian religions (Hindu and Buddhist traditions) and in various theoretical approaches to the study of religion.

He is author of *Two Sacred Worlds: Experience and Structure in the World's Religions* (Nashville: Abingdon Press, 1977), co-author of *Lustful Maidens and Ascetic Kings: Buddhist and Hindu Stories of Life* (New York: Oxford University-Press, 1981), and is Associate Editor of the *Abingdor Dictionary of Living Religions* (Nashville: Abingdor Press, 1981).

Several years back, Dr. Shinn's long-term interest in the religions of India blended together with his interest in the nature and role of religious conversion to inspire an active curiosity about the American-based Hare Krishna movement. In 1980, he received a grant to spend a year studying the psychology of religion and decided, in addition, to do some field work among the Hare Krishna devotees—work that would serve to ground his psychological studies. Over the following year, he spent a sum of more than two months intensively studying the movement and its members, visiting and living in centers throughout the United States and India. During that time he collected more than three-hundred hours of recorded interviews involving a wide cross-section of Krishna devotees as well as parents of devotees and various supporters and detractors of the movement. In addition, he observed, participated in, and filmed various rituals and activities within the numerous communities he visited. "I thought I was just acquiring data to enhance my study of conversion. Instead, through this back door, I have entered a mansion of many rooms which I expect to explore over the next three to five years"—explorations which will comprise the foundation for future publications on the movement. He currently is at work on a book which will introduce the Hare Krishna movement in the context of current controversial issues surrounding new religious movements in America.

The following interview took place at the North American headquarters of the Hare Krishna movement in Los Angeles, in mid-February 1981, just before Dr. Shinn returned home to his family in Ohio after an intensive three-week study of several Krishna communities in America.

Becoming a Hare Krishna Devotee: Who, Why, And How

SJG: First, could you describe your own academic background and trace the development of your interest in the Hare Krishna movement?

LS: My own background, as you know, includes theological training which actively explored the relationship between my own Christian faith and the faith of others. My first encounter with other religions was in courses on Burmese Buddhism and related topics, taught by Paul Clasper at Drew Theological Seminary. Clasper often raised issues of conflicting truth claims on the part of various religious traditions, especially in terms of which traditions tend to claim exclusivity and which make claims for inclusiveness. The first tend to be Western claims and the second, Eastern religious claims for the most part. So, certain questions raised in this context have dogged me for the last sixteen or eighteen years.

Now, when I went to graduate school at Princeton, I studied the religions of India, primarily focusing with Kenneth Ch-en on early monastic Buddhism and with Philip Ashby on Hindu *bhakti* traditions. There I did my dissertation on

Krishna-*līlā*, the stories of Krishna as found in the *Bhāgavata Purāṇa*. While working on that dissertation, I had my first serious encounter with Vaiṣṇava tradition. But there are really two aspects to my interest in studying Vaiṣṇavism. One is Vaiṣṇavism in its traditional Indian context, and the other is in the Hare Krishna movement, which is a missionary movement that comes out of the Gauḍīya Vaiṣṇava tradition of Bengal. I was very curious to see what kinds of adaptations have been made as the Krishna tradition came west—as the Hare Krishna movement became a missionary movement of Bhakti Hinduism to the West.

Another feature of my interest in the Krishna tradition is the current study I'm doing in the area of psychology of religion which dovetails with all the contemporary furor over "brainwashing," as well as "deprogramming." So in my study of the Krishna movement, what I'm really doing is blending some long-term interests in the religions of India and its missionary thrust to the West, with more methodological interests, raised long ago in seminary, in the nature and role of religious conversion. So, essentially, that's my two-fold interest.

SJG: What special value do you see in studying the Hare Krishna movement?

LS: What I think makes the Hare Krishna movement particularly important, other than the issue of trans-cultural adaptation, is that it's a movement under fire. It's being called a "cult" when, in fact, it's very clearly a religious tradition whose roots go back at least to sixteenth century India as one sect of Hinduism. It seems to me that its importance in being studied is to deal as much with the social furor it has raised as with its religious impact. I think these are two separate issues.

SJG: So, let's start with the basics. What sort of people become Hare Krishna devotees and what are their reasons for joining? The movement, coming out of an Eastern context, appears quite exotic, and its life style is centered on a certain degree of religious asceticism, regimentation and communalism—values which the average Westerner finds rather unappealing. In your experience of interviewing Hare Krishna devotees throughout the United States and in India, what sort of people do you find joining the movement and why?

LS: First of all, it's very clear (and I'll talk more about this later on) that "brainwashing"—if we mean by that "mind-control," "coercive persuasion," or "thought reform"—is clearly not, in any sense, an explanation of how people get into the Hare Krishna movement. What is the case is that among people who join this movement, almost all had been in a state of crisis before they joined the movement. By "crisis" I mean most often psychological crisis: a sense of identity confusion, not being quite sure where to place one's values, search for meaning, religious crisis. These crises have taken a variety of forms and degrees of intensity—from simple frustration with vocational direction to deep existential dissatisfaction.

This is not surprising though, because the psychological studies done in earlier generations have shown that dramatic changes in life direction, such as religious conversion, are usually preceded by some kind of anxiety, general or specific. Starbuck's study, at the turn of the century, of several hundred young Christians revealed that their conversion experience was generally preceded by some degree of anxiety or some crisis-like situation. So, it's clear that many people face a personal crisis prior to joining religious movements. That phenomenon appears to be ubiquitous.

The interesting question is, among all those people of the counterculture generation who were uprooted by social turmoil in the late-sixties, why did some choose the Hare Krishna movement? And it's in the answer to that specific question that you do find similarity in background among people who join the Hare Krishna movement. Number one, you find—

and here I'm repeating something Stillson Judah noted in his book *Hare Krishna and the Counterculture*—you get people who are fully disenchanted with the materialistic world because they've been so deeply involved in it. There's a very strong sense of wanting to turn away from materialistic self-gratification and finding something different, something better. Clearly, the devotees' life style is a radical repudiation of that kind of existence. And so, to a large extent, that is a common feature of those who join, judging from those whom I've interviewed so far. A second factor is that most people who join the movement were vegetarians before they joined.

SJG: Most?

LS: Most were, far more than fifty-percent, some for many years. And what is significant is that the theology provides a rationalization for that. So, it's not as if someone joins the movement because they want to become vegetarian or are convinced of vegetarianism by the philosophy. It is that they are already largely vegetarians, some knowing why, some not quite sure why. Some just didn't like meat. There were four or five instances of this in my interviews, where devotees indicated that they simply didn't like meat and refused to eat it as a child; some would even throw up when they ate it. And so they became vegetarians almost out of physical necessity. But the theology provided an avenue for them to express this particular life choice they had already made and to make sense of it.

Another common background variable in people attracted to the Krishna movement as opposed to other movements during this process of searching and looking for answers is that most of them, almost without exception, were people who had already explored Eastern philosophy or Eastern thought. They are people who had some contact with ideas like reincarnation, *dharma*, *karma*, yoga, and so on. In fact, many of them used these terms loosely or already accepted them as meaningful prior to coming to the movement.

SJG: Had they come into contact with these terms and concepts from sources outside the Hare Krishna movement?

LS: Sure. A lot of devotees practiced Transcendental Meditation and many visited spiritual centers and ashrams like Swami Satchidananda's Integral Yoga Institute, Yogananda's Self-Realization Fellowship, Sivananda Yoga Centers, and so on.

SJG: Did you find that many had gone through several different Eastern approaches, or was contact usually limited to one or two?

LS: Well, that varies tremendously from person to person. Some people encountered the movement quickly on in their search, after only one or two other kinds of general musings or readings. Sometimes the reading was merely a superficial exploration of the spiritual and the exotic, the "wisdom of the East" kind of thing, in which Alan Watts, or Allen Ginsberg or some other western cultural interpreters of the "East" would be their first exposure. Some encountered the *Bhagavad-gītā*, some read books on Zen, meditation, or yoga.

As far as actually joining or becoming committed in a serious way to other traditions—that happened very seldom. That is, people who would join a Zen monastery or something like that and then later on come to Krishna consciousness—that's rare. A number of devotees went through TM and had a TM mantra. One I spoke with was a TM teacher. But TM is a mild and, one could almost say, innocuous kind of meditational practice, not really requiring very much commitment. What it did do for some was provide a sort of general ideological setting in which the assumptions of Bhakti Hinduism, devotional Vaiṣṇavism in this case, made sense.

SJG: I think you've dealt with the question of who becomes

a member of the movement. Now, what attracted them? What were their reasons for coming to the movement?

LS: As I've asked the question, "Why have you joined the movement?," people have given a wide variety of reasons. Some were attracted, in fact many were attracted, by the devotees themselves, the community of devotees—the warmth, the feeling of community, the sense of being wanted, the sense of being cared for and appreciated in a way that they hadn't been cared for or appreciated previously. Some were attracted by the *prasāda*, the sanctified Indian vegetarian food. A very common answer, an answer that is almost consistent in its expression, is that the philosophy, that is, the teachings themselves, were attractive. But what I've discovered is that while many people said they were attracted by the philosophy, by their own admission they didn't know it very well when they joined.

SJG: What then did they find attractive about the philosophy?

LS: Well, that's the point you see. They use the word "philosophy" in a very general and non-specific sense, simply to mean some basic *ideas*—ideas which they agreed with. One very basic idea is, "You are not your body; you are a spirit soul."

SJG: Why was that particular idea attractive to newcomers to the movement—the idea of the non-materiality of the self?

LS: Well, most of them had already gone through, as I mentioned, a crisis in struggling for meaning and happiness and of not finding it through materialistic pursuits. For whatever reason, they found materialistic pleasures simply to be void of any kind of basic meaning. Hence, a religious tradition which argues that sensual or sensory enjoyment is ultimately empty in meaning, will be appealing. Undoubtedly, when I begin to draw final conclusions from my interview data, I'll be talking about the process of identity formation that people go through—everyone goes through—and how crises may occur in that process. And one way to solve an identity crisis is to make a strong commitment to a certain identity role or model. And it seems that what your tradition provides is a sense in which I can know who *I* really am: *I* am not my body. *I* am a spirit soul. And this is particularly meaningful to people whose own sense of identity, socially speaking, is a little up in the air.

SJG: But why would the notion of spiritual selfhood be particularly attractive to those who are confused about their identity?

LS: Well, now you're asking for almost a psychoanalytic analysis of motivation. What I've reported to you is what was said. People have said, simply, that this aspect of the theology was appealing. When I asked, "*Why* is that idea appealing?" the answers that were given often indicated that people hadn't really thought about why that was attractive. If you want my initial assessment, I would say that many of them have chosen to drop out of the struggle to find identity in the social-psychological world, that is, the world that defines for me a role in terms of relative material contingencies. Others have chosen that role because it makes sense *spiritually*, because it makes sense *religiously*. So, you have two sources of attraction to a spiritual self-concept. Some have rejected the struggle to find identity in the conventional social-psychological context and have chosen a community in which they are accepted as they are and don't have to deal with what they view as irrelevant social constructs of identity. They now can understand themselves primarily in terms of the notion of "spirit soul." But to draw an important contrast, there are other people who blend notions of "I-ness" in the social sense with their own sense of spirituality. And those are the people whom I would call spiritually integrated.

SJG: Of course, it may sound good, in theory, that some people who have difficulty in forming a self-concept will fit well into a movement which provides a clear and simple sense of identity, and thus alleviates problems in ego-development. But in fact, as I'm sure you've experienced, there is a rather complex social reality within the movement. Inter-personal relationships and contacts within the movement do not always necessarily fit into neat, simple patterns. In the movement, one finds a great variety of different sorts of people, doing a great variety of different things, in a great variety of different ways. In this setting, the devotee ultimately does, in fact, have to deal, in a very practical way, with interpersonal relations and the demands upon self-imaging these relations make.

LS: Yes, but that is always understood, you see, in terms of your tradition, which distinctly defines the meaning of various social roles within the community. The process of submission to spiritual authority is the key one here. One is making a conscious, deliberate decision *not* to compete "out there" in the broader social structure, but to submit oneself to the sacred authority of guru, *śāstra,* and *sādhu,* that is, the teacher, the scripture, and the tradition, which define your social role. When I speak of some devotees as having rejected the secular social reality, I don't mean to put a negative judgement on that act. That act, that choice may, in fact, be a wise choice. So, you see, in the context of the religious community, the roles of men and women, of *brahmacārīs, gṛhasthas* and *sannyāsis,* are not roles that you get to experiment with and to redefine. The tradition has already defined them. In fact, there's a great deal of conformity of expectation.

SJG: As you know, authoritarian social structures are found within most religious traditions—at least monastic, community-oriented dimensions of religious traditions. It's not something which is a unique characteristic of marginal religious movements.

LS: Yes, of course. That's why almost anything that I'm saying now about authoritarian religious social structure in the Hare Krishna movement would be equally applicable to a Catholic or Buddhist monastery, or a variety of yoga ashrams in India. So, of course, this is not something which is a "cult" feature. And that's why I said early on that I'm treating this movement very much as an authentic religious tradition, but one which has taken some interesting turns as it has come to the West.

SJG: Are there any other significant reasons why people join the Hare Krishna movement?

LS: People join the Hare Krishna movement, it seems to me, for a wide variety of reasons. But the central one is that its basic ideas—the self as spirit soul, vegetarianism, the necessity for ethical guidelines—made sense and were attractive. But, from my point of view, commitment is always as much emotionally as it is intellectually motivated. Krishna consciousness "felt good." Many devotees say that "it just *seemed* right," or "I felt like I was *home,*" or "It seemed to me that I had never experienced such peace before," "I could just tell that the devotees were happy," "I felt exuberant, blissful." These are the kinds of responses people gave for why they joined. And that makes sense to me, because anytime one makes a radical commitment of life style, it will always be at least as much an emotional commitment as it will be an intellectual or a conceptual commitment.

SJG: You've talked about who joins and why; what about *how* people join, that is, recruitment. What is the process by which people get involved in the Hare Krishna movement?

LS: Well, they come into contact with devotees chanting on the street, or encounter a devotee involved in public book distribution, or they come to the Sunday feast at the temple. There are probably more people who have joined the movement through contact with a Sunday feast than through any single recruiting structure. It's not that the Sunday feast is some sort of intense session of coercive persuasion by devotees directed towards individual, lonely guests. People who attend the Sunday program are genuinely attracted by the food, which is excellent Indian vegetarian fare, or to what you call the association of devotees—interaction with the devotees. Other people like the lecture; others found it boring. There are a variety of responses to the Sunday feast. So it's primarily through the Sunday feast that people come into contact with the devotees. It's important to note that people make their way to the temple on their own, on their own legs or in their own cars. No one is kidnapped or pulled off the street and dragged into the Hare Krishna movement.

A second way that people come into contact with the movement is through close friends or through spouses. Sometimes a person is influenced by a close friend who has joined the movement and eventually follows suit. In some cases someone who is married or soon to be married comes into contact with the movement, gets involved in it and gets their spouse or fiancee involved. In other cases, a devotee who has dropped out of the movement for a while meets someone on the outside, gets married or engaged, and then returns to the movement with their mate.

Probably the third most common way that people come to the movement is directly through the books. In at least two cases that I know of, people exploring Eastern philosophy were rummaging through library stacks looking for a copy of *Bhagavad-gītā* and came across Prabhupāda's translation. They read it, became attracted by it, and found out the temple on their own and joined it. But this kind of situation—someone joining a temple directly from having read the literature—is less common.

SJG: Is that really so uncommon? I think that if you asked devotees if they had had some contact with Prabhupāda's books before coming to the movement, most would answer in the affirmative. In the early days of the movement many more, perhaps, came through contact with street chanting. But in more recent years, most seem to have come due to contact with the books. Whether or not their coming was a *direct* result of reading the books, that might be hard to say. But most had, to some degree, read the books or *Back to Godhead* magazine before coming.

LS: That's a different matter. I would say that most of the people I've interviewed, including even the older devotees, had had previous contact with some publications—if not the books, then the magazine—and, very often, had given great attention to them. But the point I'm making is that if that were the *only* impetus they had had, they would not be in the movement now. In fact, many of them had received books previously and had read them and put them away on their bookshelf. But it wasn't until they personally encountered a devotee in public—often a book distributor—who invited them to a Sunday feast or went to a Sunday feast on the prompting of a friend, or after seeing an ad for the feast in a *Back to Godhead* magazine, that they had an occasion to actually visit a temple and come into the active association of the devotees. I would say that in the vast majority of cases, maybe as high as eighty or ninety percent, it was a particular devotee who was most influential in bringing the person to the movement. Someone preached to them effectively enough that they decided to join. So, in most cases, one of the important variables, if not *the* important variable, is personal contact with a single devotee.

I guess I haven't said this earlier, but it's the case that for many of the earliest disciples in the movement, one of the things that was most attractive to them was Prabhupāda himself. Many of the earlier devotees came to the movement through simple, intimate contact with this man, who they viewed to be a deeply pious and spiritual being. I think it's very clear that that's a primary reason for many of the people who joined the movement early. Though among the early disciples, many didn't meet Prabhupāda when they first joined and so there are certainly other reasons even for those early disciples.

SJG: Among those early disciples who came to the movement chiefly due to personal contact with Śrīla Prabhupāda, what was it about him or their experience of him that brought them into his new movement? What were their perceptions of him? How were they touched so deeply by him?

LS: Well, I think their testimony can be summarized by saying that they saw him as a saint, a pure devotee. They *experienced* him as a saint, and they *heard* him as a saint. They perceived that he was a man who knew God, and they wanted what he had. That's a summary of many of the comments devotees have made to me. I've heard literally hundreds of effusive praises of Prabhupāda, such as that every movement that he made seemed to be sacred and pregnant with meaning—even brushing a fly off his forehead, or cooking in the kitchen. It was not just in his formal religious behavior such as singing *kīrtan* or lecturing that they could sense his great power as a holy man. It was in his normal, everyday activities that they saw his purity and deep spirituality as well. So, it's clear that for some of the earliest devotees, Prabhupāda was *the* reason they came. Now, for almost all the early devotees, those who joined during his life, he *became* the reason after they had already joined.

The Role Of The Guru: Historical And Contemporary

SJG: Let me ask you about one issue which a lot of people, especially in the West, have difficulty with: the notion of submitting oneself to a spiritual master, a guru. Perhaps you could first put this issue in a historical framework: What is the purpose and the significance of the guru in Hindu tradition?

LS: Let me preface my comments about the role of guru in

the Vaiṣṇava-Hindu tradition by saying that it's probably the one feature of Vaiṣṇavism that I find most difficult to relate to personally. That being the case, I think I'm a fairly good mirror of our western culture which tends to be extremely individualistic and rationalistic and thus a little uncomfortble with notions of absolute spiritual authority and submission to spiritual authority figures. My attempt to understand the role of guru, hence, is the attempt of an outsider who doesn't himself have any inclination for finding a spiritual master. So, I want to set my comments in that frame so that you understand that it's something which I have tried very hard to understand as I've talked at great length with gurus in the Hare Krishna movement and with disciples—disciples of the living gurus or disciples of Prabhupāda. As an outsider, I've been trying to gain insight into the role of guru and the necessity of that role.

As far as the historical tradition is concerned, well, we'll just have to admit that the notion of guru is a very Asian concept, and I would say Indian concept in its particular Vaiṣṇava form. However, the notion that one can achieve knowledge or experience of the divine through another human being is an age-old notion in many, many religious traditions. You have this notion in the ancient Hebraic context, wherein the prophet sits in the council of God, and when the prophet speaks, it's God's words that he's speaking. Hence, even in translation, the prophet's words are put in quotation marks. The prophet speaks on behalf of God in the first person.

SJG: What does it mean that he "sits in the council of God"?

LS: It means that he is someone who has the ability to encounter God directly—through visions, through dreams, in the interpretation of visions, and so on—and hence speak on God's behalf.

SJG: Could you give some examples of situations that approximate the guru-disciple relationship in the Christian tradition?

LS: In the Christian tradition, the notion that Jesus is the Messiah, the one who comes directly from God's right hand and is God in person, has been a notion that Christians, of course, have fought over for centuries. That is, *what does that mean*? At the least it means that he was a human being whose words and deeds were directly inspired by God Himself. At the most it means that he was God Himself, that he was God who chose to take a human form, that he was God-man. And Christians have, as I said, disagreed over the proper interpretation of that notion for a long, long time. But the important point I'm making is that however Christians resolve the divinity-of-Jesus question, they all do assert that they can come to know God's will by listening to the words of Jesus and by observing Jesus in action, by observing his life. So he serves as a mediator between a divine which cannot be seen and human beings. In the words of one of the hymns of the early Christian community, a statement attributed to John, "No man has seen God. But Jesus, His only Son, has made Him known." So, the idea is that God is so transcendent that people cannot aspire to know Him or to see Him directly, but He can be known and understood through Jesus who is God in human form.

SJG: Other than Jesus himself, are there other examples of the role of guru in Christian tradition? For instance, what about the role of the Abbot in the Catholic monastery? Isn't he the spiritual leader or guide of the community of monks?

LS: No, the Abbot does not play that role exactly. Of any personages in the Catholic tradition, the saints come closest to playing the role of guru, because one can appeal *through* the saints to God. But one does not pray *through* the Abbot to God.

SJG: I'm thinking of the Abbot in this regard not exactly as one through whom the monk reaches God in prayer, but as one who provides spiritual guidance.

LS: Yes, but then it's always assumed that the Abbot can make mistakes. The Abbot is not thought to be infallible in his role as spiritual guide. Also, Abbots are replaced; it's not a role that one has forever.

SJG: I suppose my concept of the Abbot as guru related merely to his practical function as spiritual director and guide.

LS: Yes, but in that sense the meaning of guru becomes too broad. The minister in the Protestant Christian tradition also, in a sense, serves the role of Abbot for his congregation in that he provides spiritual instruction and guidance. But when we speak of the idea of "guru," we mean one who acts as a channel between the worshiper and God. The Abbot is not the one who presents God directly to the various monks of the monastery. It is Jesus who does that. There's no confusion over that role. The monk never assumes that the Abbot is in the disciplic line of Jesus. For the Catholic, the Pope comes closer to the role of guru, inasmuch as he sits in a kind of disciplic succession from Peter, the disciple of Jesus. When the Pope speaks *ex Cathedra*, he is understood to be revealing authentic Christian wisdom. In that sense, he comes closer to the role of guru.

SJG: Can you think of examples from other religious traditions?

LS: In the Islamic tradition, you have the Messenger of God, the *rasūl*, or the Prophet as He is sometimes called. *Lā ilāha illā 'llāh wa-Muḥammadan rasūlu 'llāh:* "There is no God but Allah and Muhammad is His Messenger." That's the *Shahāda*, the confession of faith that is spoken by Muslims five times daiy. It confirms that one comes to know Allah's word directly through His Messenger, Muhammad. And, hence, since the *Qur'an* is the message of the *rasūl*, the Prophet, it is not different from God's own message. So you have this sense in which, again, a human has served as a messenger between God and His people.

So, the whole notion of the role of guru in Indian tradition—the notion of a human being serving as a mediator between humans and the divine—is not unique to the Indian tradition. It seems to me that the distinction between guru, as it is understood in the Vaiṣṇava tradition, and these other figures—prophet, messiah, and messenger—is that the guru becomes the *sole* channel through which one approaches the divine. When I say the "sole channel," I mean that the devotee, in effect, *must* have a guru in order for his worship and love to be carried to God. The disciplic succession, the continuous succession of guru to disciple, is viewed as being a spiritual succession from Krishna through—in your tradition—His *avatāra* Caitanya, down through those who stand in the direct line of Caitanya. The notion is that the guru *is* the channel. He is, as the devotees say, the mailman to which one gives the letter of devotion and who delivers it to Krishna.

SJG: I don't exactly understand how that is different from your description of Jesus or Muhammad who both are, within their traditions, viewed as the channel to God, the channel through whom one can approach God.

LS: Well, they aren't necessarily viewed as exclusive channels to God. They are ones, rather, who serve as messengers of God's word, and hence to follow their teachings is what's critical.

SJG: But then what is the meaning of Jesus' alleged statement, "No one comes to the Father except through Me"?

LS: There are different interpretations of the phrase "through Me." Christianity is not a monolithic tradition. Some Christians interpret "no one comes to the Father except through Me" in very literal terms: that Jesus came as a sacrificial lamb whose blood washed away the payment of all previous and future sins. I have no idea what the percentages are, but my suspicion is that those kinds of Christians are in a distinct minority—those who view him as "the way" in terms of blood payment. But, you see, having made that payment, their prayers and their worship are directed entirely to God, not to Jesus—except for those few who have divinized Jesus to the point where Jesus and God become almost synonomous. But I would say that those Christians are in the minority. A more common understanding of "I am the way, the truth, and the life, and no one comes to the Father but by Me," is that one comes to the Father through the *example* of Jesus—walking in his footsteps one comes to the Father. "If you continue in my word, you are truly my disciples, and you will know the truth, and the truth will make you free." (John 8:31) In that sense "through Me" is understood metaphorically, not literally. In practice itself, there is seldom worship of Jesus as being, somehow, the only channel through which one can reach God. In the largest Christian tradition, Catholicism, Christians pray through Mary and through the various saints. There are many channels in that sense, but those channels are never understood to be exclusive channels—that without them one cannot approach God directly in deep prayer. The Reformation, in fact, made this point: we all are priests to our brothers. The fellowship of priests, in which we all, in a sense, have that same task of directing others to God directly, becomes a strong theme in Christian piety. So, again, Jesus becomes, for some, an *only* channel through blood payment, or an only channel in the sense that we must somehow approach him as an intermediary to the Father. But that is rare in Christianity. The more common understanding is that one can and must approach God directly in prayer; one doesn't depend on Jesus as the only conduit.

Now, the guru tradition, in the Vaiṣṇava context, does insist that the guru is, in fact, the channel to God. One doesn't approach God directly, but through the guru, who is viewed as the direct representative of God. One can pray to God; one can sing and dance in praise of God, but the devotee never forgets his position subordinate to the guru. One's immediate surrender is to the guru, and through him, to God. So, to that extent, the guru becomes an indispensable channel of faith and worship in a way that it does not in these other traditions.

SJG: What you say about the guru as channel to God is, in substance, correct, yet you've put it in a way that strikes me as being a little misleading. Here, perhaps, your western or Christian bias comes in. That bias, in its extreme form, would repudiate the role of guru on the grounds that the guru somehow stands between the devotee and God as an unnecessary middleman, a middleman who in some sense appropriates for himself worship that is really meant for God. In Vaiṣṇava tradition, the idea is that although the disciple worships God through the agency of the guru, his worship is still direct. The fact that the disciple worships and serves God under the guidance and instruction of the guru—and further, that it is the guru who conveys his disciple's worship and service to God—does not mean that the disciple's worship and service aren't direct. The disciple worships and serves God directly, through the guru, just as one sitting indoors may view his garden directly—through the window. That person's line of vision may proceed through the window, but still the vision is direct. In Vaiṣṇava spirituality, the guru is a completely transparent medium. The idea is that without the aid of a spiritually realized person, a devotee is as yet unable to see and approach God independently, due to his own material limitations. The guru can lead others to the path and along the path to God because he himself has traversed that path. He acts as a model, preceptor, and guide. The guru's guidance is not one of mere dogmatic affirmation, but of leading the disciple gradually to direct spiritual experience and communion with God. There is a traditional saying that by the grace of God one finds a guru, and by the grace of guru one finds God. To be able to perform this function of transparent conduit, of course, the guru must himself have attained an exalted state of spirituality, and he must be free from all personal motives in the execution of his role. I don't mean to lecture you, but I thought that this matter of "transparency" deserved some clarification.

Aside from the historical and theological aspects of the notion of guru, what have you discovered about the practical role of guru in the Krishna consciousness movement in your speaking with the devotees and observing life within the movement? In what sense and in what ways is the guru-disciple relationship central in the spiritual lives of the devotees you've spoken with?

LS: In many interviews that I've had, devotees say emphatically that their relationship with their guru is *the* reason that keeps them in ISKCON. Even when it became, for some, difficult to keep the regulative principles, or when they had disputes with other devotees or conflicts with authority figures, very often it was their commitment to Prabhupāda, to their spiritual master, which served as the sustaining force for devotees. And I would even argue that for many older devotees, Prabhupāda still serves, even years after his death, as the sustaining force in the midst of change. That is true also of the new devotees. The new devotees of the movement, who are attached to one of the present eleven initiating spiritual masters likewise view that relationship as being critical. In terms of joining the movement, contact with a guru is often the critical factor. That is, many came to the temple and were not particularly attracted to temple worship or chanting or the philosophy per se. But, when they saw and came into contact with the guru, that was the clincher in terms of helping them to make their decision to join.

SJG: Why was it the clincher?

LS: Well, as I mentioned, many of the people whom I've interviewed so far came to Krishna consciousness out of some personal crisis—vocational, spiritual, or otherwise—and experienced a sense of being uprooted. It would seem that one of the attractions of the guru figure is that one is able to submit to him one's own uncertainties about how to proceed on the spiritual path. One needs some kind of rudder in this sea of pluralism, this sea of confusing and conflicting claims about what is meaningful, and the guru appears to be that kind of rudder. Others are attracted to a guru precisely because they are convinced by the argument that one cannot approach God directly and so they accept a guru because of his position of authority as one standing in the line of disciplic succession. Some devotees found their particular guru attractive because of that guru's powerful spiritual presence. A couple have viewed their gurus as great debaters of their tradition. These are some reasons why people are attracted to gurus in the movement.

There are some devotees who don't have a particularly close relationship with their guru. Although they may see him as absolutely necessary, the guru is not, for them, the key to their being in the movement. There are some people who are not comfortable with being submissive. Some have tried for several years to become submissive and still haven't made it. There is, for many, a constant struggle between one's desire to do what one wants to do and one's responsibility to be submissive to one's spiritual or even administrative authority.

Now, let me put this all in context of my original statement, that for someone like myself, coming out of the Western tradition, it may be difficult to understand the concept of guru. Concerning *guru-pūjā,* the worship and adoration of the guru, although the theology clearly says that this worship ultimately goes to God, there are some people whose adoration and whose simple faith seems to almost end with the guru. Krishna is always there in the background—Krishna is ideally and theologically there—but experientially, they're attached to that guru.

Now, the reason that I myself still have trouble with that, after all these interviews, is because I know what can happen if a guru goes astray. He can lead people into very unfortunate circumstances in terms of their own spiritual development, regardless of the social or institutional consequences of his deviation from the norms of his tradition. When a guru has that kind of authority and misues it for one reason or another, this creates a very difficult situation for those who have submitted to him.

Now, in your tradition, you have checks against that: the guru must speak and act in line with *sādhu* and *śāstra,* with the line of disciplic succession and the scripture. But many of the newer disciples don't know the scriptures and the tradition well enough to consider them in the context of following the guru's injunctions. Consequently, he may become, for some, the sole immediate presence of the Divine Will such that his word will never be questioned even though the traditional checks are there. Now, this sort of thing will not happen with the more mature devotees. But it seems to me that for some novices especially, there is potentially some danger if a guru falls from a high spiritual standard.

Let me say though, that I think the role of guru in ISKCON has an additional feature that it has not always had in India. That is, because the GBC, the Governing Body Commission, was established by Prabhupāda as the over-arching organizational structure within which the gurus play their role, the various gurus of the movement have to work together in a way that is not typical in India. In India, gurus pretty much go their own way, even if they're in the same *sampradāya,* the same sect. They have their own temple or ashram and their own disciples. They have almost full authoritarian reign both spiritually and institutionally. It seems to me that what ISKCON has done with the position of guru is to put some checks and balances into the system, which has the ultimate effect of down-playing that role in the sense of putting the guru in proper perspective to the movement as a whole. This, I would hope, should alleviate some fears of casual bystanders who become worried about gurus being autocratic people who are going to lead their submissive disciples down wrong avenues. In ISKCON, there is a check for gurus who take that tack.

SJG: That check is that all of the gurus in ISKCON are themselves disciples of Śrīla Prabhupāda who founded the movement within which they are functioning as gurus. So, naturally, there is a sense of loyalty, on their part, to the institution founded by their own guru, and its organizational structure, the GBC. Prabhupāda used to say that the real test of his disciples' love for him will be whether they will be able to cooperate together in maintaining and spreading the Krishna consciousness movement after he passes away.

LS: Although that's the principal view of the relationship between the gurus and the GBC, I don't think that it's the only one. Traditionally, when one has that seat of authority as the guru, one has a certain independence in interpretation and action. Because the theology says that the guru is in a direct line of spiritual succession, some wonder whether the institution as such can dictate to the guru how he should interpret his tradition. The GBC, it seems to me, might be viewed by some as an institutional intrusion into the spiritual line, while at the same time it might be an absolutely indispensable organ of the institution itself.

SJG: The orthodox view would be that the GBC, far from being an institutional intrusion into the spiritual line, is an important expression of that line inasmuch as this particular institutional structure, the GBC, was established by Śrīla Prabhupāda himself, the previous guru in that line, as a means for keeping the movement on the track spiritually. The whole concept of spiritual succession, *guru-paramparā*, is that the guru must act in accordance with the instructions of his own guru and of the previous gurus in succession. In this sense, submission to that institutional structure can be viewed as an act of obedience to the disciplic succession, at least insofar as the GBC remains loyal to Śrīla Prabhupāda's moral and spiritual imperatives.

LS: The real test of the GBC, then, is whether it remains an organ of vital spiritual direction or becomes merely an instrument of institutional control. Let us hope that the former remains the case.

The Role of Chanting

SJG: I think you've summarized the issue well. Now, unless there's something you'd like to add about these points, I'd like to hear what you believe to be the role that chanting of the Hare Krishna mantra plays in the movement. Perhaps you could look at it historically and theologically, and then talk about the significance of chanting in ISKCON.

LS: The whole notion of chanting, in the Indian context, is based upon a fundamental theological assumption that goes back to the earliest Vedas—that there is a homology between sound and reality. Sounds have spiritual significance. They can function not merely as metaphors, but as direct links with the sacred realm. Throughout Indian religious history, it has been the case that the mantra, or the sacred sound, has been one avenue through which one could directly experience God, or the Divine. We find this concept not only in both theistic and non-theistic Hinduism, but also in other religious traditions originating in India, such as Buddhism and the Sikh tradition. So, meditation on or recitation of sacred sounds is a very ancient tradition in India and is clearly not new to the Vaiṣṇavas.

Now, what the Vaiṣṇavas have done, in the Caitanya tradition in particular, is to make the recitation of the Divine Name the central religious activity. As Caitanya would exclaim, "The name of Hari, the name of Hari, the name of Hari alone liberates one in this age." The point is that the name or names of God, as you have explained in your recent article on the subject,* are non-different from God Himself. Chanting is, in effect, an alternative kind of prayer. It is

*"The Nectar of the Holy Name." *Back to Godhead* 15 (3-4): 21-28, 1981.

similar to, and has many of the same functions as, meditation in its more quiestistic forms. It is similar to prayer in the Christian tradition and to devotional singing and dancing in some other traditions.

Now, the role of chanting in ISKCON follows very closely that handed down from Caitanya's day. Caitanya's movement was a chanting movement. Very much as John Wesley is said to have sung Methodism into England, Caitanya danced and chanted Vaiṣṇavism into Bengal and even beyond Bengal. And you could say also that Prabhupāda chanted Vaiṣṇavism into America and the western world. So chanting is definitely a primary religious activity, and a central theological feature of the movement.

Devotees have realizations and deep spiritual experiences from a number of devotional activities other than chanting, of course. Some find it in the worship of the forms of Krishna in the temple. Some find it in studying the scriptures. Others find their highest satisfaction in book distribution. They feel that they experience Krishna's presence in the act of transmitting Krishna's words, the scriptures, to non-devotees.

But for some, to be sure, chanting is the center of their spiritual practice. In some cases, it's clear that devotees have had their greatest experiences and insights from chanting. Some spoke of "tasting" the words of the mantra. Some spoke of experiencing the presence of Krishna, if not in the immediate sense, in a general sense of feeling the divine presence, or they develop a very acute religious-aesthetic sense of the presence of Krishna in the Deities, the temple images. Clearly, in these cases, the chanting is providing for these devotees what the tradition and the theology claim it will.

Spreading the Word: Book Distribution

SJG: One of the activities you mentioned as being a major source of inspiration for some devotees is the distribution of religious literature. Throughout the ISKCON world, devotees daily go out into public places such as airports and downtown areas, distribute the movement's publications and collect donations. Some people tend to condemn this as a commercial enterprise meant to raise large sums of money from the innocent and unsuspecting public and to use those funds for increasing the personal wealth of the movement's leaders. Now, you've spoken with a number of devotees who have been involved in literature distribution for varying amounts of time. What is the devotees' own perception of what they're doing? What is the theological significance of book distribution over and above the financial purpose it serves?

LS: I may surprise you because I tend not to separate the economic dimension from the religious dimension, because I think theologically the understanding is that both are necessary and are interconnected. Theologically, it is understood that the words of the authentic guru are a genuine transmission of the words of Krishna Himself. Hence, the publishing and distribution of Prabhupāda's books is the distribution of God's word, especially inasmuch as Prabhupāda's books are viewed as authoritative editions of traditional scriptures. And it is felt that in this age, the printed word is perhaps the best form of spreading Krishna consciousness. That is the theological underpinning.

But it is likewise Prabhupāda's teaching—as he is interpreted by many of the movement's leaders—that "Just distribute God's word (in the form of books) and don't worry about your livelihood; it will automatically come to you." It is assumed, theologically, that there will always necessarily be a connection between the spreading of God's word and the receiving of Krishna's support both in terms of basic sustenance, food and lodging, and also various ISKCON projects such as temple construction. Beyond mere sustenance and development, though, much or in some cases most of the money collected from the distribution of literature is turned right back into books which are then distributed. Some funds are used for distribution of *prasāda*, sanctified food, to the public. So my point is that this movement has chosen to theologically wed the spreading of God's word and the receiving of money as God's support of the people who spread His word.

SJG: Of course, the consciousness with which the devotees distribute books certainly is not "let us distribute these books so that we can live comfortably."

LS: No, of course not. I agree. Let me give you an idea of how some of the people who distribute books view book distribution, and this will make it clear. I spoke to a devotee recently—one of the devotees who feel that they've received some of their highest spiritual realizations through book distribution—who said that if he goes out selling books with fruitive intents and his primary motive is to raise funds and make himself look good by bringing back lots of money to the temple, he usually has a terrible day, and the members of the public respond with a degree of distrust and suspicion. But, on the other hand, when his *sādhana*, his spiritual practices, are strong (when he chants his morning rounds conscientiously and attends the full morning program) and he goes out into public in the proper frame of mind—the frame of mind of sincerely trying to spread Krishna consciousness through these books—the money just seems to flow in. So when you just try to get money, it doesn't happen. The times when the money does come in is precisely the times when you see yourself distributing God's word. I get some fairly consistent points of view among those people who find book distribution to be a very important part of their spiritual lives.

On the other hand, it seems to me that there are people in the movement for whom book distribution is a problem. It's a problem either because, in some cases, they simply don't like to do it, in which case they will get involved with some other kind of service within the movement or, in other cases, because they question some of the tactics that have been used sometimes in book distribution. They feel that even slightly misrepresenting their identity or their purpose is unnecessary or counter-productive. Some people love to distribute Prabhupāda's books but dislike selling items which in themselves may have no direct spiritual significance but are products that bring in money, such as incense or candles. So I think that within the movement itself there are a good variety of experiences of, and opinions about, book distribution itself and money-making ventures on the whole.

It is my impression, likewise, that the movement has undergone some relatively important changes recently in trying to improve its dealings with the public. I spoke with one new devotee recently and I asked him what he was being taught to say on the streets. What he was being taught to say was a fairly faithful rendition of the theology of book distribution. He was taught that he is distributing Krishna's word and that he should not focus upon the amount of money he was receiving, that that was not the important thing. The important thing was distributing the word and getting it out to as many people as possible and, further, that in order to do so, his spiritual practices, his *sādhana*, had to be strong. If he did so, and if he acted purely and honestly in public contacts, the money would automatically come. So that seems to me to be a very good direction. I would say that at present, cases of dishonesty in dealings with the public are rare. Most people who go out and do book distribution find they can't do it day after day acting on some kind of "lower platform," in your language. The ones who continue to do it year after year tend to be people who really find the spreading of Prabhupāda's words to be the critical factor.

"Brainwashing" and "Deprogramming"

SJG: Let me ask you about an issue which has engendered a good deal of public controversy over the last several years: the issue of "brainwashing." There has developed an image, reflected in or even defined by the popular press, of the "brainwashed cultist" whose mind is controlled by nefarious cult leaders and who becomes a sort of non-thinking "zombie." This stereotype has at times been applied to the Hare Krishna movement. Now, what is the source or sources of this image? How did it develop?

LS: Well, they get it from a number of different sources. One source is the media. The media have exposed certain kinds of recruiting techniques which seem to be similar to the so-called brainwashing techniques used during the Korean War by the Chinese Communists. For example, some reporters have gone incognito into one group in particular and have discovered what appeared to them to be techniques of coercion: sleep deprivation, food deprivation, and so on, and have then come out and written exposés. Because the public is largely ignorant of the great differences between the various groups referred to as "cults," it's assumed that if one group is doing that then they all are. So there's guilt by association.

The groups which the media generally present as the major cults are the Unification Church (the Moonies), the Hare Krishnas, Scientology, the Way, Guru Maharaj Ji's Divine Light Mission, and the Children of God. Those are the six that come up again and again and are linked together. Now, anybody who knows anything at all about those six groups, knows that there are tremendous differences in the way they each recruit new members, yet the public, out of ignorance, lumps them all together. So one thing that "brainwashing" means as an active or verbal term is the process of coercing someone who has one point of view to accept another radically different point of view, against their will. I don't think that is happening in any groups of which I'm aware.

A second reason the public has this impression is because there are some former members of these groups—people who have been "deprogrammed" out of them or have left for any one of a variety of reasons—who will describe life in these groups in very bleak terms. Such people, of course, often don't want to accept responsibility for having joined those groups in the first place and thus they find it convenient to attribute their involvement in them to a coercive outside influence, such as brainwashing. Under the auspices of anti-cult and deprogramming organizations, such people will often describe how they lived in a brainwashed state while in the group.

This brings up a second dimension of brainwashing which I call the "nominal" aspect, that is, brainwashing as a state of mind—not as the process by which one hypothetically comes to the brainwashed state, but the state of mind itself. In that hypothetical state of mind, one has been divested of free will and has lost the power of critical thinking and decision making. One becomes "zombie-like," "spaced-out," while living in the tightly-controlled, regimented world of the cult. Now, from my experiences of the practices and life style of the Hare Krishna movement, far from conformity, I find non-conformity much more the norm. I could explain that at great length, but let it suffice for now saying that there is a tremendous variety of different modes of life and behavior in the movement. It just seems to me, therefore, that one of the causes of the popular brainwashing stereotype are the allegations of extreme regimentation and conformity coming from people who have left the movement, people who, for a variety of reasons, have questionable motives for the way in which they describe life within the movement.

A third reason—and this perhaps is the most important and most complex reason— is that parents of new members encounter their children whom they thought they knew, and have experienced virtually new people. Now that's not necessarily a misperception on the part of the parents. In the early years of the movement, there was not, in some cases, a great deal of encouragement for devotees to keep up communication with parents. So already, because of this, a parent feels a sense of distance, a feeling of "What are they doing with *my* child?"

But when there is an encounter, and the son or daughter in the movement begins to speak—as I saw on one episode of the Lou Grant show about a young man becoming a devotee—what does he say? "Hare Krishna." The mother starts talking with her son who identifies himself by his new Sanskrit name: "I'm Śubhānanda now, I'm not Steven." The parents try to appeal to the child's logic and in response they get preached at from a very enthusiastic and, to a great extent, yet uninformed point of view. So, what are the parents hearing? The parents are hearing their child who has given up the name that they had given him, a child who, because of his inexpertise and his apprehension about the parents' response to the radical step he's taken, sounds nervous, who is preaching a strange philosophy which he has only partially absorbed. If I as a parent were to hear one of my children come at me with that kind of approach, I would feel that I was encountering a very different person.

How does one explain, then, that radical transformation? One way to explain it is, "Somebody has done this to my child. Somebody brainwashed him." I would say that this is probably the most immediate reason why many people find brainwashing a believable notion—because what they encounter is, in fact, a person who has changed radically.

Now, let's point out immediately that throughout religious history, parents have made the same kind of response to their children who have made those kinds of choices. In the early years of his ministry, the Buddha had to make a requirement that every underage member had to have a written consent from his parents, because the parents were absolutely up-in-arms that he was taking away their children, often from middle-class or upper-class economic surroundings, the royalty classes, from lives of leisure and luxury into an austere, ascetical lifestyle. That was a real problem for parents. It was also a problem in the days of Jesus. It was a problem in the early days of some of the early Muslim saints. And so I don't think we should find it surprising that parents—who in most cases have invested a tremendous amount of psychic energy in their children and who love them dearly—feel threatened by their children joining the Hare Krishna movement. Loving them dearly, they wish for their children things which they as parents view as being valuable and meaningful, and thus can almost totally misunderstand their child's adoption of a new and different way. So, I think those are the main reasons why the notion of brainwashing seems plausible to some people outside the movement.

SJG: Is there anything the movement could do to minimize parents' fears in this regard?

LS: I think one thing that has gone a long way to minimizing these fears has been the movement's encouraging contact between the new devotee and his parents from the very beginning, both by inviting the parents to the temple, and by having the new devotee return home to visit his or her parents, at least unless the parents have expressed such extreme adversity to the movement that it seems likely that they may try to kidnap and deprogram the devotee. It's been much more the case in recent years that young people have kept closer contact with their parents all the way along the line.

It might also help if you were to instruct new devotees about how different they will appear to their parents and urge them to minimize that difference initially, especially by not coming on too strongly with preaching. Preaching to their parents will accomplish nothing except encourage the parents to believe that their son or daughter is brainwashed, and it certainly is not going to convert any parents. There have been no parents who have been converted to Krishna consciousness by their kid's preaching to them on the first phone call home. The most that one could hope to do, initially, is to rebuild bridges of communication, which would allow that new member to convince his parents that he's still thinking for himself and simply has found something that he's very excited about and wants to share. That sharing often does happen eventually.

SJG: We've been discussing why the idea of "brainwashing" comes up at all in the public mind. What is your personal view of the matter?

LS: As far as I can tell, "brainwashing"—in the classical or technical sense of taking a person who holds one set of attitudes and ideas and forcefully eradicating those attitudes and ideas and supplanting them with others—simply is not common anywhere. I take this from people who have studied brainwashing extensively such as Robert J. Lifton, J. A. C. Brown and others who argue also that even in cases where you find radical changes in attitudes or ideas, there was an inclination to accept those changes in the first place. So, I'm adopting that as a basic assumption. From this point of view, "brainwashing," in the sense of wiping out previous memories, clearing the slate of the mind and imprinting something totally new, just can't be done.

What you *can* do, is to exert various kinds of persuasion on people, and that persuasion can be coercive. That's what happens in the case of some political indoctrination as was found, for instance, during the Korean War. In these classical cases, persuasion becomes coercive because it is accompanied by imprisonment, food deprivation, sleep deprivation, fear of potential loss of life, punishments and even torture. Under that sort of physical and psychological pressure, the attempt was made to have people "confess" their previous mode of thought and behavior as being terrible and wrong, to have them accept as a tutor the person who had subjected them to that coercive process who then re-educates them in a new mode of thought and behavior. Even with all these forms of extreme coercion, "brainwashing" or coercive persuasion is effective in less than thirty percent of the cases, according to Lifton and Brown.

So, it's ludicrous to talk about "brainwashing," even in the least restrictive sense, in regards to the new religious groups in America, at least any of whom I'm aware, even the ones which I find to be destructive cults. Brainwashing just is not taking place. I think persuasion, a milder form of indoctrination, does take place—persuasion which does involve convincing someone that the view they've held is wrong and that another is correct. But, as I've said, now we're talking about someone making a personal decision to change his way of life and his view of the world. That happens in a wide variety of circumstances including the Hare Krishna movement, and we discussed that earlier in terms of how people come to the movement and why, in many cases, they stay in the movement. Your movement happens to be among those which I would call the "low-key movements"—low-key in terms of recruiting people into the movement. The attempt to bring someone from the outside into the movement does not involve any of the classical features of political indoctrination or any heavy kind of coercive persuasion. It's just not present here. But, more importantly, the style of preaching tends much more to be just that: preaching—certainly preaching hard and preaching enthusiastically, preaching with all the powers of intellect on full throttle, but it's just that, it's preaching.

SJG: Have you found any other evidences against the notion of "brainwashing" as applied to the Hare Krishna movement?

LS: As I said, "brainwashing" means two different things. One is the process itself, the process by which someone becomes "brainwashed," and that's what I've been discussing thus far. Secondly, you have the supposed state of mind that is achieved through the process. And that's the state referred to when people speak of "glazed eyes," and so forth. Well, I don't see any "glazed eyes" in the Hare Krishna movement. I shouldn't say I don't see any. I see very few "glazed eyes." When I do see "glazed eyes," it's often when devotees are chanting on the streets or in the temple during the *ārati* ceremony and are sort of lost in the ecstasy of dancing and chanting and singing. Sure they are lost in their dancing and singing, just as people can get "lost" in a Beethoven symphony or in watching football on television. What might be misinterpreted from the outside as being a symptom of a brainwashed state might be, in fact, the joy of someone who is just really deeply into their religious music or dance. From the outsider's point of view they may seem to have "glazed eyes," but from the insider's point of view, they are experiencing ecstasy derived from intense religious worship.

SJG: Now, what about the much publicized attempts at "rescuing" people from brainwashing through what is popularly called "deprogramming"?

LS: I'll be brief. If anything approximates the process of brainwashing, in the sense of coercive political indoctrination—those processes which include inducement of fear for one's own emotional or even physical well-being, and which also include intense verbal haranguing and harassment—deprogramming fits that description. Likewise, the state that people achieve after having been deprogrammed, if that deprogramming is successful, is very much a zombie-like state, if by "zombie-like state" we mean parroting what your master has told you to parrot. Deprogramming, certainly, does not mean giving one the ability to "think freely again," as its proponents often claim. It means making people think the way you think they ought to think, again. And so, to that extent, deprogramming comes the closest to brainwashing of any of the processes and any of the results I've seen in these new religious movements.

One interesting point is that those people who are engaged in deprogramming have a much tougher time, for the most part, with Krishna devotees than they do with members of most other groups, because few of the deprogrammers know anything about the movement's theology and very little about what actually goes on in the movement. So, when they make exaggerated allegations to the devotee whom they are trying to deprogram, such as that the Hare Krishna children are pulled out of bed at two in the morning and thrown into cold showers and forced to dance before idols, the devotee is just sitting there laughing to himself or herself, because these things just don't go on. So the deprogrammers often come off looking like total buffoons because they don't know what in the devil they're doing. It's almost a humorous situation in which people who are terribly paranoid about the Hare Krishna movement have so exaggerated their claims against the movement that they become ineffectual in trying to deprogram someone out of it. Deprogramming will continue to be mostly unsuccessful, I believe, among those people who have any serious level of commitment to the movement. My suspicion—and it's a suspicion which I think can be borne out by the evidence—is that those people who are successfully deprogrammed are people who would probably have dropped out anyway, somewhere along the line.

ISKCON: Its Development as a Religious Institution / The Future

SJG: In the course of interviewing devotees, you must have gotten some perspective on the historical development of ISKCON from a small cult-like group centered around one holy man, to a more complex, international religious institution. How would you characterize that development and what are the implications of those institutional developments?

LS: First of all, I would not use the word "cult" any longer. It used to be a word that one could use without having pejorative connotations attached to it. Anyway, ISKCON has never been a cult. It has been a sect. It is a sect in the sense that it is a *sampradāya*, a denomination. It's one of the important strands of Bhakti Hinduism. It came to America and formed a new missionary movement.

ISKCON is a religious movement that is in the throes of

becoming a religious institution. And that's one of the reasons I'm excited about the study that I'm doing at the moment because I think we're seeing right before our eyes the attempt to codify, to regularize, and to institutionalize religious faith, religious practice—in fact, the attempt to govern a whole religious way of life. All "institutionalization" means is habitualization, that is, beginning to do things in regular ways, in such a way that there is a certain conformity required in organizational structure, in leadership, in religious practice, in publishing requirements, and in role models. What began initially as a group of counterculture youth who had decided to drop out of the drug scene and to drop into getting "high" on chanting, who were a fairly loose rag-tag organization—not even an organization but a group of people attached to an elderly guru who had come from India—has developed into a fairly complex and sophisticated institution. I can hardly attempt to summarize the history of that remarkable evolution in a few minutes, but let me point out some of the important changes.

One development is in the ritual expression of the movement. What began, in the earliest days of the movement, as a fairly simple and informal spiritual program consisting of *kīrtan*, *japa*, and altar worship developed, over the years, into a much more evolved and regularized spiritual regimen. Deity worship itself became standardized throughout the movement, with old Sanskrit religious texts becoming the foundation for a proper performance of the *ārati* ceremony.

One of the things that developed gradually as the movement grew—and this happens with all new religious traditions—was that the founder of the movement, Prabhupāda, no longer could be every place at once, and thus he began to distribute authority. About seven years before he passed away, Prabhupāda established a Governing Body Commission, the GBC, consisting of a number of senior disciples each of whom became responsible for overseeing ISKCON's activities in a particular part of the world. Through the GBC, Prabhupāda distributed authority in the realm of management—management which had to attend to economic, political, and public relations matters. Beginning with his establishment of the GBC, Prabhupāda began gradually to divorce himself from these sorts of ordinary institutional operations so that he could spend more of his time translating, traveling, and teaching.

With Prabhupāda's passing away came the next stage, the stage not only in which all managerial responsibilities passed completely into the hands of the GBC, but now in which spiritual control—or better yet, the spreading out of the responsibility of keeping the movement on target in terms of its spiritual practices—was disseminated among eleven particular disciples who took on the role of guru and began to initiate new members as disciples. At present, the movement is having to make critical decisions about how it's going to exist in a world that demands that tax laws be followed, and that religious practice and proselytization be kept within certain bounds according to the laws of the land. One magnifies that manyfold when one looks beyond America to various other countries where there are different sorts of legal, political, economic, and other kinds of restrictions that one must be aware of.

So, what began as a fairly simple organization characterized by spontaneous expression of devotion to one guru has become a complex institution with various leaders responsible for various parts of the world—a situation of institutional complexity which can easily give rise to factionalism and fragmentation. It seems to me that ISKCON is right now at the point of recognizing that this kind of fragmentation can be self-destructive to the institution itself, and hence the question, "Who is really running the show?" Is it the various initiating gurus who guide the spiritual lives of their own suborganizations of disciples, or is it the Governing Body Commission which has, as its task, to hold the whole of ISKCON on a similar and unified course? ISKCON, right now, is going through the growing pains of trying to find a way to accommodate its institutional form and its spiritual inside direction. It seems to me that the tension is in trying to keep vital the spiritual dimension that was there from the very beginning, which is represented in the guru-*śiṣya* relationship, in a context where the gurus are now several, where disciples claim allegiance to a plurality of gurus yet, nevertheless, have to claim a common allegiance institutionally.

SJG: From your point of view, what are ISKCON's chances of survival as a religious institution?

LS: It seems to me that one of the advantages that ISKCON has as an institution is that it has built into its institutional structure and into its religious life an emphasis both on the conceptual dimension of religiosity as well as the experiential dimension. Rather than relying entirely upon *convincing* people of its truths, the movement has allowed them to experience those truths in living—the truth about the world, about the soul, about Krishna, and about the path to Krishna. So, I think ISKCON has, at least in its initial formation, tried to incorporate both the cognitive and the affective dimensions of the religious life. Many institutions in the West have tried to capture only the cognitive side and have failed to develop the affective dimension and, hence, have become relatively lifeless.

The history of institutionalization in other religious contexts has shown that once a movement has become institutionalized, it may become difficult to sustain the original spiritual enthusiasm and spontaneity. Most sociologists and psychologists of religion simply don't take seriously enough the extent to which religious institutions are a product of religious enthusiasm and the extent, ultimately, to which the institution tries then to regulate and control the enthusiasm. To use the sociological language of Peter Novak, human beings must live with institutions, but the very moment they create institutions they feel uncomfortable with the very institutions they've created. Now, I think ISKCON is going to discover that it's increasingly difficult to sustain the original vision and the original enthusiasm of Krishna consciousness as years and decades and generations pass, when someday the members of ISKCON will be three or four generations removed from anyone who had direct contact with Prabhupāda, when future gurus will not themselves be direct disciples of Prabhupāda. It is with the passage of time that the institution will have its test of vitality. I think the movement will fare well precisely to the extent that the leaders adhere to the spiritual practices taught by Prabhupāda and have achieved the kinds of levels of spiritual advancement that come with those practices. To the extent that the institution and its leaders cannot keep the spiritual life of Krishna consciousness vital, the institution will become moribund, as other religious institutions have in the course of history.

I think the future of ISKCON will be as bright as its leadership. The institutional and religious practices are in place for vitality. But the key will be, from my point of view, how effective the leadership is—the leadership of its gurus and of the GBC. And I don't mean leadership in the economic, political, and administrative spheres. I mean its leadership in the spiritual dimension. The gurus, especially, must *be* pure devotees, if the guru-disciple relationship is to bear real fruit. It is spiritual integrity and purity that is going to provide the key to the durability of the movement.

Srīla A. C. Bhaktivedanta Swami Prabhupāda (1896—1977), the founder and spiritual master of the International Society for Krishna Consciousness.

The Divine Couple: Lord Krishna (the "Supreme Personality of Godhead") and Rādhā, His eternal consort.

Śrī Caitanya, sixteenth century saint and divine incarnation whose life and teachings are the inspiration for the Krishna consciousness movement.

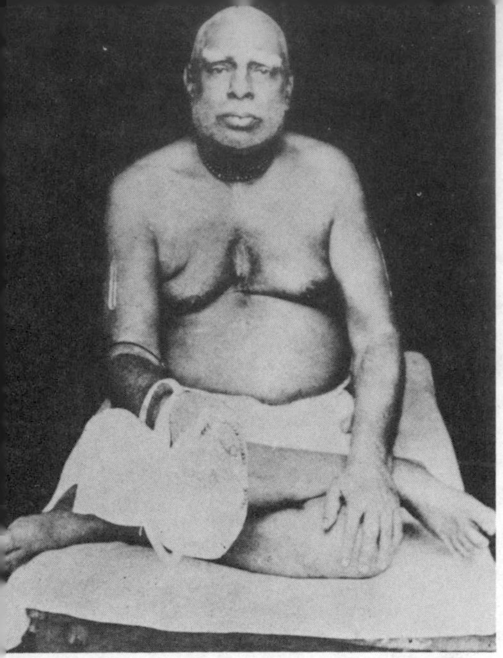

Bhaktivinoda Ṭhākura (1838-1914), pioneer of a revival of the Caitanya movement in the late nineteenth century.

The brothers Sanātana and Rūpa Gosvāmī, two of the "Six Gosvāmīs of Vṛndāvana"—chief scholars and theologians of the Caitanya movement.

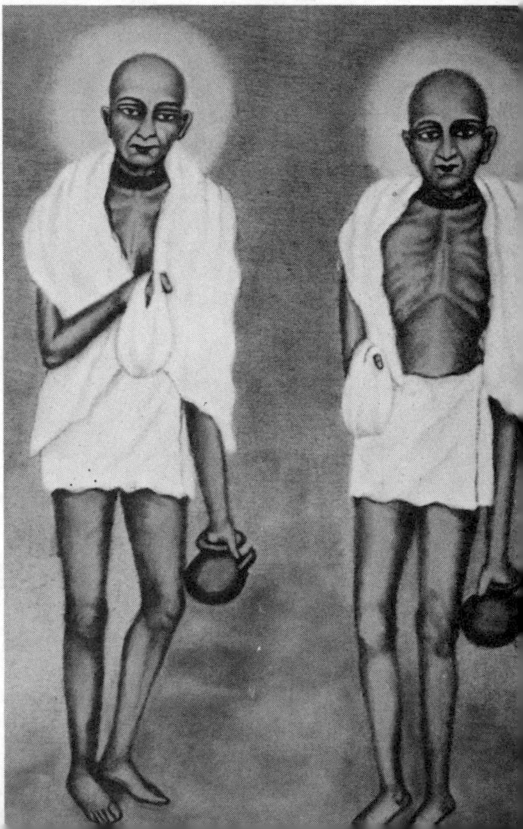

Devotees gathered in the temple to hear an early morning discourse on the *Bhāgavatam*.

Śrīla Prabhupāda dictating English commentary to the *Śrīmad-Bhāgavatam*.

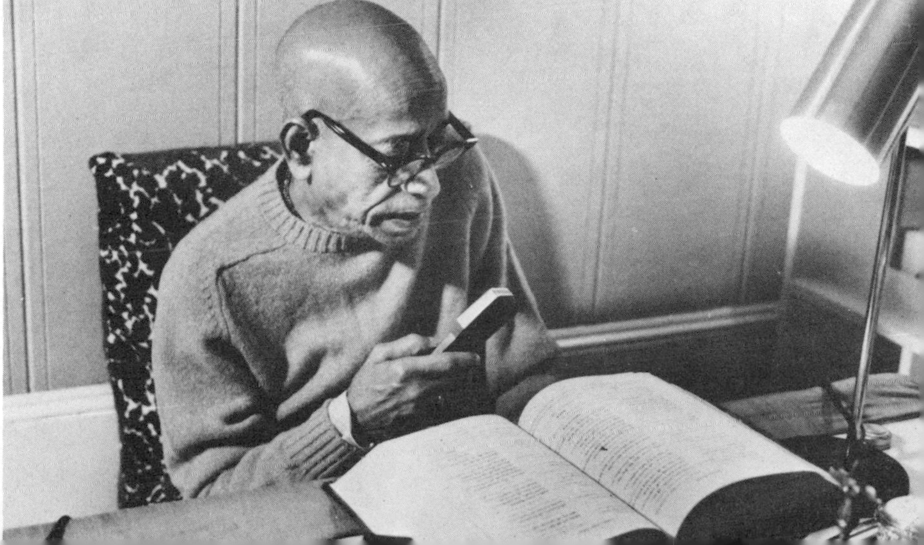

Bhaktisiddhānta Sarasvatī, Bhaktivinoda's son who continued his father's mission and who commissioned A.C. Bhaktivedanta Swami (Śrīla Prabhupāda), his disciple, to spread Krishna consciousness to the West.

Śrīla Prabhupāda with a group of enthusiastic disciples.

INTERVIEW WITH THOMAS J. HOPKINS

Dr. Thomas J. Hopkins received his doctorate in comparative religion from Yale University, and is currently Professor and Chairman of the Department of Religious Studies at Franklin and Marshall College in Lancaster, Pennsylvania, where he has taught since 1961. A teacher of Asian religious traditions, he specializes in Hindu devotional movements, Purāṇic and popular Hinduism, and the *Bhagavad-gītā* and its interpreters. His research interests also include "new religions" in America, yoga, meditation, and altered states of consciousness. His publications include the widely-used college text *The Hindu Religious Tradition* in the Religious Life of Man series (Los Angeles: Dickenson, 1971), "The Social Teachings of the "*Bhāgavata Purāṇa*" in *Krishna: Myths, Rites and Attitudes* (Chicago: University of Chicago Press, 1966), and articles on "Bhakti Hinduism," "Vishnu," and "Pūjā" in the *Abingdon Dictionary of Living Religions* (Nashville: Abingdon, 1981).

Professor Hopkins was the first professional scholar to take an active interest in the Hare Krishna movement. In the spring of 1967, he heard that there was a holy man from India who had founded a Vaiṣṇava devotional center in New York City. Having done his doctoral thesis on popular Vaiṣṇava devotional movements and the *Bhāgavata Purāṇa*, and desiring to continue his research in this field, he paid a visit to the center and thus came into contact with the newly incorporated International Society for Krishna Consciousness and its founder, A.C. Bhaktivedanta Swami Prabhupāda. Intrigued by this first encounter, he applied for and received a grant to study the movement first hand. Not long after he began his research, his interest shifted from viewing the movement merely as an access point to India's devotional tradition, to an interest in the movement itself and how it was transplanting the Vaiṣṇava devotional tradition to the West. He found himself also intrigued by Bhaktivedanta Swami himself, especially in his role as holy man and religious leader. Since that time, Dr. Hopkins has continued to monitor the growth and development of the movement with keen interest.

The following interview took place in Dr. Hopkin's office at Franklin and Marshall College in October, 1979 (with a supplemental telephone interview in September, 1981). Here, Professor Hopkins focuses most of his attention on the problem of cross-cultural transference of the *bhakti* tradition, and on the role of Bhaktivedanta Swami in that unique historical process.

Bhakti Tradition And The Task Of Cross-Cultural Transference: Krishna Consciousness Comes West

SJG: Your experience of the Krishna consciousness movement goes back to its infancy in the Lower East Side of New York, doesn't it?

TH: I believe I was one of the first outsiders to take a serious scholarly interest in it.

SJG: How did you first come into contact with the movement and what was the movement like in those early days?

TH: Back around 1960 and '61, I was doing research for my dissertation at Yale on the Vaiṣṇava *bhakti* movement in the *Bhāgavata Purāṇa.* As part of an effort to understand the meaning of the *Bhāgavata Purāṇa,* I had to look at a variety of devotional movements which draw inspiration from that text, such as the Ālvār tradition in Tamil Nadu, the devotional movements of Maharastra, and also the Caitanya movement of Bengal. I became interested in the Caitanya movement particularly because a friend of mine, Ed Dimock of the University of Chicago, was working in that area.

After I completed my thesis, I wanted to pursue the devotional movements in further research. I continued to correspond and talk regularly with Ed Dimock about the nature of the Caitanya movement. But because I was not a Bengal scholar as Ed was, I had to find alternative means to gain access to this material. Now, during this period, I heard (I don't even recall now how I heard or where I heard) that there was a *sādhu* from India who had come to New York City and had started a Vaiṣṇava devotional center there. Since I couldn't visit India at that point, I was really excited at the prospect of finally having access to someone who knew something about the Caitanya movement in Bengal.

So in the spring of 1967 I went to New York to visit the temple at 26 Second Avenue. I approached a group of the disciples who were there at the time, and I said, "I'm here to try to find out something about Caitanya." And I just got all these totally blank looks, and they said, "Caitanya? Who is Caitanya?" And I said, "Well, Caitanya was a saint in Bengal, a great religious leader." "Oh, that's very interesting," they said, "we didn't know about this." So, I gave them a mini-lecture on Caitanya and the Caitanya movement. And then I said, "Well, isn't there anyone here who knows anything about this?" Back then, of course, all the devotees were very new—the movement was in its infant stages—and there wasn't anyone who had much background in the tradition. One of the people who had been there a little longer than the others said, "Well, I think I've heard that name before. I believe that Swamiji has mentioned that name, 'Caitanya.' "

So I said, "Well, how about the *Bhāgavata Purāṇa*? I did my dissertation on it, and I'm really interested in finding out more about it." So they said, "Oh, you mean the *Bhagavad-gītā*." I said, "No, not the *Bhagavad-gītā*, the *Bhāgavata Purāṇa*." And they said, "Well, we know about the *Bhagavad-gītā*, but we're not sure about the *Bhāgavata*

Purāṇa." Then somebody spoke up and said, "Oh, aren't they those volumes that we have for sale out there on the table?" And I said, "Well, let me take a look at it and I'll see." So, sure enough, there was a three-volume set of Bhaktivedanta Swami's translation and commentary on the *Bhāgavata Purāṇa*. Bhaktivedanta Swami had brought them over with him from India and they were for sale, so I bought them.

In spite of the fact that the movement was in such an undeveloped form at that time, my curiosity was sparked, so I made subsequent visits to the temple. I was able to do so because in the fall of 1967 I applied for and received a grant from the Research Committee of Franklin and Marshall College to study the movement. Between the fall of 1967 and the spring of 1969, I visited the temple perhaps a dozen times, both at its original location at 26 Second Avenue and at its next location further up Second Avenue. My study of the movement from the inside was greatly aided by a student of mine, Eugene Hall, who lived with the disciples for some time and recorded their activities as part of an independent research project carried out under my direction.

SJG: Did you get a chance to personally meet Bhaktivedanta Swami during any of these subsequent visits?

TH: During the first year I was visiting the temple, Bhaktivedanta Swami was seriously ill and inaccessible for private meetings most of the time. The following year he was seldom in New York because of extensive traveling to other centers of the Society. So I was not able to speak with him individually during that period. I did, however, see him on several occasions, as when I attended a wedding which he performed in the temple for two devotee couples in May of 1968. In May of 1969, I completed an agreement with Bhaktivedanta Swami for him to teach a course on the *Bhagavad-gītā* at Franklin and Marshall the following spring, but unfortunately he became ill during the fall of 1969 and could not go through with the plans. I thus missed that chance to spend extended time with him, and there was no further opportunity to see him for several years. My last contact with him was in July, 1975, when I had an extended interview with him in Philadelphia, at the temple there. As you can see, my personal contacts with Bhaktivedanta Swami were generally brief and sporadic, the longest direct contact being the meeting in Philadelphia. I was nonetheless impressed by him from the beginning, and perhaps especially impressed by the influence which he exerted on so many people whose careers I've followed over the years.

SJG: Did you have substantial dialogues with any of the devotees during these early visits?

TH: I had a number of rather frustrating and abortive conversations, because as soon as I would pursue any kind of technical question the devotees would blank out on me. They really didn't know anything about the Indian background. They didn't know anything about Caitanya, they didn't know anything about Bengal. The *Caitanya-caritāmṛta* was a text they had never heard of. At that stage everything was at such a minimal level that the chanting of the Hare Krishna mantra was about all that most of them really knew. Newcomers were taught the mantra and were given chanting beads and taught how to use them. That was about it as far as ritual practice is concerned. This was back in the eclectic stage of the movement, when the *bhajans* were more imaginative than authentic. People would come in off the street bringing whatever instrument they happened to play and simply dive into the *bhajan*. There were guitars, banjos, saxophones, harmonicas—whatever people were able to play. There was an Indian drum—a *mṛdaṅga*—in the temple, but of course there weren't any *mṛdaṅga* players. There were western drummers, and so they were doing a kind of jazz-rock drumming on the *mṛdaṅga*. So it was kind of catch-as-catch-can. Very few really knew at that point that there *was* a formal structure. No one really had much of a sense of what the India connection was. India was just a mysterious, far-away place. The fact that Bhaktivedanta Swami had brought his teachings from India really didn't connect, for most people, to the fact that there was a tradition in India that he represented. The devotees' attention was fixed on Bhaktivedanta Swami himself, whom they saw as a highly evolved holy man who was introducing a kind of simple ritual chanting.

So, that should give you some idea of the devotees' level of understanding and involvement in Vaiṣṇava culture in those earliest days, and where the movement was, at that point in time, in terms of its actual manifestation of that tradition—it hadn't progressed very far. That's fairly obvious. I was nonetheless intrigued, so I kept returning to that little storefront temple over a period of time, and each visit I would talk to various people at the temple.

In the course of those visits, however, things began to change. I discovered that each time I went back (or whenever I'd receive reports from students or others who visited the temple), the devotees knew more and more about the religious and cultural background of what they were doing. And so I kept seeing, if not month by month then certainly season by season, that more and more of that tradition was being put into place. When my student Gene Hall returned from his stay with the devotees, he reported with great excitement, "Every evening when I go up to the dormitory someone is reading from the *Bhāgavata Purāṇa*," which was the only thing that was available to them at that point. The next time that I personally visited the temple, I could see that they were just beginning to practice a simple form of temple worship—worship of consecrated images with the traditional *āratī* ceremony. Previously, temple worship had consisted simply of chanting the Hare Krishna mantra and offering flowers and food on a crude altar, but now I was witnessing the beginning development of a formal ritual structure. I expressed this sense of discovery in an interim report I presented in the spring of 1969 to the research committee which was funding my study.

I have it right here—I'll read you a section from it:

> The Society for Krishna Consciousness has changed and become a much more significant organization than it was even a year ago. . . . The leadership of the Society has always been good, but there has recently been a great increase in the depth and quality of the membership as a whole. The core group of disciples has been considerably enlarged in the past year, and training of disciples has been intensified. Disciples in general now know far more about the Vaiṣṇavite scriptures than they did a year ago, and their ritual practices have become much more complex and sophisticated. A major effort has been made to introduce and perfect the full range of traditional Hindu rituals associated with the worship of Krishna. Disciples now celebrate daily worship with morning *pujā* to the image of Krishna in their temple shrine and with evening *kīrtan*, celebrate Hindu holy days, perform regular daily chanting of rounds of Krishna mantras using their bead rosaries, have learned Indian musical styles and adopted Indian food and dress, and in an amazing way for such a short period of time have assimilated their living patterns to a Hindu model.

What became evident was that Bhaktivedanta Swami did, in fact, have a plan which he was gradually implementing—a plan that clearly involved bringing more and more of the authentic tradition over from India and putting it in place in the American, or western, movement. He made his students more and more familiar with the philosophy. This I was expecting. What I did not expect, and what really surprised and pleased me, was the degree to which the ritual tradition was also brought over and put into place. That's something that no other movement has succeeded in doing, nor even really tried to do: transplanting a traditional Hindu ritual structure into a Hindu religious movement in America.

SJG: Aren't there any other examples of this sort of thing?

TH: I really can't think of any good parallel examples because I don't think there *are* any parallel examples. The Transcendental Meditation movement, for instance, has transplanted only the initiation ritual or *pūjā*. Even at that, they try to deny that this is a religious ritual, when it's obviously a *pūjā* celebration. That's really the only aspect of the tradition that they have maintained, and that's simply because even as Americanized or westernized as TM is, they can't get away from the traditional idea that a disciple must be initiated. There is something irreducibly minimal about that initiation ritual, because it's essential to the transmission of the tradition. But that's a pretty minimal component. I did some work several years ago on what I called the "shifting paradigm in Transcendental Meditation," that is, the efforts over a period of time to translate the language of TM out of Śaṅkara's Vedānta philosophy into western scientific jargon so that it could become more intelligible or more acceptable to the common American. The Krishna consciousness movement simply did not do that. Bhaktivedanta Swami, on the contrary, was very, very concerned that the tradition be presented in its fullness, as it became more and more clear that the authentic tradition was irreplaceable, that the cultural tradition out of which Krishna consciousness came was essential to the purpose and practice of Krishna consciousness, and that any attempt to translate it into purely Western cultural terms might only serve to convolute it.

SJG: So, you feel that Śrīla Prabhupāda's success in establishing the movement on western soil has a lot to do with the fact that he didn't separate the teachings of Krishna consciousness from the cultural and experiential dimensions of the tradition?

TH: Yes, I think the vision which Bhaktivedanta Swami had of a community dedicated to Krishna consciousness was a vision of a community which would be pervaded by the whole spirit of the tradition, not merely a western accommodation of the tradition preserving only a veneer of Indian spiritual culture. He really had a sense of the tradition, and he wanted to put that whole tradition into place.

And the opportunity to do that increased when there was enough support that he could begin to think of establishing rural farm communities in addition to storefront temples in cities. That was an opportunity to do what no one else had done in any serious way: to create a community in the fullest sense of the term. There may be some examples of this from some non-Indian traditions. I think some of the Zen movements have tried to set up authentic Zen communities. You also have Tibetan Buddhist monasteries in the U.S., but most of these are simply transplanted Tibetan monasteries, and largely inaccessible to most people. To become seriously involved, you have to be willing to learn Tibetan and go through a rigorous training process. But as far as something that is both authentic and at the same time accessible to a large number of people is concerned, I don't know *any* non-western tradition that has ever managed successfully to do that or has even tried to do it in any significant way.

It's mostly philosophical traditions, as such, that have been transported to the West. If you're going to trace the history of Hindu influence in the U.S., you have to go back to Thoreau and Emerson who read *Bhagavad-gītā* and, oddly enough, a translation of the *Harivaṁśa*, and thus knew about Viṣṇu and Krishna and about devotion. But their interest was merely intellectual and they had little concept of the cultural setting out of which these texts came. Nor could they have cared less about the cultural setting. Later, of course, you have Swami Vivekānanda who established the Vedānta Society. But this was largely an intellectual and quite self-consciously eclectic movement which sought mainly to prove that Indian philosophy was as good as anybody's.

So, I really can't think of any other tradition that has managed—certainly in the way the Krishna consciousness movement has—to carry over something other than an intellectual structure. Some groups, of course, bring over some sort of practice, in the very limited sense of attention to a particular yoga or meditation technique, or even some kind of limited ritual practice, but never a complete system: philosophical, spiritual, and cultural. That's what gives Krishna consciousness the kind of strength and power that it has. It does not isolate any one component of the spiritual life and make *it* the exclusive religious practice. But rather it does what I think the Hindu tradition in general has tended to do, and certainly devotional traditions have tended to do, and that is to make all of life a religious practice. So being Krishna conscious means having Krishna in one's mind *all* the time, not just twenty minutes in the morning and the evening. Every act is an act of devotion, every thought is a thought of Krishna, and so forth. That's the goal; that's what you're working for.

Most of these groups that promote some particular yoga or meditation technique, such as TM, very self-consciously back away from challenging lifestyles. TM will say, "In time, if you practice this technique your life will get better." But if you ask, "*How* will it get better?" they'll say, "Well, you'll just know. You'll begin to put this new consciousness, this 'Being Consciousness' into practice in your life, and your life will get better." But they don't give any guidelines as to *how* you put this "Being Consciousness" into practice, or how one should live one's life, or what a better life is.

In the Krishna consciousness movement you have a sense of a complete structure gradually being put into place—a sense of what a society, a culture, a community ought to be like, how it ought to function, what kinds of occupations people should be involved in, how they should relate to each other within their occupations, what a family is and how a family should relate to the religious tradition and to the rest of society, how the *sannyāsis* can relate to the *gṛhasthas*, and the parents to the children, and so on. A whole cultural system has certainly by now been well established in the Krishna consciousness movement in the U.S. I don't think anybody else has ever tried this with anywhere near the high degree of seriousness and success that your movement has.

One significant implication of the fact that the Krishna consciousness movement is presenting a fuller picture of Indian spirituality and culture is that its very existence is an implicit challenge to the notion of western cultural superiority. During the British rule in India, the British systematically denigrated Indian culture as being inferior to English or European civilization. The British left the Indians with something of a cultural inferiority complex by teaching them that anything Indian was second-rate: Indian culture, Indian traditions, Indian values, Indian anything. You have someone like Macaulay saying, "One shelf of English books is worth all of the literature of India." It was the famous Macaulay's Minute back in the nineteenth-century that was the force behind the decision to make the educational system in India English-based. It was based on a negative judgement about the value of traditional Indian culture as over against British culture. To the culturally-imperialistic British, India was simply backward. The Indians, in their view, might have had something at one time, but probably not much. They might have had something for people in the beginning stage of cultural evolution, but obviously the future is in terms of the West: western science and technology, western values, western literature, western philosophy, and so on.

So when you're trying to put the Krishna consciousness movement into some kind of historical context and trying to understand what Bhaktivedanta Swami has really accomplished by having people like you wearing your robes on the streets of American cities, and having whole groups of Americans adopting Indian culture, you really have to look at it not just within the context of American attitudes toward nonconformists, but within the broad context of that whole intellectual tradition which views the West as the Supreme fountainhead of wisdom and value, and in which India and other non-western cultures are viewed as culturally and intellectually deprived. Your movement puts out a very clear challenge to American and western values. In a sense it's saying, "Hey, you know *that's* no way to live—living for limited, self-centered materialistic goals. Live a good, spiritual life. Live this kind of life which is healthy, which is clean, which is intellectually stimulating, which is personally satisfying, and which is religiously challenging and rewarding."

To think that western values are self-evidently right and that westernization and modernization are the only way to go is, I won't say "self-evidently" wrong, but close to it. I've known many Indians in America who on the surface are as westernized as they can be—more American than the Americans—and yet they still have a guru and they still have a little *pūjā* room in their homes, and they still follow the traditions taught to them by their parents. But they think that there's something wrong with themselves. They think that it's due to some defect in themselves that they still cling to these traditions. What the Krishna consciousness movement is doing is making these westernized Indians aware that keeping to their traditions is not incompatible with the modern world, that it's not a foolish thing to do, and that they don't have to do these things in the closet.

SJG: The same thing is happening, even more so, in India itself. It's ironic that at a time when many Indians—especially educated cosmopolitan types—are embracing western lifestyles, young Westerners who have enjoyed all the fruits of modern western society are rejecting that society and traveling to India to live the lives of renounced Hindu *sādhus*. That's had a powerful impact on many in India, and it's begun to cause many Indians to take a second look at their own spiritual roots.

TH: I have nothing but admiration for the effort to bring the experience of the movement back into India and to revitalize the tradition there. This kind of thing has happened historically. Missionaries of devotional movements have gone out and swept up large numbers of people and brought them back to the home community, where they've acted as a revitalizing force. This is very significant.

The Krishna consciousness movement is significant in another sense as well. There have been a great many utopian communities established in the U.S. If there's anything that U.S. history has been characterized by, it's been a succession of experimental utopian communities, starting, I suppose you could say, from the Pilgrims—who certainly had a sense of what a community should be. Later, in the nineteenth century, you have Owens and the Oneida community, and there are many others. The nineteenth century is just studded with utopian communities, movements, farms, and so forth. But the main problem with all of them, looking at them all in retrospect, is that they were all *ad hoc* experiments; they had never been tried before. They were all based on somebody's idea of how an ideal community ought to work. They all began with some sort of idealistic theory, and then had to face the task of trying to put that theory into some kind of practical form, and in the course of doing so had to encounter all varieties of unexpected problems and difficulties. This translation of theory into action usually required a great deal of time and effort, and, in spite of that, most ultimately failed.

What is significant about your movement is that it has taken a social system, a cultural tradition which has been tried for two-thousand years or more, and which has proven to be stable and workable, and which has been debugged probably like no tradition has ever been debugged, and brought it to western soil. I'm not suggesting, by any means, that Indian society has always been ideal. But the same social system has been in place for a very long period of time and has been made compatible with religious life, especially in the context of the medieval *bhakti* movement.

It's not as if Indian religious culture—what you call "Vedic civilization"—is a single monolithic tradition with no variance at all. It's a tradition with a great variety of available options. But those options have all been tried out. So, you've got an enormous reserve of tried experiments which you can go on. You're not starting off merely with a theoretical idea; you're starting off with something that's been proven in practice and which now can be established in a different geographical setting. It's now a matter not of adjusting the tradition to the capabilities of western converts, but of adjusting the western converts to the tradition.

SJG: Does the fact that a good number of people outside India have "adjusted" to this particular tradition indicate, perhaps, a kind of trans-cultural or even transcendental quality of Vedic or Vaiṣṇava culture? People are attracted to the Krishna consciousness movement, it seems, not due to some quaint fascination with Indian culture (in your early experience, the devotees knew practically nothing of the "India connection") but because they are touched on a very deep level, a spiritual level. Why the universal appeal that seems to transcend relative cultural orientation?

TH: Interestingly, one of the earliest archeological evidences of the worship of Krishna in India is a monument to Krishna erected by a Greek named Heliodorus at a place called Besnagar. This monument, called the "Besnagar Column" or the "Heliodorus Column," is usually dated at the mid-second century or first century B.C., and was erected by a Greek who was an ambassador to one of the regional courts of India. In the inscription on the monument, he describes himself as a *bhāgavata,* a devotee of Lord Vāsudeva, Krishna. It's interesting that this evidence of Krishna worship comes through the medium of a foreigner who was converted to the worship of Krishna.

If you look back in history, the two traditions which generally have been access points for foreigners seeking entrance into Indian religious tradition are the Vaiṣṇava devotional movements and Buddhism. If you look at the period between the second century B.C., the post-Mauryan period, up to the Gupta Empire—when the ancient Vedic culture and the popular devotional culture merged, producing a tremendous burst of cultural development—India was invaded or moved into by a number of foreign peoples. You have Greeks who were successors to Alexander's original conquest, you have people called the Yüeh-chih, you have the Śakas and the Hunas, and later the Kushans who came out of central Asia. While residing in India, all these peoples were attracted to various forms of Indian religion, but they had no access to the formal brahminical tradition because that tradition was extremely purist and elitist. But they were accepted by movements such as the Vaiṣṇava devotional movement wherein they could worship Viṣṇu and Krishna ,and they were also accepted by Buddhism.

And it's intriguing when you look at the twentieth century A.D. and see which movements have successfully moved into the West—again it's Buddhism and a Vaiṣṇava devotional movement. These two traditions, historically, have been to a very large extent culture-free, in the sense that they have not depended upon a particular cultural setting to make them work. They are, in a sense, self-contained cultural units which are transportable across national boundaries. This issue of transferability or portability of tradition is a fascinating one. Some traditions have not been able to make that kind of cross-cultural move.

It's noteworthy that the form of Buddhism that has traditionally been the most exportable—the form you find in China, Japan, and Korea—is salvation Buddhism, what you might call "*bhakti* Buddhism" which involves devotional worship of Amida Buddha, the compassionate Buddha who grants salvation and elevates his worshippers, who devotionally recite his name, to a heavenly "Pure Land."

SJG: So, it seems that what makes Vaiṣṇava devotionalism and "*bhakti* Buddhism" so attractive, and therefore exportable, is their inherently devotional character.

TH: Yes, I think so. That whole orientation toward a personal deity of compassion and concern, and of love, who is not just some kind of absolute, impersonal reality in the Vedāntic or Advaitic sense, but a Personal Being of infinite compassion, one who is concerned for those suffering in the world, appeals to something very deep within the human spirit. Krishna Himself describes in *Bhagavad-gītā* that whenever the world is threatened by unrighteousness, "I enter the world and restore righteousness, *dharma*." It's that kind of personal quality, it seems to me, that appeals to human beings across all cultural lines.

The kind of universal accessibility and attractiveness that we see in Vaiṣṇava devotionalism owes much to the fact that it does speak to very basic human needs and it speaks to those needs in terms that are both powerful enough and simple enough that people can connect with it at a variety of different levels. So, the fact that this tradition has a universal spiritual appeal and that it also has tended to be inherently egalitarian—this presents a very powerful combination, and people are very easily brought into its fold.

A good example of devotional Vaiṣṇavism's egalitarian character is found in a famous story from the early life of Rāmānuja. When he was first given his initiation, his guru taught him the mantra *oṁ namo bhagavate vāsudevāya:* "I offer my obeisances unto the Supreme Lord Vāsudeva (Krishna)." His guru told him that he must never speak this mantra aloud, because that was the custom. Rāmānuja then asked his guru, "Why shouldn't I speak it aloud? What is wrong with that?" And the guru said, "If other people should hear it, then anyone will be able to use it and attain salvation easily." So, according to this story, Rāmānuja immediately climbed to the top of the highest building in the town and shouted the mantra out in all directions. He thought that if it is possible for all people to be saved by knowing and reciting this mantra, then obviously the thing to do is not to keep it a secret but to let everybody hear it, so no matter who they are or where they are they can be saved. Whether this story is historically accurate or not, it ought to be because it certainly expresses the spirit of the devotional movement—that salvation or love of God is not to be confined to a small elite, it's to be given freely to everyone.

Have you ever been to Paṇḍharpūr in Maharastra?

SJG: No, I've never visited Paṇḍharpūr.

TH: Oh, you'd like Paṇḍharpūr, because it's pervaded by much of the same quality of genuine devotion to Krishna that you find in a place like Vṛndāvana. There's a simple, popular movement there which draws on people from a very wide range of backgrounds—college professors, professional people, peasants from farms—all brought together in a conscious community of believers. You really see the power of devotion break through all of these ordinary barriers of caste and education and bring people together for worship. When I was there in 1969 during the festival period, one of the most popular *kīrtan* leaders was a Muslim woman; she was absolutely fantastic. I have some marvelous recordings of her singing. It's the power of the devotional spirit, obviously, that drew her into this from outside the Hindu tradition. Both of us Westerners there at that festival were welcomed with open arms. There was no question of separation or difference due to caste or nationality.

That's the quality that this tradition has had all along. Historically, it has cut across all kinds of caste lines, educational lines, regional lines, and national lines. In India, it's always been the means of accepting foreigners. That's why Krishna consciousness, Vaiṣṇava devotionalism, could be brought to the West in the first place, and why it could flourish among people to whom Indian and Hindu tradition was a completely foreign element. Heliodorus presumably was not the only foreigner who was converted to Vaiṣṇava devotional practice (although he might have been the only one to erect a column, at least one that's still extant). Certainly, there must have been many others. The point is that there were no barriers to a foreigner's becoming a Vaiṣṇava. If you committed yourself to the path of devotion, if you had real devotion, you were accepted as a genuine *bhakta*, a genuine devotee. There was no further qualification needed.

SJG: You may know that when Western Krishna devotees first began to visit India back in 1970, many Indians were a bit incredulous at the sight of American and European Vaiṣṇavas, and the Indian press had a tendency to characterize them as faddists or as experimentative hippies. But as time went on and the "fad" persisted, the Indian public as well as the press began to take the movement quite seriously and to view the western devotees as authentic. At present, the Krishna consciousness movement in India has a very broad and substantial base of support, and increasing numbers of Indians are participating in it along with the non-Indian devotees.

TH: You know more about the contemporary reaction to the movement in India than I do. I know only second-hand from hearing reports from various people. But what you say doesn't really surprise me. It would have surprised me in the beginning, when the American devotees were largely uninformed and inexperienced. It doesn't particularly surprise me now because there is a strong emphasis on authentic practice among the American Krishna devotees whom I know, and conformity to right practice has always been the standard of brahminical tradition. Although the tradition places considerable importance on who you are by birth, that's really something that can be negotiated. Conformity to correct practice cannot. If you're not doing the right thing, then it doesn't make any difference who you are; you're not going to be accepted. It's been often said by scholars of the Hindu tradition that the tradition is not one which emphasizes orthodoxy so much as it does *orthopraxis*, correct practice. This has always been the ultimate test of acceptability in the tradition. The Vaiṣṇava devotional texts in particular emphasize personal attributes and behavior over status by birth. The *Mahābhārata* says in at least one place—and the tradition says in many places—that a person is a brahman who acts like a brahman and a person is a *śūdra* who acts like a *śudra*; it's behavior that counts, not the conditions of birth.

SJG: There's a strong indication of that in the *Bhagavad-gītā* where Krishna states, *cātur-varṇyaṁ mayā sṛṣṭaṁ guṇa-karma-vibhāgaśaḥ:* "I created the four occupational divisions of human society (the *varṇas* or "castes") on the principles of *guṇa* and *karma*, personal quality and work." He distinctly does not mention birth *(janma)* as a determinant of social status. This theme is, of course, elaborated in many Purāṇas.

TH: It's not very often recognized just how revolutionary a statement that is. There's a real tension in the tradition, as you're undoubtedly aware, on this point. The Vaiṣṇava devotional tradition has pushed the orthodox Hindu tradition to the limits on this question. It has always insisted that the quality of a person's life and the quality of his or her devotion is what really counts in the final analysis. It wouldn't surprise me that consistency of experience with Krishna consciousness members would eventually win over even the orthodox brahmans, or at least a lot of them. I suspect, however, there are still some who are going to hold out and say, "If you're not born a Hindu, you're not Hindu," or "If you're not born a brahman, you're not a brahman." But even if the movement were not acccepted by the orthodox caste-brahmans—and many of the devotional movements were not accepted in their early stages—consistency of behavior, in terms of correct, authentic practice, will still bring about a wide general acceptance. And of course there's no question but that your movement's rules, practices, and codes of behavior are the ones of the authentic tradition.

So, the fact that the tradition is in the business of accepting people of widely varying cultural backgrounds is nothing new in the twentieth century. This is the tradition of the *bhakti* movement, and it has been from the very beginning. The only problem has been not barriers to acceptance, but accessibility. Most people couldn't go to India to join devotional movements. Furthermore, devotional movements sometimes fade from view for periods of time. Traditions get senile; they lose that sense of spontaneity, openness and acceptance. And when they do, no matter how much they may still say the words and go through the motions of *bhakti*, real *bhakti* isn't there, and lives do not become transformed. Then there is need for somebody to come along and revitalize the tradition. Historically, this is what's often happened to devotional movements: a holy man, a saint, a poet, or a mystic emerges and brings new life to the tradition. I think that's one of the reasons why traditions tend to lose their vitality—there aren't that many genuine holy people around in some periods of history. In any case, it is interesting that a religious tradition has the capacity to revitalize itself. For me, this is one of the most intriguing aspects of the Indian devotional tradition—that it has always had that innate capacity.

One of the most interesting examples of the reviving of a devotional tradition, or of any religious tradition, comes, in fact, right from your own Gauḍīya Vaiṣṇava tradition, in the figure of Bhaktivinoda Ṭhākura.

SJG: All of us in ISKCON know the name of Bhaktivinoda Ṭhākura as one in the line of teachers before Prabhupāda, but most don't know much more about him. Have you had access to any good biographical material on Bhaktivinoda?

TH: I don't know of any good, comprehensive biography of Bhaktivinoda, even in Bengali, but I've been able to piece together a composite overview of his life from a number of different sources, and I'm beginning to understand the magnitude of his achievement as a religious reformer and revivalist. He's a fascinating figure. In the course of my learning about him, I've come to view Bhaktivinoda as one of the towering figures of modern Indian religious history.

SJG: What particular role do you see him playing as a religious reformer within the context of the Caitanya tradition?

TH: To appreciate Bhaktivinoda's contribution, it would help to understand something of the state of the Caitanya tradition at his time. In the centuries following Caitanya, the devotional movement he had founded, Gauḍīya Vaiṣṇavism or Caitanya Vaiṣṇavism, declined somewhat, and by the middle of the nineteenth century, the movement had lost much of its vitality. It lacked leaders who could raise it above the level of popular religiosity based largely on heredity and habit, and it lacked articulate theological leaders. Furthermore, the tradition had become tainted by various tantric influences which sometimes turned the devotional mysticism of Rādhā and Krishna into a kind of sex mysticism. As a result of all this, few educated people took the tradition very seriously. Here's where Bhaktivinoda came in. It was this situation that he sought to remedy. It was he, more than anyone else, who made possible the resurgence of Gauḍīya Vaiṣṇavism in late nineteenth century India, and it was he who set into motion the chain of events that lead to the establishment of the Krishna consciousness movement in America in the next century. Let me go back a bit and talk about his life and his own personal religious development to put this all in context.

Bhaktivinoda Ṭhākura was born into a wealthy Caitanyaite family in 1838, but characteristically for that time and place he had an English and Western education, and he completed his education at a Christian college. So he's typical of that group in Bengal who had high social status, an intellectual orientation, and an English education that prepared them for life under British rule. After finishing college, Bhaktivinoda started teaching in Orissa, where he was one of the pioneers of English education, and he also began to study law on his own. He passed his law examinations, took employment as a civil servant with the government of Bengal, and eventually was appointed a magistrate within the provincial civil service. He stayed with the Bengal civil service, rising within its ranks until his retirement in 1894.

SJG: For some time during that period he was also the British-appointed overseer of the famous Jagannātha temple in Purī, Orissa.

TH: Yes, that's right. Now, according to his own testimony, Bhaktivinoda's interest in his own religious tradition was, for the first thirty years of his life, strictly personal and was largely a matter of cultural nostalgia rather than intellectual conviction. In his day, even people in Bengal hardly had access to their own Caitanya Vaiṣṇava tradition. Bhaktivinoda apparently couldn't find a copy of *Caitanya-caritāmṛta*, which is written in Bengali, because most of the manuscripts—as well as other written documents of the tradition—were in private collections or stored away here and there; nobody was doing anything with them. As a young man he also had not yet encountered the *Bhāgavata Purāṇa*, either the text itself or the important Vaiṣṇava commentaries like those of Śrīdhara Svāmī and the Gosvāmīs. So, Bhaktivinoda had little contact with the real religious and intellectual core of his own tradition.

This situation changed dramatically in 1868 when he received from a friend a copy of both the *Caitanya-caritāmṛta* and the *Bhāgavata Purāṇa*. He studied these two texts in depth, was overwhelmed by their wealth of theological and spiritual teaching, and experienced a personal transformation. At that point, he decided not only that he should work to preserve the Caitanya tradition, but that he should promote it publicly and restore it to respectability. Throughout the rest of his career, he dedicated himself to doing just that. He wanted to bring about not only intellectual acceptance, but a full-scale religious revitalization.

Up to that time, there was very little attention being given to the great writings of the tradition. His first job, as he saw it, was to make as much of this tradition accessible in published form to as many people as possible. He did a tremendous amount of translation of Sanskrit works into Bengali and some translation of Bengali and Sanskrit works into English. He published some hundred books during his career—most of them translations, commentaries, and expositions of Vaiṣṇava theology—for the purpose of recovering and promoting the Caitanya tradition. He did all this, amazingly, while carrying a full load of responsibility as a court magistrate and while raising thirteen children!

In 1881 he founded a journal called *Sajjana-toṣaṇī* to disseminate the teachings of Caitanya. Several years later he established a printing press at Bhaktibhavān, his home in Calcutta, to make possible even wider distribution of Vaiṣṇava works. It's clear that Bhaktivinoda considered printing and publishing the key to successful promotion of the cause and this was a distinctive feature of the movement from this time on. In 1888, after conducting extensive scholarly and field research, Bhaktivinoda discovered the actual birthplace of Caitanya, which had long been forgotten. He promoted the building of a temple at that site and used that promotion as a way of generating enthusiasm for his mission. When he retired in 1894, he spent most of his time working on that project, which was successfully completed the following year. Finally, in an effort to begin to promote the Vaiṣṇava cause on an international level, Bhaktivinoda sent copies of his books to scholars and academic institutions in Europe and America.

SJG: Could you say something about his view of caste in relation to religious matters?

TH: Bhaktivinoda refused to acknowledge caste distinctions among devotees, and apparently he opposed the wearing of the sacred thread by brahmans as a sign of caste superiority. To support his position, he argued from traditional Vaiṣṇava religious beliefs, especially the example in the *Bhāgavata Purāṇa* of the saint Nārada who, although raised as a *śūdra*, was given brahminical status because of his learning and devotion. And I think the Caitanyaite tradition was clearly on Bhaktivinoda's side on this issue. Caitanya himself had argued the same case, and his close associate Nityānanda, whom he engaged in preaching to the masses in Bengal, had created a minor social revolution by his total disregard of caste background in the recruiting of devotees.

SJG: How, eventually, did Bhaktivinoda pass on the responsibility of leadership of the Gauḍīya Vaiṣṇava movement to his son and successor Bhaktisiddhānta Sarasvatī?

TH: Bhaktisiddhānta, it seems, was drawn into this rather early. His education was guided personally by his father. He was taught Bengali, Sanskrit, and English all at an early age, and his father farmed him out to pandits and teachers who would give him the best possible education in the classical tradition as well as in the more popular devotional tradition. And his father personally imbued him with a powerful sense of the mission to spread Krishna consciousness. He was also brought by his father into the publishing enterprise very early. My understanding is that Bhaktisiddhānta Sarasvatī was serving as a publishing assistant to his father from a very early age—editing and preparing texts for publication and so forth. His father gave him a clear sense of the importance of this mission to publish and to make available as many texts as possible.

One of the first things that Bhaktisiddhānta did after his father passed away in 1914 was to set up a printing press in Calcutta, the Bhagwat Press, to expand the publishing operation beyond even what his father had done. Bhaktisiddhānta would refer to the printing press as the *bṛhat-mṛdaṅga*, "the great *mṛdaṅga*," because the drum-beats of an ordinary *mṛdaṅga* can be heard for only a couple of blocks, but the printing press can be heard around the world. So that mission to publish and to make literature available to people was probably his most important task.

SJG: Aside from his work in scholarship, writing, and publishing, what about his organizational role?

TH: Bhaktisiddhānta Sarasvatī became very actively involved in the organization of the religious community, a task which his father had been largely unable to do because he was employed, full-time, as a district magistrate. Bhaktisiddhānta was not employed in any official position, and so he was able to devote his time entirely to the cause. You know, of course, that he founded and organized an India-wide Caitanya Vaiṣṇava institution, the Gauḍīya Maṭha. I believe that Bhaktivinoda had put together the idea for such an organization, but it clearly was the organizational role that he bequeathed to his son. Bhaktisiddhānta, with the able assistance of his disciples, did an enormous amount of organizational work during his lifetime—getting the Gauḍīya Maṭha organized on a local basis, establishing a regional organization, traveling extensively with his disciples, and sending disciples out to other places to try to organize local units, and so on. You find a lot of this story in the first volume of Satsvarūpa dāsa Goswami's biography of Bhaktivedanta Swami, *Śrīla Prabhupāda-līlāmṛta*.

SJG: Didn't Bhaktisiddhānta also maintain and further his father's policies of social equality?

TH: Yes, but with a reversed ritual symbolism: where his father had refused to acknowledge the sacred thread, Bhaktisiddhānta gave the sacred thread to every candidate accepted for initiation regardless of his caste background, on the grounds that if he qualified religiously he was as good as any other brahman.

Now, what I see as particularly significant about Bhaktivinoda Ṭhākura and Bhaktisiddhānta Sarasvatī is not only that they were familiar with western thought, which many people in their cultural situation were, but they were also adamantly determined that they would not water-down or alter the Caitanya Vaiṣṇava tradition in order to make it available. Bhaktivinoda has some really powerful passages in his marvelous little book, *The Bhāgavata: Its Philosophy, Its Ethics and Its Theology*, in which he argues for the universality of the Vaiṣṇava tradition. He states there that the religion of the *Bhāgavata* "is not intended for a certain class of Hindus alone but it is a gift to mankind at large in whatever country he is born and in whatever society he is bred. In short, Vaiṣṇavism is the absolute love binding all men together into the infinite unconditioned and absolute God." And the corollary of that is that it doesn't have to be altered to make it accessible to people; it only has to be made available. The emphasis is not on changing the content of the tradition to make it intelligible to people, but on simply making it available—through translation and publication and other forms of propagation—because it is inherently accessible; it deals with the lives of people in a way that is universal. The relationship between God and man is not culture-bound. It crosses all cultural boundaries. Bhaktisiddhānta Sarasvatī actually laid the foundation for an international Vaiṣṇava mission by his directive to his disciple A. C. Bhaktivedanta Swami that he should carry the message of Krishna consciousness to the West.

Bhaktivedanta Swami: An Indian *Sādhu* in America

SJG: Now, what about Bhaktivedanta Swami? How does he fit into all this historically?

TH: Bhaktivedanta Swami was the inheritor of a revitalized Caitanyaite tradition as it came down from Bhaktivinoda and Bhaktisiddhānta. Let's backtrack a bit and take a quick look at his life in India before coming to the United States. He was born in Calcutta in 1896 and received an English education at Scottish Churches' College in Calcutta. After college he went into business and ran a pharmacy for many years in Allahabad. After his initiation in Allahabad by Bhaktisiddhānta Sarasvatī, he turned his attention increasingly to the religious duty set by his teacher: to preach the message of Caitanya to English-speaking people. He founded the magazine *Back to Godhead* in 1944 to serve as a vehicle for this purpose and produced a series of English expositions of sacred writings. His long-term goal, however, was a translation and commentary on the *Bhāgavata Purāṇa*. He began work on this project after being initiated into the renounced order, *sannyāsa*, in 1959, and by 1965 he had completed and published the First Canto of the *Bhāgavata* in three volumes. At that point, armed with a message and a mission, he set sail for New York City to bring Krishna consciousness to the West.

Bhaktivedanta Swami's success story is an unlikely one to say the least. He was seventy years old when he arrived in America. It was his first trip outside India, he had no money, and no local means of support. But he did have a revitalized and spiritually rich Gauḍīya Vaiṣṇava tradition that had been imbued, by both Bhaktivinoda and Bhaktisiddhānta, with a spirit of universality and of relevance to the modern world. But it must be admitted, certainly, that not anybody could inherit and transmit that legacy. Other disciples of Bhaktisiddhānta had tried and failed to bring the devotional message of Caitanya to the western world. And after Bhaktisiddhānta passed away, his organization, the Gauḍīya Maṭha, was torn asunder by internal power struggles and other kinds of upheaval. Bhaktivedanta Swami, obviously, was a very special person, a spiritual leader of rare power. His success in bringing the message to the West and planting it in a place where it took root and flourished without compromising his tradition has to be seen as largely an effect of his tremendous personal spirituality and holiness, and his incredible determination.

It's an astonishing story. If someone told you a story like this, you wouldn't believe it. Here's this person, he's seventy years old, he's going to a country where he's never been before, he doesn't know anybody there, he has no money, he has no contacts. He has none of the things, you would say, that make for success. He's going to recruit people not on any systematic basis, but just picking up whomever he comes across and he's going to give them responsibility for organizing a worldwide movement. You'd say, "What kind of program is that?" There are precedents, perhaps. Jesus of Nazareth went around saying, "Come follow me. Drop your nets, or leave your tax collecting, and come with me and be my disciple." But in his case, he wasn't an old man in a strange society dealing with people whose backgrounds were totally different from his own. He was dealing with his own community. Bhaktivedanta Swami's achievement, then, must be seen as unique.

Bhaktivedanta Swami's personal example of devotion was not only impressive, but it was compelling, as evidenced by the way in which so many young Westerners were drawn to him. What got people chanting the Hare Krishna mantra in the beginning was confronting Bhaktivedanta Swami and being just overwhelmed by the man and feeling, "I want to be near this person; I want to know this person; I want to learn from this person; I want to become like this person." And his approach was one of taking people on and saying, "Here's how."

I don't think any devotional tradition has ever really been successful without some kind of model devotee to provide an example of devotion and of holiness. The role of the holy man is really inseparable from the devotional traditions. There's just no way you can convey the quality of devotion without an example of devotion. Devotion, in the sense of spontaneous devotion, is not something you can teach people intellectually or convey by reciting a set of abstract principles saying, "Now, being devotional means being such and such. Number one you do this and number two you do that." Being devotional means being *like* someone who is a devotee.

Of course, devotion does not arise out of nowhere. The devotional path is indeed a *path*. The devotee follows various religious regulations and disciplines which gradually revive the natural devotion of the soul, of the heart. But it is difficult to adhere to such disciplines, or to know *how* to adhere to them, if there is no good example of a devotee to follow. The devotional tradition makes this point constantly: that association with saints inspires saintliness, association with devotees inspires devotion. The association of genuine devotees can exert a powerful effect upon one's consciousness. I can still not just remember, but almost hear the singing of certain devotees at Paṇḍharpūr, for instance. I can still clearly remember the quality of those devotees. I can clearly remember the quality of Bhaktivedanta Swami. He wasn't a great singer in the sense of having a superstar's recording voice; his was the voice of a man seventy years old. Yet when he chanted and when he sang, the whole enterprise took on a different quality, and he would shape the experience for other people. You could *see* him shaping the experience for other people. If the chanting became routine, if it began to lose its spirit, he would change the beat, change the meter, or introduce some new element into the *kīrtan* to bring people's minds back to what they were doing. So you could see him very consciously and very patiently shaping people's devotional practices and their sense of who they were, and bringing them to the standard. He would guide people not by saying, "That's wrong" or "We don't do it that way in India," but by providing, as people became ready, new examples and new levels of attainment so that one never reached the end of the process. There was always another level to reach. No one ever seriously expected to reach his level, and yet he never set that level so far beyond where people were that they would view it as unattainable. He was a master at making that kind of contact.

Bhaktivedanta Swami is certainly one of those people who had that capacity to guide and direct and to discipline. He wasn't afraid to set standards. In talking about his effectiveness in dealing with counterculture youths, from the very beginning it seemed to me to be obvious that he was providing a sense of direction to people to whom no one had ever really given that kind of guidance. Their parents and other authority figures had simply told them, "Do whatever you want. It's your life; go out and do whatever you want with it." That's not much to go by. Bhaktivedanta Swami's approach was quite different. If you wanted to live your life the way you wanted to live it, that was all right with him, but not where he was!—and not in the temple and not in the community of disciples. In the temple there were standards, and there was a wise, compassionate, and understanding person who knew what was what. There was never any question of where he stood on things. He never pulled any punches or watered down his position to lull people into submission or acceptance.

SJG: The concept of submission to a spiritual master is, of course, very deeply rooted in Eastern spiritual traditions. But in the West there's a very strong distrust of the very idea of guru—a spiritual authority to whom one submits oneself for spiritual guidance. The typical western response to that is to view that kind of submission as a sort of abandonment of rational, critical thought and of personal autonomy. How is it, then, that Bhaktivedanta Swami's young disciples were able to transcend the western apprehension about absolute spiritual authorities and accept his authority as a spiritual master?

TH: I think it's partly because that fear of submitting oneself to an authority is not really fear of submission to authority per se. Rather, it's a fear of being taken, of submitting to a false authority, or a deficient authority. All three of the major American religious traditions have some emphasis on the notion of submission to authority. Roman Catholic tradition involves submission to the authority of the Pope, and to the priest as an immediate authority. The Jew makes his submission to the Law, and to the Rabbi who interprets and speaks for the Law. In the Hassidic tradition, one makes submission to the Rebby, who certainly is a respected spiritual authority—no question about it. He has authority and he enforces discipline. In the Protestant tradition, you have submission to the Word of God, the Bible. The idea of submission is certainly not absent in the western religious tradition.

What I think most of the young people in the counterculture were rebelling against was the fact that authority had let them down. Authority was not doing its job, as it were. Their parents were saying one thing and doing something else. The government was saying one thing and, Lord knows, doing all sorts of other things. The principles of democracy were being contradicted by what was happening in American society. If there's anything that Americans—especially—are afraid of, it's being taken. If there's anything that bothers an American, it's being sold a bill of goods. And when you find out that every authority figure in your life has sold you a bill of goods, you begin to question the whole idea of authority. But even though many young people in the counterculture might have viewed themselves as rejecting authority per se, in fact they were rejecting false or imperfect authority. When they finally found somebody who had a kind of authoritative quality and who could be trusted, their attitude towards authority changed. Bhaktivedanta Swami came across to them as someone who really did live the way he said you ought to live and who really did follow the standards that he said were the standards to follow. And he did so in a way that was not just up to par, but was beyond par. The actual quality of his life tended to alleviate their distrust and rejection of authority.

I feel that many adults made a mistake by taking the counterculture youth at their own word when they said they wanted no authority, direction, or discipline. Bhaktivedanta Swami never made the mistake of taking that seriously; he never catered to that spoken statement. He always saw what people really needed and spoke to that.

Over a period of time, I've changed my views on the need for implementing authority. Reflecting back on that period, I think that many of us who were in some kind of position of authority as teachers disgraced ourselves by reacting to the protest against authority by telling our students, "You want to do away with rules and requirements? Okay, let's do away with all the rules and requirements." We thought that acquiescence to their demand would bring more respect and that the lines of communication and our ability to teach would be enhanced. But that is not at all what happened. The real effect was that students came to feel, "Well, you don't have any standards, so why should we take you seriously?" Bhaktivedanta Swami never got caught in that trap. He understood the problem for what it was—a deep need for some kind of meaning and structure.

SJG: Unlike Bhaktivedanta Swami, most people who have come to the West in the role of spiritual mentors have tended to demand very little from their followers in the way of submission and obedience, and to set very low standards of personal conduct and discipline. Their attitude towards the personal morals of their disciples is generally laissez faire—as it often is to their own personal morals. Very few, for instance, have even attempted to set up or enforce strict rules encouraging sexual restraint or abstention from intoxicants (as is considered important in most of the traditions and disciplines these teachers represent). Why is it, then, that Bhaktivedanta Swami was able to demand, and receive, from his students a high standard of personal conduct and spiritual discipline?

TH: I think what he did was simply to say, "Okay, here is something that is of value, and here's what you have to do to get it." And, what he offered was genuine and sufficiently attractive so that people were prepared to pay the price. Many of his students had previously sought spiritual life elsewhere and had been disappointed—especially with the form of religion handed to them by their nominally Christian or Jewish parents. I had a number of conversations with devotees about their home synagogues, for instance, in which they described surrealistic encounters with their Rabbis. When they tried to raise the question of spiritual life and spiritual experience, they only got blank stares and responses like, "What is that? We don't do that here." So they didn't feel that they were getting much from their Rabbis. When they finally found someone who offered them tangible spiritual life, they were prepared to pay the price to receive it. For most people, those who were serious, the price wasn't too high to pay.

There were, and there probably still are, a lot of people who have always been disciples on the outside—friends of the movement, interested participants, but never willing to make the movement to discipleship for one reason or another. For many people, the demand of discipleship was more than they could meet. But I never met anyone who was anything but respectful of that demand, and who didn't view the problem not in terms of what was demanded, but in terms of their inability to meet the demand.

SJG: From what you observed during your various visits to the temple in New York in its early days, is there anything you remember in particular about Bhaktivedanta Swami's dealings with his disciples? Anything which particularly stands out in your mind?

TH: The one thing that I remember, the thing that I am constantly struck with, was the total confidence with which Bhaktivedanta Swami had people doing things. Take the example of his disciple Brahmānanda. Bhaktivedanta told him, "Go and start a magazine. Start a printing and publishing enterprise." And Brahmānanda replied, "I don't know how to do it." And Bhaktivedanta said, "Well, find out. Krishna will help you." This sort of exchange occurred numerous times, with numerous disciples. He inspired a sense of confidence in people because he himself was absolutely confident and convinced. He had no doubt that what he told people to do they would be able to do. He had much more confidence in people than they had in themselves, to say the least.

His confidence, however, was not in others or in himself

exactly, but in Krishna. That's the other thing that was so impressive about the man himself. He never put himself forward as having the power to make things happen. He never said, "Go and do this because I will give you the power. I will inspire you to do great things." He always said, "Krishna will give you the power. Krishna will guide you." It was a confidence not in himself or in the other person, but in Krishna, and that was effective. He wouldn't have been so effective, I think, if he had said, "You've got to have confidence in yourself," because that's pretty hard to do if you don't have confidence in yourself; nor if he said, "Have confidence in me," which, although better, you don't quite know how that works. But, on the other hand, "Have confidence in the Lord of the Universe"—well, that's a different matter.

Bhaktivedanta Swami's success as a religious leader of the institutional kind, as distinct from a religious leader removed from any institutional context, lies largely in his ability to engage people in religious activities of a practical nature or, conversely, practical activities with a religious purpose. This is one of the strengths of the whole *bhakti* tradition. It has tended not to become otherworldly in the sense in which the term is very often taken: utter indifference to the world and to action within the world—reclusiveness, inactivity.

SJG: This is a real problem: how do you reconcile the fact that we are spiritual entities, not of this body and not of this material world, with the reality of being within a material body and living, for now, within the material world? How can we live within the world and not become affected by worldliness? Can one live within the material world in a spiritual way? Can one be "in the world but not of it"?

TH: That is, of course, the classic problem.

SJG: On the surface, it appears that one has only two alternatives: to act in a worldly manner or to not act at all. But to act in a worldly manner means to come under the control of the law of *karma* and thus to deepen one's entanglement and suffering in the material world. As far as inactivity is concerned, that's not even possible. In the *Bhagavad-gītā,* Krishna tells Arjuna that one cannot remain detached from the world merely by abstaining from activity, because the soul is by nature active. One cannot sustain a state of inactivity for long, because it's unnatural. Ultimately, one is compelled to act, and to act in accordance with one's own psychological make-up. The *Gītā*'s solution is Karma-yoga or Bhakti-yoga: performing action in the world in accordance with one's own nature, dedicated to Krishna, and performed in devotion. One can act according to one's own nature yet not suffer *karmic* reactions to that work. One's work or activities become liberating rather than binding.

TH: The *Gītā* really is one of the great theoretical and practical statements on how to resolve that conflict. The Hindu tradition in general has managed to combine the religious and otherworldly concern for salvation and release from the world, with the need to perform worldly action. The *Gītā* is one of the great solutions. What Bhaktivedanta Swami did was to take that theoretical solution and apply it practically within a religious institution in a way that most other movements or traditions have not tried to do or have not been able to.

He often cited the example from the *Bhagavad-gītā,* wherein Arjuna wanted to leave the battlefield, go off to the forest and become a mendicant. Krishna then tells Arjuna, "That's not your duty. Your responsibility is to be here performing your own duty in accordance with your own nature—that of a *kṣatriya,* a righteous warrior. If you act under My direction and perform your *dharma* in service to Me, your activities will not incur *karma* and ultimately you will come to Me." To help people to discover what their own nature is, what their own psychological proclivities are, what their natural abilities are, and then to put them to work in some kind of practical way, and to perform those activities with devotion to God, is what the devotional tradition is all about.

Bhaktivedanta Swami never tried to construe the teachings of the *Gītā* to encourage some kind of otherworldly religiosity. His teachings were always in practical terms: one can worship Krishna by starting a magazine, one can worship Krishna by producing devotional art, or by cleaning the temple, or by cooking a feast for public distribution, or by repairing the temple car. It is activity performed as devotional service to Krishna which is the practical essence of the devotional tradition and which releases enormous amounts of energy once you get over the hurdle of thinking, "How can *I* do this?"

One thing that I haven't touched on—and it seems to me important particularly in recent times—is the question of institutional organization. In the beginning, Bhaktivedanta Swami was clearly *the* leader of the community. Lower-level leadership and organizational structure were fairly informal and flexible, based largely on the particular devotional qualities and practical skills that people had. But it's clear that he was quite concerned, early on, about the problem of organization. In America, there wasn't any pre-existent Vaiṣṇava community. There weren't families with a tradition of involvement going back generations who could provide a stable community for the continuity of the tradition. He wanted to create, therefore, a stable organizational and administrative structure which would allow for a continuity of the movement beyond his own lifetime. The need for creating a stable structure must have been a particularly acute concern for him because he didn't establish the movement in America until he was seventy years old, so he could not look forward to having an extended period of time in which to be personally present, directly providing leadership.

It is my sense that in creating an organizational structure, he was drawing largely on the experience of the tradition, both positive and negative. He had seen what happened when Bhaktisiddhānta Sarasvatī passed away and the Gauḍīya Maṭha did not follow his recommendation to create a leadership council. Instead, various leading figures in that movement immediately started competing for leadership and the Gauḍīya Maṭha was split up over all kinds of rancorous disputes concerning leadership and the possession of properties—politics and economics. I think that Bhaktivedanta Swami was very concerned to avoid that kind of problem, and it was out of that concern that he created the Governing Body Commission—the GBC—as a vehicle for stable organizational leadership.

SJG: Could you say something about Bhaktivedanta Swami's attention not only to devotional practice but also to the philosophical and theological foundations of devotional practice—the balance between devotion and scholarship?

TH: One of the things that originally attracted me to the Hindu tradition, and to the devotional movements in particular, was that they never did separate the devotional life from the intellectual life.

One of the things that is most striking about the *Bhāgavata Purāṇa*, for instance, is not just the quality of its devotional statements, but also the rigor of its thought. It is not just a kind of romantic devotionalism devoid of intellectual content. It's a very systematically conceived, very scholarly statement of the devotional life. That combination of emotion and intellect, which has been so often separated in religious traditions, is very consistently kept together in the devotional movements, and particularly the Vaiṣṇava devotional movement.

Many traditions lack this balance. Take, for instance, Śaṅkara and his intellectually powerful Advaita philosophical tradition. There you have a very strong intellectual tradition, but almost no concern for the development of spiritual emotion. On the other side, you have certain Christian, especially Protestant movements—charismatic or pentacostal movements—which have tremendous emotional engagement, but very little attention to the life of the intellect. The

Vaiṣṇava devotional movement, on the other hand, has always kept these two things together.

The best example I can think of is Caitanya and his followers the six Gosvāmīs. Caitanya was the devotee *par excellence*. His biographers describe the incredible intensity of his devotion to Krishna, his dancing and chanting in spiritual ecstasy, his visions, his deep mystical raptures. Yet he also traveled throughout India and debated—successfully—with some of the leading religious intellectuals of his day, and he also held long discourses on devotional theology with certain followers, including Rūpa Gosvāmī, Sanātana Gosvāmī, and Rāmānanda Rāya.

The six Gosvāmīs themselves were great devotees of Krishna and great mystics in their own right, yet simultaneously they were tremendous intellects. They collectively wrote a great number of theologically and philosophically sophisticated texts on *bhakti*, among which are some of India's greatest spiritual classics, such as Rūpa Gosvāmī's *Bhakti-rasāmṛta-sindhu*. Jīva Gosvāmī was probably the greatest devotional philosopher among them, and his contribution is acknowledged universally.

The intellectual and theological achievement of the Gosvāmīs was to give a rational, intellectual structure to spiritual emotion. Their writings systematically analyze the different stages of the devotional path, such as *vaidhi* and *rāgānuga*, and the various levels and nuances of spiritual devotion and devotional ecstasy—the various *rasas* and *bhāvas* and so forth. They gave these things meaning within a broad intellectual and theological context, rooted both in the popular and the classical traditions. There is an intellectual integrity and rational structure to the practice of *bhakti*, of devotion. It's not just a gut, emotional thing. It's mind and emotion together in a spiritual context. Historically, the real power of the Vaiṣṇava devotional tradition has been in its refusal to separate the intellect and the emotions.

If you look at the points at which any religious tradition is really powerful, they are usually those points at which these various elements have been kept together. If you look at the lives of the great Hassidic Rebbys, for instance, you see that they were people of intellect and spirituality, and also practical wisdom. They didn't separate these different elements. Also look at the greater saints of the Roman Catholic tradition, someone like St. Theresa. She was certainly a great mystic, certainly a person of deep spiritual emotion, but she was also just one hell of an organizer! She put together an entire monastic order with its own complete institutional structure. She knew not only how to pray to God, she knew how to keep books—and she didn't see any conflict between them. This is the quality that certainly came across with Bhaktivedanta Swami. I was in a conversation with him one time where he was really doing all of those things at once: he was giving a disciple some practical instruction in the devotional life, he was explaining some devotional point and summoning up a philosophical explanation for the devotional life, and at the same time he was explaining to someone how to keep tax records straight. And those were not contradictory things; they were all part of the same devotional process.

Any movement or any tradition that loses hold of one of those strands is going to have difficulty. And if it loses hold of more than one, it's in real trouble. It becomes rudderless, free-floating. If the tradition becomes exclusively intellectual, then you lose a whole sense of emotional life and practical action. If you're strictly devotional, you lose a sense of the coherent meaning of what you're doing, and it becomes an emotional trip that isn't likely to have much staying power. Nobody can stay on an emotional trip forever. And if you're strictly practical, you lose a sense of what it's all about in terms of inner meaning.

The Transmission Of Sacred Tradition: Bhaktivedanta Swami's Scholastic Contribution

SJG: While we're on the subject of integrating devotion and

intellect, perhaps you could say something about Bhaktivedanta Swami's own literary and scholastic contribution, particularly in the form of his many writings—translations, commentaries, and summary studies on the important texts of the tradition.

TH: As far as his scholastic and literary work is concerned, the first point that should be made is that he has made certain important texts of the Indian devotional tradition accessible to the western world that simply were not very accessible formerly. This is very significant. What few English translations there were of the *Bhāgavata Purāṇa* and the *Caitanya-caritāmṛta* were barely adequate and were very hard to get hold of. When I was working on my doctoral dissertation and wanted to get hold of a copy of the *Bhāgavata Purāṇa*, the only place where I could obtain a copy of the text and translation was from Harvard's Widener Library. I had to borrow it from inter-library loan and have a microfilm copy made of it. Nowadays if you want to take an airplane trip anywhere, you go to the airport and there's somebody trying to sell you a copy of the *Bhāgavata Purāṇa*. Bhaktivedanta Swami has really made these and other major texts of the Vaiṣṇava tradition accessible in a way that they never were before, and so he's made the tradition itself accessible to the West. This is an important achievement.

SJG: You say that he made Vaiṣṇava tradition accessible through his books. In what way did he do that? What I mean to ask is, to what degree do you see him presenting the tradition verbatim, as it were, and to what degree do you see him interpreting the tradition, in the sense of updating or modernizing it?

TH: He does both. He is very loyal to the tradition, yet he communicates the tradition in terms that are comprehensible to a contemporary Westerner. As far as fidelity to tradition is concerned, Bhaktivedanta Swami's commentaries are very traditional. His commentaries very closely follow those of the important Vaiṣṇava commentators, and the Gauḍīya Vaiṣṇava commentators in particular. His commentary on the *Bhagavad-gītā*, for instance, is based largely on the *Gītā* commentary of Baladeva Vidyābhūṣaṇa, to whom he dedicates his work. His commentary on the *Bhāgavata Purāṇa* relies heavily upon several major commentaries such as those of Śrīdhara Svāmī, Viśvanātha Cakravartī Ṭhākura, and Jīva Gosvāmī, all of whom he quotes and cites frequently. His commentary on *Caitanya-caritāmṛta* is based on the Bengali commentaries of Bhaktivinoda Ṭhākura and Bhaktisiddhānta Sarasvatī. This is something that needs to be stressed because unless you know the tradition you won't realize the extent to which he's representing it. What you're getting in Bhaktivedanta Swami's commentaries is a lot more than what appears: you're gaining access to the whole classic tradition of Vaiṣṇava scriptural commentary. It's clear that Bhaktivedanta Swami is not commenting on these texts off the top of his head. He's very strongly rooted in his tradition.

On the other hand, in the tradition of great commentaries, he takes the tradition one step further in application. When you're writing a commentary, of course, you don't just start off and do your own thing. You follow the tradition and you bring the text into the present, but you don't really give a new interpretation to it. There are commentaries which may attempt—and I suppose every commentary in some sense always attempts—a new interpretation, subtly or not. But the main purpose of the commentary is not to give a new interpretation, but to give a new application of the teaching, so that you have the same teaching applied to a new audience—an audience which may not have access to the original or earlier commentaries. It's putting the teaching into a new social, intellectual, and linguistic context so that it becomes as accessible now as the previous commentaries were in their time. A good commentary brings the text into the present. It's classically been the purpose of commentaries to take the text and to give it meaning in terms of people's lives so that they're not just dealing with mere intellectual statements. Writing a commentary is not a merely intellectual or academic exercise—it has a practical goal: to engage people with a living spiritual tradition.

SJG: In this light, then, what is significant about Bhaktivedanta Swami's commentaries?

TH: What is significant is that his commentaries are the first that have been written specifically for the comprehension of Westerners and others not familiar with the total Indian cultural and theological context. If you try to read the commentaries of Jīva Gosvāmī or Sanātana Gosvāmī or any of the great teachers, you find that you have to know quite a bit in order to read them with understanding. They contain a good deal of technical terminology, and they were written with the assumption that the reader has familiarity with traditional Indian philosophy, culture, and aesthetics. Anyone who doesn't come out of that particular cultural background is going to miss at least half of what's being said. Bhaktivedanta Swami has managed, successfully, to bridge an enormous cultural gap and to give practical application to teachings that were originally designed for people in a very different cultural setting. That's not easy to do, by any means. I think he's been very successful. The very existence of a genuine Vaiṣṇava movement in the West is compelling evidence of his success as a commentator.

SJG: Apart from his work as a commentator, what about his work as a translator—from a linguistic point of view?

TH: The translations are done accurately from a scholarly point of view. He leaves no tracks obscured. For each verse of the original he presents the Sanskrit text, its Roman transliteration, a translation of each individual word of the text, and a full English translation. There's no sleight of hand there. Everything is out front so you can see what's going on. You might not agree entirely with every choice of terms for translation, but at least you know what you're dealing with. It's all there available to work with

SJG: Occasionally, I've heard the criticism, or the comment, that Bhaktivedanta Swami's translations are less concerned with literal meanings than with the devotional spirit of the texts he's translating. Could you comment on this whole issue of literal versus interpretive translation and apply it to the case of Bhaktivedanta Swami's work?

TH: This is, of course, a long-standing problem in translation in general. Entirely apart from the religious context, the problem of translating a text from one language to another, whether poetry or prose, is the tension between the endeavor to give a strict, literal translation and the endeavor to convey the spirit of the original. That's the classic problem for anyone attempting translation work. It's commonly recognized that it's not possible, in a sense, to translate any text literally because the only thing that conveys the text purely as it is, is the text itself. Any translation is, in that sense, a change in the meaning of the text.

I have looked at Bhaktivedanta Swami's translations from that standpoint and I think, again, the fact that I have had a fair amount of experience with commentaries has helped me understand what it is that he's doing. A lot of his translations are based on a combination of literal text and commentary. He's involved in a tradition of interpretation which does not look at the Sanskrit text in isolation from a tradition of commentaries, as if he were translating it for the first time ever. He's translating out of a tradition of translations where over a period of time there's developed an agreement on what the significance of various terms is. This goes back a long way. If you look, for instance, at Śrīdhara Svāmī's commentary on the *Bhāgavata Purāṇa*, you'll find that a lot of his commentary consists of describing what devotees do, so that one can understand the meaning of the text.

SJG: I don't follow.

TH: Well, you have a verse, for instance, that says, "The forms of devotion are this, and this, and this, and *sevā*." *Sevā* literally means "service," but in isolation that doesn't really convey anything. So, in his commentary he explains that there are different kinds of service the devotee can render, such as bathing the temple images, preparing food for the devotees, repairing the temple building, cleaning the temple compound, and so forth. Obviously, he's drawing on his knowledge of what devotees of his own time did as acts of service. So, if you translate the term *sevā* literally as "service," you lose a sense of what the term means in the context of the devotional community. So, to translate the term with specific reference to the various examples of devotional service is really more true to the original sense of the term than simply to translate it as a single word. There's a good deal of that style of translation in Bhaktivedanta Swami's work, but in every case that I'm aware of it's done for the sake of making the meaning of the original more clear, rather than obscuring it.

To give another, more important, example: from a strictly scholarly, historical standpoint, the Krishna who appears in the *Bhagavad-gītā* is the princely Krishna of the *Mahābhārata* and not the pastoral, playful Krishna of Vṛndāvana. But from the point of view of orthodox Vaiṣṇava tradition the Krishna of the *Gītā* and the Krishna of Vṛndāvana are one and the same. From the tradition's point of view, there is not a great deal of significance to the princely Krishna in isolation from the other aspects of His life. It's not Krishna the historical prince and charioteer of Arjuna who is really important religiously; it is the Krishna of Vṛndāvana—the transcendental Lord enjoying loving dealings with His most intimate devotees—that is important religiously. If you look at Bhaktivedanta Swami's translation and commentary on the *Bhagavad-gītā*, you can understand that it is the *Bhagavad-gītā* as seen through the perspective of the *Bhāgavata Purāṇa*. He's not trying to deal with the *Gītā* in isolation from the whole tradition. He's dealing with it as it has meaning within the context of the tradition. That's no more distorting, it seems to me, than to read back into the teachings of Jesus the recognition that he is the resurrected Lord. The believing Christian reads the Bible with that understanding. To the Christian, words spoken by the Master are important not because they're an accurate transcription of what somebody once said at some point in time, but because they're spoken by a person whose later achievement is so important that everything he said takes on a new significance. Every tradition operates that way. As a Sanskritist, one can argue that in Bhaktivedanta Swami's translations there is expansion of meaning and added interpretation, but from the point of view of a religious Sanskritist, his approach is the only one that really conveys the meaning of the text.

SJG: This raises the basic hermeneutical question: How is a religious text best understood? That question implies another closely related one: *Who* is best equipped to understand a religious text? From the point of view of orthodox Vaiṣṇava tradition, religious texts such as the *Bhagavad-gītā* and *Bhāgavata Purāṇa* are sacred, revealed knowledge which can be understood—in the way that they are meant to be understood—only by entering into the devotional mood of the texts themselves. Intellectual and scholastic skills may be indispensable for understanding speculative concepts, but deep spiritual truths can be understood, according to the tradition, only through faith (*śraddhā*) and devotion (*bhakti*). Or, God Himself reveals the spiritual truths of the scripture to those who approach scripture with faith and devotion. This theme comes up in the *Bhagavad-gītā* where Krishna tells Arjuna, "I am explaining this knowledge to you *because you are My devotee and My friend,*" and elsewhere where Krishna says, "This knowledge cannot be explained to anyone who lacks *self-discipline and an attitude of devotion and service.*" This, of course, is not distinctive only of Vaiṣṇava tradition. Wasn't it St. Anselm who said, *Credo ut intelligam:* "I believe, in order that I might understand"?

TH: Yes, I think any religious tradition would make that point. It's an insistence certainly that the Christian scholar or theologian would make. He would say, "What right do you have to interpret this teaching when you have no sense of the spirit of the teaching?" You can't translate religious texts mechanically. Translation depends too much on an understanding of the spirit and the experience that lies behind them.

SJG: So what does that do to secular Hindu studies?

TH: What it does to a lot of it, is to make it—I won't say questionable, but of secondary importance. I think, however, that the current generation of scholars of the Hindu tradition are by and large people who do have a strong sense of what the religious component of that tradition is about. They may not be Hindus, and they themselves may not, in any very obvious or overt way, be religious people, but they do have a sense of what it means to be religious. Many scholars of religion recognize that unless you do have some sense of what it means to be religious, you have no business messing with religious texts—that they're not intended to be read simply as philosophical statements but as expressions of a series of experiences which have meaning only in the context of some kind of shared experience.

SJG: Doesn't the phenomenological approach to religion—quite influential nowadays—say that one should try to understand a religious tradition on its own grounds, so to speak, and in its own terms, rather than to simply interpret it from an external, judgemental point of view?

TH: I think phenomenology of religion as an approach has made us much more aware of the degree to which an awful lot of distortion has taken place in the study of religion or, more importantly, that some significant dimensions of religion have been neglected. There are a number of different schools of thought that go under the general heading of "phenomenology of religion," and I won't try to summarize all of them. I don't even understand some of them all that clearly. But phenomenology of religion, as I understand it, means essentially that you try to understand phenomena in terms of the phenomena themselves. It involves a kind of inductive scholarship, rather than deductive scholarship. This is true of many other kinds of scholarship in modern times. In the textual approach to poetry, for instance, you don't just take a piece of poetry and read into it anything that you damn well want to. You've got to respect the intentions of the poet and take what he says seriously. Or, if you're trying to interpret Greek drama, you have to assume that what the writer says is what he means to say. You can't say, "Well, he wasn't really thinking at that point," or "He didn't really say what he wanted to say." You've got to take what is said seriously.

Now, if you're dealing with a religious tradition, you've got to take what the people within that tradition say and especially *do* seriously and assume that there's enough integrity in the tradition, or in the people of the tradition, that what they're doing religiously all fits together in some way, even if you can't see how it fits together. Rather than observing from the outside and saying, "These things that they're doing don't connect with each other, but I'll make a connection," you've got to say, "There must be some reason why this thing and that thing and the other thing all appear in the same context, and I've got to keep working at that until I can see the total picture." In a religious tradition, there is some kind of internal coherence and integrity which has to be recognized and not violated.

SJG: But apart from developing a healthy, empathetic respect or appreciation for the internal coherence and integrity of a religious tradition, what about understanding the tradition as a living spiritual phenomenon based upon experienced truths? Vaiṣṇava texts say quite clearly that empathy isn't enough. Apart from analyzing Vaiṣṇavism as merely a historical, cultural, and sociological entity, Vaiṣṇavism as a spiritual phenomenon—one based upon certain distinctive kinds of spiritual insights and experience—can be understood only through undergoing particular ascetical, spiritual, and contemplative practices. The core of the tradition is spiritual, and one can reach that core only through spirituality, per se. How would you as a scholar of religion respond to that kind of challenge from the texts themselves?

TH: Well, I think one has to respect that. I wouldn't stay away from the texts, but I would approach them with an appreciation that there are certain levels of religious meaning which I might not be able to fully understand. Even if one is not religious oneself, or does not have an explicitly religious motive for studying these texts, one should at least acknowledge that the texts derive, at least in part, from real religious experiences and that they aim to bring the reader to those experiences. When these texts describe modes of religious perception and experience, these descriptions should be taken literally, not metaphorically or symbolically.

A good example of this sort of thing is the contemporary understanding of meditation, as over against a generation ago. In the past, scholars read texts on Hindu or Buddhist meditation and translated and interpreted those texts. But if these scholars had never themselves had any actual experience with meditation, their interpretations lacked depth. Much of what they said simply didn't make a lot of sense. Without recognizing that meditation experience does, in fact, bring about altered states of consciousness, one cannot understand, much less interpret, a text on meditation. Talk of altered states of consciousness is not just a literary device. There are some real things that happen when you meditate. When you're in an altered state of consciousness, you perceive things differently; the world appears differently. If one doesn't understand that, he can't understand anything that's being said about the practice of Buddhist meditation, or about the practice of yoga or, for that matter, about the practice of Christian meditation.

A text on meditation is not just intellectual argument or philosophical discussion. These texts are written by people who are talking about real things that happen when you do certain things, and those experiences are universal enough that anybody who's had them will understand what the texts are talking about.

Taking this same principle and applying it to the devotional tradition, or to any religious tradition, you'd have to simply say, without being metaphysical about it, "If you ain't had the experience, you can't talk about it!" That is, if you haven't yourself experienced the sorts of spiritual insights and states upon which the religious text is based, you can't really understand the text itself fully. If you haven't had those experiences, or aren't at least following the spiritual practices which lead to those experiences, then you will have great difficulty understanding theological statements about those experiences. Otherwise, it's like saying, "*I* can understand what childbirth is about. I'm a sympathetic, open-minded person, and I can read about childbirth and watch people in childbirth and so I know what you're going through." The hell you say. You simply don't. There's an element, a dimension, of that experience which is simply uncommunicable to someone who has not been through it. To someone who has been through it, you only need to mention it casually and they say, "Yeah, sure. I know about that. I experienced that."

SJG: Earlier, you stated that in his presentation of the texts of the Vaiṣṇava tradition to Westerners, Bhaktivedanta Swami had bridged an enormous cultural gap, and you suggested that one evidence for his success as a commentator is that his writings have been attended by the development and growth of a genuine Vaiṣṇava movement in the West. In light of what you've just been saying, the fact that he did successfully establish a Vaiṣṇava spiritual movement outside of India seems to indicate that he bridged not only an enormous cultural gap but also an enormous experiential gap, and that he was able to do that because he presented these core

Vaiṣṇava texts not only as a scholar who understood them but as a devotee who *experienced* them. I know for a fact that, for him, translating and commenting upon a text like the *Bhāgavata Purāṇa* was not merely an academic exercise, but a process that absorbed him fully, both intellectually and spiritually. He'd do his work usually late at night or during the early morning hours in quiet and solitude. After translating any particular verse from Sanskrit to English, he would study the various important Sanskrit Vaiṣṇava commentaries on the *Bhāgavatam* in depth, and after meditating on their meaning for some time, and contemplating how to relate the material to time and circumstance, would proceed to dictate his own commentary into a recorder. The whole process involved intense intellectual and spiritual concentration. If there was ever anything disturbing his mind, such as problems relating to practical institutional management, he simply could not work. He once related, intimately, that his "Purports," his commentaries to individual verses of the texts, were his "spiritual ecstasies."

TH: So, what you end up with is not another theoretical expression of Hindu religious philosophy, but an indication of the experiential, spiritual depth of the tradition. Whatever one might think of the philosophy or theology that is being expressed, or of the particular arguments that are made, you certainly have the sense of being in the hands of someone who knows whereof he speaks. He talks about things that he has had personal experience of, and you can't help but feel confidence in this. I had an instructor at one time, a professor at Yale, who used to start off one of his courses by saying, "You know, there are going to be days when I'll be talking about things that I really understand, and there are going to be days when I'm just lecturing—communicating things that I've been told—and you'll be able to tell the difference."

SJG: An honest man.

TH: The kind of teaching that really makes an impact is the kind where you *know* that someone is speaking out of his own experience. You certainly get that sense with Bhaktivedanta Swami. You get that same sense with any great spiritual person. It's not a question of simply taking your collection of classic Vaiṣṇava commentaries, mechanically balancing out the various viewpoints and saying, "Well, in general, they seem to agree on such-and-such." When that wealth of knowledge and insight is processed through the mind and the experience of a holy person, it emerges as a statement of his own understanding.

**The Krishna Consciousness Movement:
Its Development as a Religious Institution**

SJG: At this point, I'd like to focus on the Krishna consciousness movement itself, as a contemporary social reality. Earlier, you were describing the movement in its beginning, when it was functioning within the social milieu of the 60's counterculture, and you explained how the movement provided answers and direction for many young people who had been involved in the counterculture. Looking at it from the other side, one might say that through its radical rejection of the Establishment, the counterculture itself helped to prepare some people for a radical alternative, like the Krishna consciousness movement. At least superficially, then, it appears that the movement depended heavily upon the counterculture for recruits. Yet we see that now, long after the demise of the visible counterculture, the movement continues to exist and grow. Why is that? What is that appeal about the movement that doesn't depend upon that particular social environment for that appeal to work?

TH: I think that appeal is the same appeal that it's had all along. People always need some kind of guidance, some kind of direction, some kind of standard to live up to, and some kind of structure to give their lives meaning. You speak as if the condition of the world that gave rise to the counterculture has suddenly disappeared and we're now in a new age in which the world and society are a great place again, where there are no abuses of authority and no injustice.

SJG: Of course it isn't like that, but I'm simply saying that now there's no broad, organized movement, as there was before, for expressing protest against the hypocrisies and injustices of society. With the counterculture—defining it in its broadest terms—you had a large and powerful social and political movement which had major issues like civil rights and the Vietnam war upon which to focus a tremendous amount of energy. There was a broad attempt to change the whole fabric of society, to change it radically. I agree that the basic conditions that gave rise to the counterculture are still in place, but now there's really no large-scale organized effort to protest or deal with those conditions. Now it seems that people are just turning within themselves out of frustration, becoming generally alienated and cynical, even nihilistic.

TH: But if you listen to what you're saying, you're saying that there is more need for the Krishna consciousness movement now than there was then. The counterculture provided a community of sorts. It was a pretty shaky community, and it wasn't awfully supportive in many cases, and certainly in many or most cases it didn't lead anywhere—but at least it was a community. At least it was an alternative to feeling totally isolated and alienated while everybody, including you, is inwardly feeling despair but outwardly acting as if everything's O.K. But now there isn't even that. The Krishna consciousness movement provides, at the very least, a sense of community, and thus it fulfills now the same kind of need, socially speaking, that it did during the counterculture.

I'm not sure, though, that the movement initially would have prospered as it did without that kind of period, because the devotional movements have always sprung up, I think without exception, in periods of tremendous social stress and change. They've always been an answer to the collapse of society. In a sense they're ideally suited to, and tried and proven in, periods of social disorder. That's what the *Kali-yuga* is all about, isn't it? It's when everything falls to pieces, when the world is no longer a secure place and a source of satisfaction.

The descriptions in the *Viṣṇu Purāṇa* and the *Bhāgavata Purāṇa* of the features of the *Kali-yuga* say that this age is characterized by a fundamental corruption of the basic institutions of society. There is upheaval in social life, religious life, the economic, political, and legal structure, education—everything. The leaders of society are corrupt and exploit the citizens. There is wholesale degradation in the quality of human life. This is a description of every age of social chaos that's ever existed anywhere in the world. In every one of those ages, or at least in many of them, there have been movements of devotional or personal experience which have moved in to fill up the void in people's lives.

The counterculture era was a period when the problems of society were so obvious and so visible that you couldn't ignore them. We were fighting a crazy war, we had a crazy president, the whole society was riddled with contradictions in values and standards, and nobody was providing any kind of guidance or discipline. So, obviously these conditions did lend themselves to creating a mood of receptivity to a movement like yours which did provide meaning, guidance, and discipline.

As you pointed out, the most prevalent problem with American society now is alienation. Sociologists speak of the collapse of the family, the alienation of family members from one another, the absence of community, the isolation of individuals from each other. And that's what the Krishna consciousness movement at this stage is prepared to offer some kind of answer for.

In fact, the movement is offering much more than it did

during its early, countercultural years. The original temples provided a healthy peer group. Everybody was more or less the same age—roughly eighteen to twenty-five years—and came from the same background. They had all been through much the same kind of experiences and they had ended up in much the same kind of place at about the same stage in their lives. And once in the movement, their experience of the movement was all more or less similar. But what the movement is providing now is a society of a much broader vision and scope, where you have an ever-increasing range of ages and backgrounds, families with children, and a much wider variety of activities and concerns. Now when someone joins the movement, there's a sense of joining a community which is not just a peer-group defense community against the world, but something that *is* a world—a world which has its own kind of lifestyle, standards, and vitality at every level. The Krishna consciousness movement is moving, in the sociology of religion sense, from being a sect to a denomination.

SJG: Could you elaborate?

TH: The line between sect and denomination is a blurry one that sociologists argue about quite a bit. A religious body is defined as being sect or denomination with reference, generally, to the degree to which it stands in separation from or is in conflict with society. A sect tends to be selective in its emphasis. That is, it tends to have a certain kind of concern, usually individual or collective salvation, and to build the community or the organization around that particular concern. A denomination, on the other hand, tends more to reflect the general range of concerns of society. Sects, sectarian groups, tend to see themselves as standing apart from and against society, and they draw people out of, or save people from, society and provide an alternative way of life to people who otherwise would be lost if they were to stay within the ordinary social structure. With sects, you find something of an "us and them" attitude. A denomination or church, on the other hand, is fully tied into the greater society and it generally shares its values; it's not really separate from the social community at large.

SJG: So, how does all this apply to the Krishna consciousness movement?

TH: The movement is becoming a denomination gradually because it has become large enough, and well-established enough, that it's having to diversify its activities in order to deal with the whole range of human and social needs of its members: educational, economic, legal, marital, and so forth. And in developing these areas, the movement is having to deal, to an ever-increasing degree, with society at large.

For instance, now that there are many married couples in the movement there are many children requiring education. Now that you're having to concern yourself with the education of children, you're having to concern yourself with the oversight that the state has over your own schools. You have to concern yourself, therefore, with having trained, qualified, and accredited teachers, and having schools that meet state standards. The movement now has a major printing and publishing enterprise, as well as other kinds of business concerns, and therefore it has to deal with a wide variety of financial and legal dealings and concerns. So you no longer can consider yourself immune from the ordinary concerns and restraints of society. And of course you have all the residential centers themselves which have to interact, to some degree, with the larger residential community. It's one thing to have a tiny storefront temple in a large city where nobody pays all that much attention to you, but it's another thing to have a community of several hundred people living in a place, whether urban or rural, where there are lots of other people already living. You have to deal with your neighbors and define and develop relationships with them. You have to become a part of the larger community, in a sense. I see a lot of these kinds of questions being raised now, and I suspect that every time ISKCON's Governing Body Commission comes together they're having to take on more and more of these issues as they emerge.

SJG: You say that a denomination is distinguished from a sect in that it has more interaction with the society at large. But is that interaction necessarily positive and cooperative?

TH: "Denomination" doesn't necessarily imply a cooperative interaction, but it tends to be more cooperative than a sect because it is having to increase its dealings with society due to the fact that its widening interests are intersecting with those of the society. The sect does not have to deal as much with society because the range of its concerns is much narrower. A sect may be formed, for instance, around the expectation of the imminent second coming of Christ. In that case, everything is geared towards preparing for that event. Lots of other things can be put aside in the urgency of the moment. They may not bother about education, for instance, or about marriage and family. Perceiving the second coming of Christ as imminent, Paul asked that people not become encased in marital relationships because there was so little time in which to focus in on preparing for the momentous event. In a sect, there's a kind of intensity of focus that a denomination, which tends to see itself more in long-range terms, can't sustain.

One effect of that sense of urgency in a sect is that its standards of membership will be more strict. In a denomination, standards of membership tend to be broadened. It's like the difference between preparing a crew for a rescue boat in a storm and preparing for a pleasure cruise in calm weather. In the first case, you're going to be very selective about whom you get on board because in a crisis situation everyone has got to do their job perfectly. In the second case, because you're not in a crisis situation you can afford to have a few laybacks, people who aren't up to standard. The pleasure cruise doesn't require that all the passengers be competent navigators and seamen. So in a denomination you have a relaxation of standards. I don't really mean that in a pejorative sense. I'd rather use it in a positive way, to indicate a broadening of perspective, a recognition that you can allow many different types of people to become members in different ways, that you don't have to focus in on a certain type of person and a certain kind or degree of membership. I know from speaking with some Krishna devotees that there is now some kind of movement within ISKCON toward establishing a lay community or lay movement alongside the more formal, disciplined movement.

SJG: Yes, that's been happening for some time now. There's a growing recognition within the movement that there are many people who are prepared to take up the practices of Krishna consciousness, but who are not inclined to leave their secular educational or career patterns and live totally within the rigorous monastic setting of the temple community or to engage as full-time missionaries. The movement is encouraging such people through such programs as "Friends of Lord Krishna" (F.O.L.K.), to practice Krishna consciousness in their own homes. They're encouraged to study the teachings of Krishna consciousness, regularly visit their local temple, and to evolve, gradually, to the point where they meet the minimal requirements for initiation: abstention from meat-eating, intoxication, illicit sex, and gambling, as well as chanting sixteen rounds daily of the Hare Krishna mantra on beads. There are ever-increasing numbers of people who are doing this. There are now serious practitioners of Krishna consciousness in practically every walk of life: medical doctors, lawyers, teachers, a model, the owner of a major furniture company in Europe, and so on. The title "devotee" now is being applied not only to the full-time, live-in members, but to the new laity as well.

Krishna Consciousness and Religious Persecution: A Historical and Psychological View

In spite of the fact that the Krishna consciousness movement is becoming more denominational and reflecting a wider range of societal concerns, it is still viewed with suspicion by a large section of the public. Why is that?

TH: Tension between new or alternative religious movements and the societies in which they exist is nothing new in history. The early Christians had the same kind of problems that you do. They were viewed by the society of their day as breaking up families—luring children away from their families, and husbands from their wives—taking people away from educational and career situations, keeping people from going to war, and generally undermining the stability of society. I have a colleague whose main area of study is early Christianity—Christianity in the Hellenistic period. Knowing that historical period so well, he's struck with the parallel between Greek society's response to the early Christian movement and the contemporary reaction to new and alternative religious movements. He can quote the accusations, the criticisms, and the claims that were made against the early Christians by the guardians of the status quo, and they sound virtually identical to the charges and accusations that are now made against unpopular new movements. The parallelism is almost uncanny.

The classic example of this kind of thing, of course, is Socrates. Why was Socrates put to death? He was given the death sentence for corrupting the youth of Athens. He had influenced many of them to question the values of Athenian society, and thus he came to be viewed by that society as dangerous. So what do you do? You give him some hemlock and get rid of him! After you've tried and failed to argue him down, you take the final solution. In China, the Buddhists were accused of keeping people from going off to war, because instead of joining the army, many of the young men were going off to the Buddhist monasteries. This was viewed as terrible because it undermined the strength of society.

So any new religious movement is likely to get accused of precisely these kinds of things because, in fact, they do some of these things. They do draw people away from their families and provide an alternative way of life with a new value system, and they do raise questions about the state of society. And because they raise questions about society, they pose a threat to those who don't want to have those questions raised because they're uncertain how to answer them. The worst thing you can do to people is to hold up a mirror and let them see themselves as they are. Many of these new religions are doing exactly that, and people don't like it. You know the reaction of the "anti-cult" parents' groups: everybody's wrong except them. Their kids are being kidnapped and brainwashed and sold a bill of goods, and so forth. You know all the accusations. The one thing that they don't like to talk about, though, is where they failed their kids or where the society has failed their kids. That's scary. If you start thinking about that you may not be able to sleep nights. So you get together with a bunch of other people, and you all agree that these are terrible people who are doing awful things.

But there's nothing new about all of this. Throughout history, new religious movements have been feared and persecuted, not only because they challenge conventional societal values, but because they often do not conform to the religious status quo. American history is full of examples of religious persecution. Joseph Smith and the Mormons were kicked out of New York State and went to Missouri. Then they were burned out of Missouri and they had to go further west. All this happened because they had strange beliefs and were following odd practices and so people simply didn't like them. Right now you're sitting here in Lancaster County, Pennsylvania, in the middle of a wide range of sectarian groups—every conceivable variety of Amish, Mennonite, and Brethren—all of whom are here because they were run out of some other place. They came because it was safe here.

SJG: New religious groups are persecuted, it seems, not only for being different in terms of variety, but also in terms of degree. It's all right to be religious, but not *too* religious. Krishna consciousness is often attacked, for instance, for its strict ascetical and contemplative practices: vegetarianism, celibacy, chanting, and "otherworldliness" in general. What's ironic is that most of those who are doing the accusing themselves come out of a religious tradition whose founder and scriptures insist upon a fairly high degree of renunciation and asceticism. There are very strong elements of this both in the Gospels and in the Epistles. We're told to be "in the world but not of it," to serve God rather than "Mammon," to be concerned with things of the spirit and not of the flesh, and to "pray incessantly." When a Hare Krishna devotee actually engages in this sort of world-renouncing asceticism and spirituality, he is viewed as being under some sort of insidious "mind-control."

TH: "It's all right to be religious, for goodness sake, but to be religious seriously? Now that's going a little far. You shouldn't get too caught up in it. It's simply not civil to be so religious." The people who make the kinds of accusations of which you speak are doing so, in many cases, because the seriousness and intensity of your religious practice calls into question their commitment to their own religious tradition. This is what I meant by holding up the mirror. If other people are lax and immoral, you can criticize them for being that way: "Those terrible people, they're doing all those awful immoral things. How bad." But in a sense they make you look good because they're so bad. But you can't enjoy basking in reflective morality when other people come along who are more serious, religiously or ethically, than you are. It's one thing to have a set of religious standards and to hold to the view that, "Since no one could *really* live up to those standards, it's O.K. if I don't." But it's another thing when somebody comes along who really does live up to those standards. When that happens, you have to face up to the fact that those standards are realistic, that it *is* possible for people to follow them. So if I'm not following them, it's not because it's impossible to do so, but because I'm not strong enough or serious enough.

That can be a very threatening kind of thing. That's hard to deal with. It's much easier to say, "Oh, those crazy extremists. They always try to turn this into some kind of literal teaching. I know it says, 'Thou shalt not kill,' but it doesn't *really* mean that. It just means that one is not supposed to kill in this context or that context or the other context. You know, we have to be practical about these things. We can't just go around not killing at all." And then someone comes along and says, "No, you've got to take that literally—it *does* mean what it says." Now, that's really disturbing, because if it really does mean what it says, then you've got to go back and reexamine an awful lot of things that you've been doing.

So if you look at the groups that have been persecuted in the western tradition, you'll find that almost invariably the accused have been, by their own principles, ascetical and world-renouncing, following some kind of very rigorous, puritanical teaching. So it is not at all surprising that a group like yours should arouse the suspicion and fear that you do.

As people get used to the Krishna consciousness movement and especially as they come to appreciate the various ways in which the movement is appealing to those outside of an ascetical and monastic setting, they'll come to accept the movement as an integral part of the contemporary religious and social scene. I think that process has already begun to happen.

Consecrated images ("Deities") of Krishna and Rādhā are worshipped in ISKCON temples.

A *brahmacārī* (celibate student) studying the sacred texts.

Spreading the word: book distribution.

Street chanting: Hare Krishna, Hare Krishna, Krishna Krishna, Hare Hare/ Hare Rāma, Hare Rāma, Rāma Rāma, Hare Hare.

A pastoral scene from New Vṛndāvana in rural West Virginia—one of many thriving farm communities established by devotees throughout the U.S. and abroad.

Passing on the Vaiṣṇava heritage to young devotees at an ISKCON elementary school.

Devotee artist putting finishing touches on a statue of Garuda for the "First American Transcendental Exhibition" (F.A.T.E.), a multi-media museum in Los Angeles.

A F.A.T.E. exhibit illustrating the *Bhagavad-gītā*'s teaching on reincarnation: "As the embodied soul continually passes, in this body, from boyhood to youth to old age, the soul similarly passes into another body at death."

The ancient Jagannātha Chariot Festival of Purī, India, reincarnated on Fifth Avenue, New York.

INTERVIEW WITH A. L. BASHAM

Dr. A.L. Basham, a native of England, retired recently as Professor and Chairman of the Department of Asian Civilizations at The Australian National University, in Canberra, where he taught for over fifteen years. As an historian, he is one of the world's most highly respected authorities on ancient Indian civilization, and has written extensively on the Hindu and Buddhist religious traditions. His most popular work, *The Wonder That Was India* (New York: Grove Press, 1959), is a standard college text. He is the editor of *A Cultural History of India* (Oxford: Oxford University Press,1975), and has published numerous articles in academic journals. He is also the author of several articles in *Encyclopedia Britannica*, including a major article on the "History of Hinduism." Currently, he is working on a comprehensive text of the religious history of India.

One of Dr. Basham's areas of interest is the influence that Hindu and Indian ideas have exerted in the West over the last century, since the time that educated Westerners like Thoreau and Emerson began to study the Hindu scriptures in English translation. Much of the history of that cross-cultural influence involves the popularity of people whom Dr. Basham refers to as the "streamlined swamis"—Indian gurus who tend to water-down and commercialize "the wisdom of the East" for Westerners who are superficially attracted to the mystique of "spiritual India." Distinct from the "streamlined swamis," in Dr. Basham's view, is the Hare Krishna movement, an authentically orthodox, theistic Hindu movement which represents "the first time since the days of the Roman Empire [that] an Asian religion is being openly practiced by people of western origin in the streets of western cities."

The following interview took place in Dr. Basham's office at The Australian National University on April 24th and May 15th, 1980. Here, Professor Basham takes a close look at the Hare Krishna movement, viewing it not only as an important historical phenomenon, but also as a significant modern social movement.

The Hare Krishna Movement: Its Historical Significance

SJG: In your conclusion to *A Cultural History of India*, you say that the Hare Krishna movement "is historically very significant, for now for the first time since the days of the Roman Empire an Asian religion is being openly practiced by people of western origin in the streets of western cities." There are, of course, many religious groups of Asian origin that have established outposts in the West in one form or another. Why do you call special attention to the Hare Krishna movement?

ALB: For one thing, the Hare Krishna movement is very definitely a religion. It's a religion which you have to believe in fully and completely. You can't be partially a Christian and partially a Hare Krishnaite. You have to adhere to certain practices and submit yourself to various rules and taboos which do not apply to the ordinary people of the western world. The numerous organizations in the past which have brought Indian ideas to the western world—organizations like the Rāmakrishna Mission, the Theosophical Society and so on—while having certain religious characteristics, have essentially been societies of people interested in mysticism, gnosticism, and so on, mostly middle-aged people who met together once a week and listened to the local swami lecturing to them, and then went back and carried on with their conventional, secular lives. But the Hare Krishna movement demands a significant change in one's way of life if one is to become a full member of it. As such, I don't think anything like it has occurred in the European context since the days of the Roman Empire when Christianity, Judaism, Mithraism, and other religions made numerous converts in the West. It is, therefore, something not completely new, but something which, I think, hasn't happened for a very long time indeed. And so I feel that it is very important historically. You notice, I said in the *streets* of western cities. We have, in fact, people of purely western blood coming from families of the Christian or Jewish tradition who are doing, in the streets of western cities, all the things and more which religious Hindus do in the streets of Calcutta. This being the case, I feel that—without making any value judgements—it is a very important historical phenomenon, and I can't think of anything like it since the Roman Empire.

SJG: In that same conclusion to *A Cultural History of India*, you write, "A new aspect of the counter-attack from the East is the importation not only of the mystical gnosis of India, but also of her simple faith. This is chiefly the work of the Hare Krishna movement founded by Śrīla Prabhupāda." What sorts of groups do you have in mind when you refer to the importation of "the mystical gnosis of India"? How is the Krishna consciousness movement different from these?

ALB: One can trace the steadily increasing influence of mystical gnosis in the western world almost from the end of the eighteenth-century onwards when the *Bhagavad-gītā* was first translated into a European language by Charles Wilkins. Indian ideas circulated rapidly among the intelligentsia, not only in the English-speaking world, but also in other parts of Europe. They certainly had an effect on people throughout the western world—Germans like Schlegel, Deussen, and Schopenhauer, Americans like Thoreau and Emerson, Englishmen like Max Mueller (an Englishman by adoption) and Aldous Huxley, Frenchmen such as Romain Rolland, and Russians like Tolstoy. But these people were in no sense thoroughgoing Hindus and they were impressed primarily by the mysticism of the Upaniṣads and of the *Bhagavad-gītā*. This movement was strengthened through various developments such as the Theosophical Society, and the publication of Sir Edwin Arnold's *The Light of Asia* in the 1870's, a book which had a significant effect on quite a number of people in developing a sympathetic attitude towards Buddhism.

Since the Second World War, particularly, there has been a great increase in the number of practitioners and teachers of Indian mystical gnosis in the western world. But these people have been essentially teachers of yoga, of mystical praxis, and of mystical ideas, but they have not been, in the same sense as in your Hare Krishna movement, *religious* leaders. Undoubtedly you do practice some form of meditation in the Hare Krishna movement, but your primary activity is not mysticism in that sense but singing the praises of Krishna, isn't it?

SJG: Yes. We do not practice any sort of silent, abstract contemplation, or any techniques of a purely mental or psychic nature. Our primary form of meditation is devotional and theistic—the recitation or singing of the *mahamantra:* Hare Krishna, Hare Krishna, Krishna Krishna, Hare Hare/ Hare Rāma, Hare Rāma, Rāma Rāma, Hare Hare. These sounds are accepted as eternal, divine names of God, spiritual sounds which are non-different from God. This chanting is performed either individually or in congregation, within the temple or out in the streets.

ALB: And so this is a different thing. It is the simple Indian *bhakti* which you have brought into the western world and not the mystical, other-worldly Upaniṣadic doctrines which you may accept in theory, at least, but which do not mean so much to you as these simple, straightforward practices.

SJG: But the *bhakti* tradition can also be accurately described as mystical and other-worldly, don't you think? By "mystical" or "gnostic" I think you are referring specifically to Indian pantheism or monism, aren't you?

ALB: Yes, that's correct. Certainly *bhakti* tradition is mystical. It leads to transcendental experience. I myself have watched—and you could almost say taken part in—Caitanya *kīrtans* in Calcutta where one does feel complete release from all the toils and worries of the world and one is carried off into a higher sphere. It's a wonderful experience and you feel better for it. This is a kind of mysticism; I'm not disputing it. But when I talk about the mystical gnosis of India I mean primarily the Advaita Vedānta of Śaṅkara and his modern supporters and followers. This has come through in all sorts of ways with the Rāmakrishna Mission and many smaller movements of one kind or another. But it isn't quite the same thing as yours, which is essentially a matter of simple faith—faith which is, of course, brilliantly articulated in a long-standing theological tradition.

SJG: In a letter you recently sent me, you briefly contrast the Hare Krishna movement with the *Vedānta* of the neo-Hindu propagandists whom you refer to as the "streamlined swamis." What exactly do you mean?

ALB: "Streamlined swamis" is a facetious phrase which I invented myself. I don't mean it with any particular ill will and I don't wish to be unduly critical in the use of this term, but I intend it as a reference to the doctrines and teaching which various Indian swamis put forth, a streamlined kind of Hindu mysticism designed to appeal to modern, jet-age disciples: levitation in a few months or even weeks, *mokṣa* in a few easy lessons—a Hinduism without class, without worship, without rigid taboos, and so forth. At the opposite extreme from your form of Indian religion or mysticism, we have, for example, Transcendental Meditation. Now, I don't want to disparage Transcendental Meditation because I know it's done people some good. It relaxes them. So I'm not unduly critical of Transcendental Meditation, but it is a typically "streamlined" form of Hinduism. It's scarcely Hinduism at all. In fact, we are told by the Transcendental Meditationists that you can be a member of their organization—you can follow their various practices, their yogic meditations and so on—and yet you don't have to give up anything you already believe in. You can belong to a church and participate in the Eucharist, have your children baptised, or you can remain an unbeliever and an atheist. Transcendental Meditation seems to have dropped all its theological and even philosophical trappings. It's just a method of mental and psychic training.

That is the one extreme. Yours is the other. You appropriate an Indian religious sect—its beliefs, its practices, all its taboos, and so on—root and branch and import it into the West. In between these extremes we have all sorts of variations, and the "streamlined swamis" are those who tend rather to the Transcendental Meditation extreme than to yours. Some of the modern Rāmakrishna people seem to be going in that direction. I don't mean it with any undue disparagement, but such people do streamline their religious, theological, and philosophical ideas in order to bring them up-to-date, to make them palatable to the twentieth-century western mind. That being the case, I think my phrase "streamlined swamis" is perhaps justified.

The Hare Krishna Movement vs. "The Permissive Society"

SJG: So, as far as the other extreme—the Krishna consciousness movement—is concerned, you see its followers as pursuing more than merely Indian mystical ideas or meditational techniques. They venture upon a path of total self-transformation, devoting themselves to a path that represents a clearly radical departure from normative western thought, behavior, and lifestyle. In your view, then, what is it about western or modern culture that they find so distasteful? Against what are they rebelling? On the other hand, what is it about Indian culture or Vaiṣṇava *bhakti* tradition that they find so attractive?

ALB: I think one of the things that they subconsciously find difficult to get on with is the "permissive society," the notion of "do your own thing": concern yourself only with the fulfillment of your own personal whims and aims. You know the Hindu doctrine of the four progressive aims of life: *dharma* [social duty], *artha* [acquisition of wealth], *kāma* [worldly enjoyment], and *mokṣa* [liberation] as the final end. The tendency of the permissive society is to leave *dharma* out altogether. And if you're one of the "outsider" types who float around among the educated youth today— quite a few of our students are like that—you might also leave *artha* out. All you need bother about is *kāma*. And that *kāma* needn't necessarily express itself in sexual activity. A lot of these kids seem to think that *kāma* just means having sex, due to the phrase "*Kāma-sūtra*." But obviously, in its broad context, *kāma* means self-gratification: just do whatever you want to do, whatever you imagine is going to make you happy.

SJG: As they say, "If it feels good, do it."

ALB: Yes, if you think it's going to benefit you and make you happy, then do it. That's *kāma*. And they find it just doesn't work. They want something to map their courses by; they want something which gives them a feeling of direction. And, of course, *dharma* does that. Psychologically, if we don't follow *dharma*—whatever our *dharma* may be—we're sunk. As you realize, in the Hindu tradition, while there is *sanātana-dharma* [the eternal codes of right conduct, applying to everybody], everyone has also their own individual *dharma*, *sva-dharma*. We've got to follow our *dharma* or we suffer from all sorts of psychological difficulties, to say the least of it. It affects our *karma* [actions] and our overall behavior as well as our future happiness. And in this way—whatever we believe about a future life—there is a lot of truth in the fundamental doctrines of Hinduism. Now, if people have no *dharma*, if they deliberately deny having a *dharma*, then their only *dharma* is just a vague sense of not bothering other people too much and getting on with "doing their own thing." But, everybody has a different "own thing." They are no longer a group; they don't really belong to anybody. They are isolated. Moreover, their life lacks direction. They drift. And for this reason, among others, we have a great growth in the use of dangerous drugs nowadays.

Sexual promiscuity or the permissive society may look all right on paper, but it has certain disadvantages which I think the world, more and more, is beginning to realize. For one thing, while the famous "pill" has largely solved the problem of unwanted children—you can now use sex as a pleasant entertainment without any great fear of consequences—it hasn't solved the problem of human jealousy. A man and a woman are not going to be very happy in their relationship when they are constantly fearing that someday somebody might come along and take their partner away from them. That is what they *are* fearing today. I know from many of my students whom I've talked to—especially it affects the women but men feel it too. The thought of losing their beloved constantly haunts them. And it's the same in marriage. A young married man has no real confidence in being about to keep his spouse until old age. And perhaps he himself will turn his eyes to another one. And thus, the lack of stability in human relationships is one of the main causes of the growth of mental and psychological trouble in the world today.

Your movement sets itself diametrically against all this sort of thing. It disparages undue sexual activity. You mustn't have sexual activity unless you definitely want to produce a child from it. One man for one woman for the rest of your life. It goes back, in fact, in a very new and different guise, to eighteenth and nineteenth century Puritanism. I might seem old-fashioned, but it seems to me that that is what the world needs. It may be that with the invention of easier and reliable contraception, the world will never go back to anything quite like the old Puritanical conception of human relationships, but it needs something a bit like Puritanism . . . not necessarily the rigid Puritanism which would brand every person who committed adultery with an "A" on their forehead or, as the Muslims do in Saudi Arabia, execute them. It should be far more tolerant than that. At least some people feel that the world needs, and that they need, a system which has taboos about it. We can't all be grown-up all the time; only *sannyāsis* and saints can do that. Many of us, for most of our lives, are children at heart, and we need some sort of guidance and control. A religious movement gives that. It is depressing that the Christian churches are doing very little in this respect now. Even the Catholics are getting almost as permissive as the unbelievers in their ideas of human relationships.

Not only does the young man or woman of this age, in many cases at least, find that the permissive society is unsatisfying, but he also finds the system of values which he is expected to follow unsatisfying. On the one hand, he has the choice of one or other of the Christian communities, most of which still expect him to believe in certain doctrines he might find difficult to accept, such as the physical resurrection of Jesus. On the other hand, he has downright unbelief, which is psychologically unsatisfying. Man needs a sense of the mystery and the wonder of the world and of his existence within it. Unbelief or lack of concern for religion—atheism, agnosticism, whatever you like to call it—just doesn't give that. An attitude of faith is really very important for human happiness: faith in something outside oneself, faith in the fundamental goodness of the world, or faith that there is good in the world and that the world has meaning. And if you can get that, you are at least some way on the road to a happier and better life. I think that is what attracts some people to the Hare Krishna movement. The movement offers them a completely different lifestyle, one which is guided and directed. Within the framework of the movement they have a good deal of liberty, but it lays down guidelines which its members are expected to follow. Many young people really need direction, guidance, meaning.

Further, there is a general feeling, among many, that the

capitalist society has made a mess of things. Communist society, which allows even less freedom than capitalism does, has also made a mess of things. Between them there is the danger of their blowing the world to bits. Many seek a third alternative, a different way of life which is neither one nor the other. Your movement presents them with an alternative which some, at least, find acceptable.

Is The Movement "Hindu"?

SJG: I'd like to get your views on the Hare Krishna movement in relation to its roots in Indian religious and cultural tradition. One of the problems that we experience when attempting to educate the public about the historical roots of the movement is that the most convenient term for us to use, and the one that the average person will relate to, is "Hinduism." Yet, we ourselves prefer to avoid the word altogether for a number of reasons, one of which is that "Hinduism" is a highly stereotyped term. It tends to bring to mind such notions as nondevotional monism and pantheism, as well as polytheism and caste, notions which we're not eager to be identified with.

ALB: It's interesting to look at the sources of those western stereotypes. I think I've already mentioned what seems to me to be the origin of the monism stereotype—the nonpersonal nature of God and ultimate oneness of souls and God. It goes back to figures in the nineteenth century like Emerson and Thoreau in America, various German thinkers, the Theosophical Society and, in later times, people like Aldous Huxley, Christopher Isherwood, and all the innumerable swamis who have come over from India and preached in the West. Nearly all of them put forward monistic doctrines. And that, of course, has built-up the stereotype of Hinduism as monism.

The stereotype of polytheism and the evils of the caste system, I think, owes more than anything to Christian missionaries. In the days before Indian independence, the Christian missions would, from time to time, send active missionary workers back to England, America, Germany, or wherever it might be, on furlough, and these people would be much in demand to give lectures in church halls, and to preach the Sunday sermon. And these people would paint a terrible picture of the miserable, suffering Indian masses who were benighted by their nasty, idolatrous polytheism and ground under by the wicked brahmans who imposed a cruel class system upon them. I remember hearing such things when I was a very little boy in the 1920's. Later on, of course, a better type of Christian missionary appeared who tried to make a real study of Hinduism from his own angle and developed a much more understanding and tolerant view of it. But the old-fashioned type of missionary was quite certain that Hinduism was the work of the Devil, and hence that it was very evil. It did all the things which Christianity, especially Protestant Christianity, said you shouldn't do, such as image-worship and the worship of many gods. Catholics were always much more tolerant of this sort of thing. Though he may be theoretically monotheistic, the simple Catholic will, to all intents and purposes, pray to quite a wide range of divinities, including the Blessed Virgin Mary and various important saints, often in the form of physical images. But Protestant Christianity was founded on the basis that there is one God only, divided into three persons, and that worship of images is sinful. To the Protestant of the old-fashioned kind, this was a terrible thing to do, almost as bad as it was to a traditional Jew or Muslim. So the missionaries, I think, are largely responsible for the polytheism stereotype and the "caste-ridden society" stereotype.

The caste-system stereotype, the evils-of-caste notion came also from the British rulers of India who, in the last fifty years or so of their power, did their utmost to prove that they were there for India's good. One of the arguments that I remember hearing against Indian independence was that India is so divided by caste that it could never stand on its own two feet while the caste-system existed, because the system destroyed the unity of the nation. And you hear the same thing being said even by Indian reformers to this day. But it certainly hasn't broken up the unity of the nation. The British in India, in any case—or many of them—liked to propagate this idea that the caste-system is a very evil thing in Indian life.

SJG: Another reason we tend to avoid applying the designation "Hindu" to ourselves is that the founder of the Hare Krishna movement, Śrīla Prabhupāda, felt that it has a distinctly sectarian implication. One is "Hindu" in contradistinction to being Christian, Jewish, Muslim, etc. Krishna consciousness, viewed from within as a universal, transcultural spiritual principle, just doesn't fit neatly into the contrived historical-cultural term "Hindu." A more appropriate term for Krishna consciousness, from our point of view, would be "*sanātana-dharma*," "eternal Religion." If truth is indeed true, it must be true everywhere and for everybody. It must transcend relative cultural orientations. But for the sake of placing Krishna consciousness on the map of the history of religions, the term "Vaiṣṇavism," signifying the cultural and theological tradition based upon the worship of Viṣṇu or Krishna, is an accurate and descriptive term for the historical tradition of Krishna consciousness. We refer to ourselves as "Vaiṣṇavas."

ALB: Yes, you can say "We're not Hindus, we're Vaiṣṇavas." That's fair enough. But the term "Vaiṣṇava" won't do for the whole complex of religious practice which goes on in India because there's a great deal there that isn't Vaiṣṇava. And if you're going to say "Vaiṣṇava," "Śaiva," "Śākta," and so on, you're going to imply that there are three separate religions which are as different from one another as perhaps Christianity is from Islam, and this is rather misleading. One needs one comprehensive term to cover the whole thing and I don't know of any other than "Hinduism." But I agree that it's not a very satisfactory term, and it includes some practices which are no longer acceptable to modern man. If you're going to say that "the Hindu performs *satī*" [the self-immolation or forced immolation of widows], for instance, this would be incorrect, because *satī* is not an essential part of Hinduism. You might say that caste is an essential part of Hinduism, and there are Indians, certainly, who say that. It's very hard to put your fingers on one doctrine which is the common denominator or common factor of Hinduism. With practically every aspect of Hindu doctrine, one can find one sect or other that rejects it. The Vīraśaivas, some of them at any rate, seem to have more or less rejected the whole doctrine of transmigration. The authority of the brahman class is rejected by some rather extremist groups of Hindus. The Vedas—that is to say the Vedas in the sense of the four original Vedas—are rejected by others. So it's very difficult to find one good term which can cover the whole thing. I agree, though, that "Hinduism" is not very satisfactory as a term.

SJG: In light of the fact that Westerners tend to stereotype Hinduism as fundamentally non-theistic, or non-monotheistic, it's quite significant that the Krishna consciousness movement has introduced the theistic side of Hindu tradition to the West. The movement has widely disseminated the major texts of theistic Hinduism in English and other European language translations; it has introduced *saṅkīrtan*, public devotional chanting, in the streets of hundreds of western cities; it has organized large devotional festivals such as the Jagannātha Rathayātrā in several major cities, and so on. Through the publications and activities of the movement, many Westerners have become aware of *bhakti* tradition for the first time.

ALB: Yes, that's certainly true. I'm sure there are many people in the West who had no idea that Hinduism involved all this. From the point of view of spreading knowledge of Indian religion, you have done a great deal in the western world.

You've done much more than the swamis of the Rāmakrishna Mission and others, because they propagate a form of Hinduism in which the devotional, theistic aspect is almost entirely cut out and ignored. Yours, you see, is the straightforward Hinduism of the common man, the best form of it. I'm sure, if nothing else, you have a great educational function in explaining and exemplifying these things, by living example, to the people of the western world

The Two Faces of Hindu Tradition: A Psychological Perspective

SJG: Let me ask you to explain a little more about the two major and conflicting schools of Indian thought which you've been alluding to in our discussion: the devotional/theistic school, versus the non-devotional/non-theistic school—that is, Indian dualism (Dvaita) and Indian nondualism (Advaita), or what might be called the Personalistic versus Impersonalistic traditions. Do you have any suggestions—perhaps from a psychological point of view—or perhaps from a sociology of knowledge perspective, why people, in fact, become attracted to the monism of the Impersonalistic school. What are such people looking for? What sorts of needs may be satisfied by that particular philosophical viewpoint?

ALB: You're referring presumably to people in the western world?

SJG: I think we can generalize.

ALB: I don't know whether it's true of everybody, but the people who take up Indian mysticism or religion in one form or another, generally take up some kind of Advaita because that is what is chiefly propagated by the people whom I call the "streamlined swamis." Then, there have been various influences of a literary and intellectual kind which have led to this phenomenon, some of which I mentioned earlier, such as people in your own America like Emerson and Thoreau who were much taken with the Advaita philosophy and spread knowledge of it. Then, in more recent decades, in the 1930's and the 40's, it was people like Aldous Huxley who was thoroughly committed to an Advaita view of life. In his *Perennial Philosophy* he tried to show that the Advaita doctrine was the only one which made sense to modern man who had lost faith in a personal God. All these influences, not only from India but also from people of western origin who had absorbed all or something of Indian Advaita philosophy and mysticism, certainly had a big effect.

But, we can suggest that there are even psychological influences at work. You see, this is an age of deep insecurity and fear—fear of serious and terrible catastrophes in the world such as a Third World War, economic depression, severe depletion of natural resources, widespread social breakdown, disintegration of human moral values and so on—fears of all sorts and kinds which derive from the "acquisitive society" and the "permissive society." And this deep insecurity and anxiety, in turn, helps towards a feeling that you've got to negate or transcend your individuality, because if you're no longer a personality, a self, you can't suffer, because there's no self to have consciousness of suffering. Moreover, the Advaita formula of "*atman* equals Brahman" [the individual soul is identical with the Supreme Soul] implies that you yourself are the whole universe and all that underlies it. But this is a refined form of egotism, if you like. It satisfies the individualist craving and at the same time, by getting rid of the specific embodied individual, it gives the person hope that he will be saved from all the sufferings of finite selfhood. And that, of course, is also at the bottom of Theravada Buddhism, which also believes that in the ultimate condition, the human personality disintegrates; there is no personality, only *nirvāṇa* is left. Thus Buddhism really has much in common with Advaita Vedānta, but with a slightly different terminology.

SJG: So there are two aspects, you're saying, of the attraction to impersonalist thought. One is the fear of a spiritual personal identity, and the other is a kind of ultimate egotism—a desire to become God.

ALB: Yes, that is how I see it.

SJG: In his commentary on one verse of the *Bhagavad-gītā*, Śrīla Prabhupāda writes, "For those who are materially absorbed, the concept of retaining the personality after liberation from matter frightens them. When such materialistic men are informed that spiritual life is also individual and personal, they are afraid of becoming persons again, so they naturally prefer a kind of merging into the impersonal void." In other words, those who have experienced the suffering of the world conclude that happiness can be experienced only when one is freed from personal identity per se, because it was as individual, personal selves that they experienced suffering.

ALB: Yes, they want to cut out their identity. If you're not an individual, you can't suffer. If you cease to be a person, you obviously transcend suffering. They want to get rid of themselves because they're frightened of being a person. It's a deep cosmic fear, a fear of the whole universe, the sort of thing that is reflected in some of the existentialist philosophers like Heidegger and Sartre.

SJG: Recently, you related to me some personal observations concerning Śaṅkarite [Advaita] *sannyāsis* [monks] in India.

ALB: Well, I don't want to do them less than justice, but Śaṅkarite *sannyāsis* and lay Śaṅkarites who claim to have gone far in the path of Rāja-yoga and Śaṅkarite meditation tend to be rather pompous, self-satisfied, and self-opinionated. I don't see any fading away of the self with them. Rather, the reverse. And this sort of attitude of pompous self-satisfaction—although I can think of many very noble and fine exceptions—is something which I think the Indian *sannyāsi* is prone to suffer from. This may happen with the Śaṅkarite teachers particularly because of the very character of the Advaita Vedānta doctrine: the self is Brahman, the supreme spiritual reality. Everything that isn't the Self, that isn't Brahman, is just *māyā*, illusion.

And there are strong logical arguments against Śaṅkara's doctrines. They hold together all right provided you accept Śaṅkara's very narrow and not normally accepted definition of *sat* or *satya*, truth or reality—that the only thing you can call real is something which is eternal and never changes, that doesn't come into being and doesn't disappear. That, in my view, is a forced interpretation of reality. *Satya*, in Śaṅkarite philosophy, isn't *satya* as the ordinary man in the street understands it. It's something quite different.

SJG: You've mentioned that Śaṅkara didn't interpret certain texts because of their theistic emphasis.

ALB: Well, I know of no Śaṅkara commentary on *Śvetāśvatara Upaniṣad*, for instance, which, as you know very well, is thoroughgoing theism. A thread of theism goes right through the Upaniṣads from the earliest to the later ones, parallel with the non-theistic Advaita. Right near the beginning of the oldest Upaniṣad of all, the *Bṛhadāraṇyaka Upaniṣad*, we read, "At first there was nothing at all but the One, and that One was in the form of a *puruṣa*, of a *Person*." What one must realize is that in ancient India there was a wide range of speculative and mystical thought of one kind or another which produced Jainism, Buddhism, theism, and Advaita of various kinds. You could even find the early elements of Tantrism in some of the Upaniṣads. Many Śaṅkarites do not recognize the tremendous wealth and richness of Indian philosophical and speculative thought in ancient India.

SJG: You seem to express a preference for the dualistic and theistic traditions. What is it about the great Vaiṣṇava theologians like Rāmānuja and Madhva that you find more attractive or more . . .

ALB: I find their teachings more attractive because they do leave room for personality in the universe: the personality of God and the personalities of the individual souls who are God's children and who are always sufficiently individualized to recognize themselves as being creatures of God. What the factual truth of the Rāmānuja picture of the universe is, I don't wish to discuss here. But it is certainly a much more attractive universe to me than the Śaṅkara one; and for me it's much more psychologically satisfying.

SJG: Why?

ALB: Well, because the world obviously isn't "one." It may all be one within the body of God, contained in God. But I'm not you and you're not me and I don't see why, when I achieve complete *mokṣa* (which I probably never shall in a thousand lives) I should be completely merged in you, and I don't think I want to be. I don't see logically why I should. I might become merged in God in that I feel that I'm almost one with God in devotion, and that I am within God, within the soul of God or that my soul is linked with God. But if I lose my individuality completely, I don't see how I can enjoy the presence of God.

SJG: Yes, that is our view also.

ALB: Well, these are all the arguments that go back to Rāmānuja and his criticism of Śaṅkara. And they are thoroughly valid. Śaṅkara might have been more clever as a philosopher than Rāmānuja, but in the final analysis I think that Rāmānuja was a better philosopher.

SJG: Theologically, our tradition is quite close to that of Rāmānuja.

ALB: Yes, I know it is. If you follow Caitanya, you're close to Rāmānuja.

SJG: The special distinctive feature of Śrī Caitanya's philosophy is the doctrine of *acintya-bhedābheda-tattva*—that the soul is inconceivably, simultaneously one with and different from God. In other words, the soul is of the same spiritual substance as God, but it is an entity distinct from God—qualitatively one but quantitatively different.

ALB: That is very clearly stated by the Caitanya school.

The Movement's Roots in India's Religious History

SJG: You've put the Krishna consciousness movement within the broad historical context of theistic Hinduism, the *bhakti* tradition. More specifically, as you know, the movement is a direct modern expression of the devotional movement founded in sixteenth century Bengal by the well-known mystic and saint Śrī Caitanya. In your *Encyclopaedia Britannica* article, "History of Hinduism," you state that "with its discouragement of ritualism, its strong ethical emphasis and its joyful expressive method of worship, the Caitanya movement affected the whole life of Bengal and was not without influence in other parts of India." With these or any other points in mind, what is most distinctive and important about Śrī Caitanya's movement within the overall context of India's religious history?

ALB: There were, of course, other movements in other parts of India during the medieval period which are rather similar, but the Caitanya movement was, perhaps, most fully expressive of certain characteristics of these movements. It dispensed with the traditional, complicated, brahminical *yajña* rituals, viewing them as unnecessary for salvation. As far as its "strong ethical emphasis" is concerned, it taught fellowship and brotherhood and the love of man for man with an intensity which many religious movements in India didn't. It tended, thus, to override caste. We're told that members of all castes were welcome into Caitanya's order and that they lived together in perfect amity and unity. I'm afraid that caste has slipped back to some extent into the Caitanya movement of Bengal of the present. But I believe it was originally intended to form a sort of casteless community of devotees. And, finally, the movement's joyful and expressive method of worship: the *kīrtan* with dancing through the streets of the towns and villages. If certain other Hindu sects do adopt this practice, I think they've done so under the influence of Caitanya. And all these things have tended to affect the whole life not only of Bengal but, to some extent, the rest of India. The Caitanya movement reaches well beyond the borders of Bengal. It is very influential in Orissa. There are Caitanyaites in Assam, and in Bihar, and of course there is a big outpost of Caitanyaites in Mathura and Vṛndāvana and throughout that whole famous sacred area of Krishnaism.

SJG: It's very strong, also, in modern Bangladesh.

ALB: Yes, there are quite a few followers of Caitanya in Bangladesh of course. But that counts as Bengal, historically. It's just a part of Bengal which, as a result of historical events, has been cut off from the rest.

SJG: You mentioned earlier that you had taken part in a Caitanya *kīrtan* in Calcutta. Can you describe that experience?

ALB: Over the years, I've observed several Caitanya *kīrtans* but I remember one in particular. It was about twenty years ago. I got off a train in Sealdah Station, in Calcutta, just about sunset, and noticed that there was a Caitanya *kīrtan* taking place in one corner of the station yard. Whenever I come across a *kīrtan* in progress, I always stop and watch and listen, but often I'm in a hurry and have other things to do, and so I can only wait a minute or two. This time I was in no hurry. I had plenty of time to spare. The devotees had erected a decorative tent in which they had set up the statue of Krishna and numerous brightly colored pictures of Krishna and Caitanya and the various saints of the order. The whole scene was lit up with bright lights and decorated with many flowers and various other decorations. Not very many people were there at first, but as I stood by watching and looking, more and more people came along and got involved. They were chanting "Hare Krishna, Hare Rāma" just as you do. They kept on chanting and chanting and chanting, until, after a while, a few of them began to dance and then nearly everybody was dancing. I don't think I got as far as dancing, but I found that I was certainly joining in the chanting and I was really carried away. I was there for at least two hours. It was a wonderful experience.

As I think you know, on a theoretical and logical level I am not able to fully accept your doctrine of the historicity of Krishna and so on, but nevertheless I do see the emotional and spiritual force of the Caitanya movement. That evening outside Sealdah Station is something which I never forget—the intense experience of exhilaration and relief, and the feeling of security and safety and inner happiness which came from it. And it was so clear that all the people were feeling it. It couldn't but affect me too. The worshipers were mostly poor people or lower-middle class and better types of working class people from the buildings and tenements of the surrounding neighborhood. They had, most of the time, very dull and difficult lives, no doubt. They worked hard and hadn't much to look forward to materially. But there was such happiness, such relief from tension and strain on their faces as one could hardly imagine. And I feel that this is a very good form of religious worship. Irrespective of the truth or falsehood of what they believe in, it does people enormous good. I'm afraid I tend to take a rather pragmatic view of religion.

SJG: The tradition is, of course, not based merely upon cathartic religious emotionalism, but on a rich and sophisticated theology as well.

ALB: Yes, of course Caitanya had a theology, and it was fully developed by his immediate and subsequent followers. We have no writings of Caitanya himself other than several devotional hymns, but he was obviously very highly educated in his own lore and tradition and he developed a cohesive theology which he communicated orally to his followers, and which was fully elucidated in their various theological commentaries and other writings. So, obviously, the Caitanya tradition has its own logically worked out philosophical and theological system, one that is based upon the *Bhagavad-gītā* and the *Bhāgavata Purāṇa* and of course Caitanya's own special insights. But this tradition is distinctive in that it gives full play to religious emotion. It demonstrates that theological rationality and religious emotion go hand in hand. Mere theology cannot satisfy the heart. That is the importance of *bhakti*.

SJG: Would you view *bhakti* as one of India's most important gifts to the world?

ALB: Yes, I would say so. Of course, from a purely quantitative, historical point of view, we'd have to say that Buddhism was India's most significant gift to the world. Buddhism became much more of a missionary religion than Hinduism ever was, and has affected the life and the way of thought of most of Asia. Whether this is spiritually the greatest gift or the greatest in the sense of the most marvelous is another matter. Although the Indian form of *bhakti* hasn't had a great direct influence on the rest of the world, we can say that this attitude of loving devotion to a personal God, as developed in Indian *bhakti* tradition, is undoubtedly one of India's greatest gifts to the world, and a very precious and a very valuable gift. Unfortunately, the world has not yet taken to it. The Christians, the Jews, and to some extent the Muslims, have developed their own particular types of *bhakti*. Whether there was mutual influence at any earlier time, whether Indian *bhakti* had influence on Christian *bhakti* in the days of the early church, is something of which we have no very positive evidence, either way. Some Indians like to think that India had a great deal of influence on the formation of Christianity and on Greek philosophy also. There are certain striking parallels right enough, but the evidence isn't sufficient to come to a final conclusion. But, in any case, *bhakti* is a very important gift of India to the world if the world will accept it.

Is It Artificial for Westerners to Become Devotees of Krishna?

SJG: Do you think that there is anything in any sense artificial about Westerners taking to the path of *bhakti* as expressed in Vaiṣṇava culture, or does this, perhaps, say something about the universality or universal appeal of that culture?

ALB: What do you mean by artificial?

SJG: Well, some people say something to the effect that, "If you're seeking the religious life, then why don't you look within your *own* religious tradition, your own western roots?"—the implication being that there is something unnatural or contrived about seeking within a different cultural context for spiritual knowledge or spiritual life.

ALB: People did just what you are doing two thousand years ago in the days of the Roman Empire because they became dissatisfied with their own culture and their own religion, and no doubt they too were criticized because they didn't look within their own religious tradition. And what came out of it? A different culture—one which obviously had some of its roots in the culture of the Roman Empire and other roots in early Palestine. And it formed a unity of its own. Something similar is happening now. Two or three hundred years ago nobody in Europe or in the western world could have become a Hare Krishnaite even if he wanted to, because he wouldn't have known anything about it. Very few people had visited India, and those who had knew next to nothing about Indian religion. Now that this is known and understood, it's bound to have some effect. Just as Christianity has had a significant effect on India, so Indian religion will have an effect on the western world.

As I visualize the future, the cultures of the world will not become exactly homogeneous, but at least they will draw closer together. As things are now, there is a great deal of difference between the values and the attitudes to life of the educated New Yorker or Londoner or Melbourner, and the simple Indian peasant of Uttar Pradesh. But those differences are not quite as great as they were a hundred years ago and they are becoming less and less. We may find one hundred years from now that the differences between the average European or American and the average Indian will be no more than, shall we say, the differences between the average Swede and the average Spaniard, brought up broadly in the same cultural milieu but with very considerable regional differences. I think this sort of thing is inevitable in a world which is getting smaller, where people are traveling further and learning more about one another.

If we're going to say that these young people in the West are unnatural and artificial in taking to Hare Krishnaism, then we must say that all the Indians who have adopted Christianity (of which there are about ten million now) and who, in earlier generations, adopted Islam, were equally unnatural. It must cut both ways. In a free world, every religion has every right to make converts where it wants to, provided it makes them by fair means and without compulsion. And people have every right to try whatever legitimate religious movement they feel will do them the most good. And if some young people in the western world are finding benefit from the Hare Krishna movement, why shouldn't they participate in it? We have to seek for the best wherever we can find it. The great majority of people of the western world probably find the Hare Krishna movement rather fantastic and bizarre. But many don't, and they are, in my view, fully entitled to do the Hare Krishna thing without being accused of being unnatural or artificial.

The Movement in Social Context

SJG: How might the movement better communicate its message to the public or how might it at least bring the public to understand it better?

ALB: I can't suggest much about that. You're engaged in a certain amount of public education as it is. Possibly you should put a little less emphasis on the priestly side and do more to encourage the lay, fringe membership. The feeling of ordinary people is that one can't belong to your movement unless one shaves his head, wears a *dhoti*, and dances in the streets. Obviously, most people don't want to do those things. The movement hasn't adapted itself very much to the customs and the habits of the local folk. I'm not saying that you should give up any of your fundamental beliefs such as vegetarianism and so on. If you can compromise to some extent on some of the less important ones, you might gain more members. You might get more converts if you made a few more concessions to the western way of life. On the other hand, though, if you keep to your rules rigidly you can be sure that those converts that you do make will be really earnest ones and not half-hearted. It's not for me to give advice. This is something your movement must decide for itself.

SJG: Śrīla Prabhupāda always stressed quality over quantity. He often used to say that he would consider his mission a success if he brought only one sincere soul to pure Krishna consciousness. I can say, however, that within the movement there is increasing acceptance of the fact that a person can participate in the spiritual life of Krishna consciousness without necessarily living in the ashram and wearing the traditional attire and so on. There are, in recent years, increasing numbers of older, socially established people who live and work on the outside—family people who participate to varying degrees in the ritual and ethical practices of Krishna consciousness, and study its teachings.

ALB: Yes, you're the priests of the movement, as it were, and you're developing a lay membership.

SJG: Yes, that's happening now. That's a more or less recent development.

ALB: If ISKCON is to become a significant factor in the world, that is what you'll have to do. But, of course, you must be careful, at the same time, to maintain very strict moral and spiritual principles within your core membership.

SJG: You wrote to me recently that you believe that the Hare Krishna movement is "here to stay." What evidences do you see of this staying power?

ALB: It's been here for quite a while now, since 1966. You've had fourteen years and you've made some impact in that span of time. Everybody in the big cities knows you and recognizes you, in many countries of the world. Much depends of course on the proper education of your children. You're training your children to be good Hare Krishnaites aren't you?

SJG: Yes. In our children's schools, in addition to all the standard academic subjects, the children learn Sanskrit and study the *Bhagavad-gītā* and so forth, and they're taught fundamental brahminical principles.

ALB: So they're getting special education in the Hare Krishna way of life. Some of them might revolt against it and turn to the secular world when they're older. Those who don't will form a core to carry the Hare Krishna movement down to further generations. I fail to see why you shouldn't survive. Also, you've got a well-defined hierarchical structure now and you seem to be financially well established. Of course the danger is that your movement will slowly fizzle out like the Theosophical Society, which at the beginning of this century was quite an active and sizable society, but is now a rather effete organization of a few elderly people. But there again, you see, you are a real religion, and the Theosophical Society is just a sort of "society"—it's "streamlined." Your movement has its roots in early sixteenth century Bengal; it's not just, to use my favorite expression, a "streamlined" thing, especially tailored to meet the needs and the interests of the western world. That may prevent you from getting a mass membership. But in the long run, it may be a source of strength.

SJG: You also state that the movement "will have an influence far beyond it's actual membership in the years to come, making for gentleness in human relationships and faith in the fundamental goodness of the world in days of increasing tensions in both social and individual life." How do you see that sort of influence coming about? Could you elaborate a bit?

ALB: It's sort of a leaven which leavens the lump. There are other movements too which exert the same influence: some Christian movements, for instance, and other neo-Hindu movements, likewise. Your movement teaches brotherhood, kindness, and generosity—you feed anybody who comes along to your temples. You teach kindness to animals. You teach honesty and sincerity in everything you do and say. It's bound to have an influence. You'll never get the great mass of the population of the world living up to your highest standards or the highest standards of any religion. But the few people who do, whatever their religious creed, are going to help the world along. That's about all I can say on that, because I'm no prophet. I can't foresee the future. But I feel that you cannot but help in some measure to stimulate these sorts of values, even in people who are not memebers or who in some way may even be critical of your movement—just as the Christians did in the days of Rome. They did a lot to improve human relations, an effect which spread far beyond their own membership.

SJG: You touched briefly on this point earlier: how does the public view the Hare Krishna movement, as far as you are aware? Is their's a fair perception?

ALB: When you say "the public," what do you mean? The average man on the street?

SJG: That's what I mean.

ALB: I can't really say because I don't know the public. You'll have to have a kind of Gallup Poll and ask selected representatives of the various cities of the world and different income groups and different educational backgrounds and so on: "What do you think of the Hare Krishna movement? Put 'X' in the box: good, bad, indifferent." You can do that if you like and then you'll find out. But from what little I can see about it, the public in general views the Hare Krishna movement as a lot of young cranks and dropouts who haven't anything better to do than make fools of themselves. Let's face it! Those who know you a little better, as I do, feel differently about it. But the people who don't know this movement, who don't really know what you're standing for, just don't understand. The public's ignorance about your movement is abysmal. I think the general view, however, is that you're quite harmless. Nobody imagines—except perhaps for a few rather alarmist types—that you're going to do any harm in the world. But people who are more knowledgeable understand your movement better than the masses. Although I could never belong to it myself, I do realize that yours is a significant movement and one which is a force for good in the world.

SJG: Among people you know personally—friends or colleagues—what sort of attitudes have you found about the movement?

ALB: I think on the whole that most people who know something about India and Indian religions share something of my view. And of course in academic circles, there is a strong attitude of tolerance.

SJG: While we're on the subject of public views and reactions to the movement, to what causes would you attribute the trouble which the movement has had to face from time to time from the public and from established authority? Are there historical parallels?

ALB: The closest parallel which comes to mind is the Salvation Army, which you probably know something about. These people started from the 1870's onwards in London and other parts of England, carrying their message on the streets with brass bands, and dressed in unusual uniforms as you are. They would stop at the street corners, start up the band and sing hymns, preach loud and soulful sermons and urge people to give up drinking and fornication and all these evil things and turn to the Lord. And as a result they had rotten bananas, oranges, apples, and eggs thrown at them. They put up with a great deal of persecution. And they sometimes got in trouble with the authorities for blocking traffic just as you do. But in the end it was found that these people were intensely sincere, and they were gradually accepted. Now they are a respected branch of the Christian faith. They do a lot of good in the world, much more good than many other Christian movements in the way of positive help to those in need. They are a rather close parallel, in some ways, to your movement.

Except perhaps in communist or fascist countries which have rigid dictatorships, I don't expect that you'll suffer any major persecution. I don't visualize the Hare Krishna movement providing large numbers of martyrs thrown to the lions as was the case with the early Christians. But this sort of minor persecution which you so often do suffer now is something which is reminiscent of that suffered by the Salvation Army and by many other genuine religious movements in their formative years.

SJG: To what causes would you attribute these minor persecutions?

ALB: Well, simply to the fact that people find you odd, strange, exotic. I think it's mostly fear of the unknown. Moreover, they hear all sorts of sensational stories about you in the newspapers. There's also, I suppose, a bit of the old scapegoat mentality at work. How much real persecution have you had so far? Have you had mobs of rather nasty, low-grade people throwing rotten eggs at you?

SJG: No, not too many eggs. The main form of persecution comes in the shape of "deprogramming." Parents of a member of the movement—usually a new member—believing their son or daughter to be in grave mortal danger, decide to remove their adult offspring from the movement by force. They hire some person who has taken up the deprogramming profession who, for ten or twenty thousand dollars or more will illegally kidnap that person, bring him or her to an isolated location and then subject him to days or even weeks of intensive psychological and in some cases physical duress, aimed at convincing the person that he must repudiate his new faith.

ALB: It's a very unpleasant thing altogether. I know of a case here in Australia—a rather extreme and tragic case—of a young man who became a religious fanatic, so to speak. He was in his early twenties. He got carried away with religious emotions, gave up his job, and took to wandering about praying to God. His sentiments were Christian-oriented, though not apparently connected to any particular sect. He obviously was following along the lines of the Christian hermits of medieval times who would go off and live in little huts in the wilds and spend their time in prayer. He'd lock himself in his bedroom for hours on end, praying and meditating, and his mother couldn't get a word out of him. She was a widow. I knew her slightly. This woman got so upset that she consulted a psychiatrist and had this poor boy admitted to a mental institution. They gave him the right treatment, and he was turned out cured. Within a day or two he committed suicide. If the boy had been allowed to follow his own bent he might have become a saint or a great religious leader, after going through a period of intense striving and inner tension. Who can tell? The mother was terribly sorry about it, and wished she had let him go on. But this is what parents do, often with the very best of intentions.

Krishna Consciousness and Christianity

SJG: Do you see any similarities between the Christian monastic tradition and the Hare Krishna movement, in the area of spiritual or moral practice?

ALB: Now, what are the three basic rules of Catholic monasticism?

SJG: Poverty, chastity, and obedience?

ALB: Yes, poverty, chastity, and obedience. Well, I think you have quite a lot in common. You take a vow of poverty. You live very simply—without superfluous material comforts and possessions. As for chastity, your monks, that is, your *brahmacārīs* and your *sannyāsis*, live strict, celibate lives. Even the *gṛhasthas*, the married members, abstain from sex unless they wish to conceive children. That certainly counts as chastity. As far as obedience is concerned, reverence for the teachings and guidelines laid down by the scripture and by the guru are certainly quite important in your order. To live in your ashrams, one must follow certain strict rules concerning diet and conduct and so on. So, you have much in common with the Christian monastic orders. Certainly you dress much more gaily though.

SJG: Can you think of any other points of comparison?

ALB: Especially in olden times, the monasteries used to feed travelers, the beggars, and the poor, and you do the same. They were religious centers of prayer and song, music, literature, and story telling, and you're doing pretty much the same thing. There is quite a lot in common between you. Something interesting, though, about your movement is that the married people, at least those who are core members, other than the fact that they live together as husband and wife, live much the same way as the monks do. They follow all the same strict ethical and spiritual rules. For all practical purposes, they, too, are living as religious ascetics. This is a very impressive feature of your movement.

In monastic life the whole world over, there are many things in common, if not in theology and dogma, then at least in moral and spiritual practice.

SJG: I certainly have found that to be so in visiting a number of Christian monasteries and hermitages in the United States, Canada, and here in Australia.

ALB: Yes, probably when you talk to these people you find you have much common ground. Usually the monastics have a good grounding in theology and they approach their theological dogmas in a rather different spirit from that of the lay person. Their involvement is obviously more experientially oriented, as is yours. Yes, I'm sure you can find quite a lot in common with Benedictine and Cistercian monks.

SJG: Because the Krishna consciousness movement, as a manifestation of *bhakti* tradition, is teaching a distinctly monotheistic, devotional, salvation-oriented ethic, some people have commented that the movement is in some sense a new competitor to Christianity in the West. Although we don't view ourselves as entering into any sort of competition with Christianity, it's interesting that they see us in that light.

ALB: That I think, in a sense, is true. The *bhakti* tradition is very close to Christianity—Christianity of the devotional type—in its psychological attitudes. It comes particularly close to some aspects of mystic Catholicism. If you read the poems of mystics such as St. John of the Cross and St. Teresa, you find attitudes rather close to those of the *bhakti* poets of medieval India. I would say, for this reason, among others, that one shouldn't look on Krishna consciousness as a rival of Christianity. Obviously, if a young man or woman joins the Hare Krishna movement, he's not joining a Christian church. If he joins a Christian church, he's not joining the Hare Krishna movement. But when all is said and done, there is such an enormous pool of non-members of any church to draw upon nowadays, that there's really no need for the Christians to look on you as their rivals. Rather you should both look on yourselves as allies in a common struggle against unbelief, lack of faith. Many Christians may feel that you are something of a rival, but there's no special reason why they should do so. I think most of the converts you make are not earnest young Christians affiliated with Christian churches. They are chiefly young men and women who have no particular faith commitment to any particular Christian or other denomination. They're in the process of seeking. Am I right?

SJG: Yes. Although many might have had a religious commitment earlier in their lives, or at least maintained (usually on the urging of their families) some degree of affiliation with a religious institution, it is almost always the case that by the time they join the movement, their earlier commitment and institutional ties have, for one reason or another, long since been severed. People join the movement, in most cases, following a significant period of searching and experimentation.

ALB: So I don't think there should be any serious rivalry in the present day and age between Christianity and the Hare Krishna movement. Your aims are very similar. Allowing for a difference in terminology, iconography, and so on, there is considerable similarity. So there should not be any rivalry.

SJG: I think that the sense of threat or rivalry comes most often from the Christian side.

ALB: I'm sure it does, because the things you preach are basically very similar to their own doctrines. And also, the historical uniqueness of your movement may disturb the orthodox. It is the very first time since the Roman Empire, as I've said more than once, when an Asian religious movement has been practiced publicly in the streets of the western world by people of western descent. The Hare Krishna movement is something unique in the West, at least in the history of the last two-thousand years. And for that reason, because of its strangeness and unexpectedness, it tends to make the earnest Christians feel a bit nervous. But they ought not to. They ought to recognize you for what you are: a movement with doctrines and ideas very close to their own, with much the same aims and rather an ally than a foe.

INTERVIEW WITH SHRIVATSA GOSWAMI

Shrivatsa Goswami belongs to a Vaiṣṇava priestly lineage which has supervised the famous Rādhā-ramaṇa Temple of Vṛndāvana, India, since the temple's founding by the Vaiṣṇava saint Gopāla Bhaṭṭa Gosvāmī in the early sixteenth century. He received his M.A. in Indian philosophy from Benares Hindu University and is presently nearing completion of his doctoral dissertation: a mammoth study of the philosophy of Jīva Gosvāmī, including a translation of *Ṣaṭ-sandarbha*, Jīva Gosvāmī's magnum opus (an editing of Gopāla Bhaṭṭa Gosvāmī's original treatise). He is the founder and Director of the Sri Caitanya Prema Sansthāna, an academic and cultural institute dedicated to Vaiṣṇava philosophy and culture, located in Vṛndāvana. During the 1977—78 academic year, he was Visiting Scholar at Harvard Divinity School's Center for the Study of World Religions. During that year, he taught a pro-seminar for Hindu Studies specialists on Vaiṣṇava practices in Vṛndāvana and helped organize a conference at Harvard on the goddesses of India.

Shrivatsa Goswami is co-author, with John Stratton Hawley, of *At Play With Krishna: Pilgrimage Dramas from Brindaban* (Princeton: Princeton University Press, 1981) and author of "Rādhā: The Play and Perfection of Rasa" in *The Divine Consort: Rādhā and the Goddesses of India*, in the Berkeley Religious Studies Series (Berkeley: University of California Press, 1982). He is a member of the Board of Editors of the *Encyclopedia of Indian Philosophies* (General Editor: Karl H. Potter), as editor for the volumes on Vaiṣṇava schools of philosophy, including those of Caitanya and Nimbārka.

During his stay in the United States, Mr. Goswami visited several ISKCON centers and was intrigued at seeing a form of his own religious tradition taking firm root on foreign soil. He met the editor of this volume in Cambridge, Massachusetts, at the home of Professor Harvey Cox, and a friendly dialogue was initiated which has continued to the present.

The following discussion took place at Mr. Goswami's home in Vṛndāvana, on March 12, 1982. Here, Shrivatsa gives a detailed account of the philosophical, devotional, and mystical tradition out of which the modern Krishna consciousness movement emerged, and reflects upon the movement's historical significance in light of that ancient tradition.

Bhakti: Its Religious And Theological Significance

SJG: Shrivatsa, when did you first become aware of the existence of the Hare Krishna movement? Was your first encounter here in India or later on when you visited the United States?

SG: I first heard about ISKCON after Śrīla Prabhupāda's return to India from America in 1970. At that time I was in Benares and I learned about the movement through my father. He had arranged, together with some of our disciples, to welcome Prabhupāda in Bombay. An institution which my father heads, the Rādhā Mādhava Saṅkīrtana Maṇḍal, arranged for Prabhupāda's public meetings and advertised them through newspaper announcements and through distributing posters throughout the city. My father was eager to help Prabhupāda, as was Hanuman Prasad Poddar, the well-known spiritual writer and editor of *Kalyān*, who worked along with my father in the arrangements. Then, when I returned from Benares to Vṛndāvana in 1971, I met some ISKCON devotees, Gurudāsa and his wife Yamunādevī, who were living here in Vṛndāvana in a small room in Raman Reti. They used to come to Rādhā-ramaṇa Temple and inquire about the temple rituals and other matters.

SJG: Did you ever personally meet Śrīla Prabhupāda?

SG: Yes I did, on two occasions—first, to invite him to a large *Bhāgavata* festival in Jaipur in November, 1972. We invited many holy men and scholars from all over India to attend. The event was held at the Govindajī Temple. For seven days, one hundred and eight pandits sat and chanted the entire *Bhāgavata* in unison. Each evening we would have various *sādhus* give discourses on the theme of the *Bhāgavata* and present-day society—how to relate the teachings of the *Bhāgavata* to our own modern Indian society. So, my father and I visited Prabhupāda at the Rādhā-Dāmodara temple to invite him to this event. But Prabhupāda's health was not very good at that time. He said he would try to come but that he might not be able to. He accepted the invitation, but ultimately he could not come. And I remember one interesting remark he made. He asked my father, "What is your son doing now?" My father said, "He has just completed his M.A. at Benares Hindu University and is now living in Vṛndāvana." So Prabhupāda said, "He is wasting his time. You give him to me and I'll take him around the world to preach." And I said, "All right, maybe someday in the future I will come with you." I took it as a loving remark from Prabhupāda.

The second time I saw Śrīla Prabhupāda was in September, 1974. We had organized a festival called *Aṣṭa-yāma līlā* wherein the *rāsa-līlās* are performed according to the *Govinda-līlāmṛta* of Kṛṣṇadāsa Kavirāja. So, I went to ISKCON's Krishna-Balarāma Temple, which was being constructed at the time, to invite him. He was living in a suite behind the temple, and we spoke together for some time.

SJG: After having met Śrīla Prabhupāda and witnessing ISKCON's pioneering days in India, it must have been quite interesting for you to observe the movement in America, where it had been flourishing for a number of years. How did you encounter the movement there?

SG: During the academic year of 1977-78, I had the opportunity to reside at Harvard University as Visiting Scholar in the Divinity School. During that year, apart from purely academic activities, I tried to acquaint myself with the very interesting and diverse religious movements in America. I visited, for instance, some Cistercian and Tibetan Buddhist monastaries in Massachusetts and elsewhere. Living in Boston, I had the opportunity to visit the ISKCON temple on Commonwealth Avenue and to develop relationships with some of the devotees there.

SJG: This is when you and I first met at Harvey Cox's house in Cambridge.

SG: You were there with some devotees from the temple who prepared a delicious feast for a number of Harvey's colleagues and students and he introduced us. I later attended a lecture you gave in Harvey's "Contemporary Religious Movements" class at the Divinity School.

SJG: I think the next time we met was in Los Angeles.

SG: Yes. After I attended a conference there, you arranged for me to stay for some days in the very large Los Angeles ISKCON community. I found that stay very enjoyable and I learned a lot about the movement in its American setting.

SJG: Before we begin discussing the contemporary Krishna consciousness movement, Shrivatsa, I'd like to take advantage of your extensive knowledge of Indian spiritual tradition and ask you about ISKCON's historical and theological roots. As we know, Krishna consciousness is rooted in the concept of *bhakti,* love of God, specifically Krishna-*bhakti,* devotion to Lord Krishna—understood as the original and supreme form of Godhead. First of all, what is the essential meaning of the term *bhakti*?

SG: The Sanskrit term *bhakti,* which is loosely translated

as "devotion," comes from the root "*bhaj*" to which is joined the suffix "*ktin*." When "*bhaj*" and "*ktin*" are joined, they become "*bhakti*." The root "*bhaj*" means "to serve" or "to love." In usage, the term "*bhakti*" stands for the notion of being devoted to someone. In the religious realm that devotion is to God. The term is sometimes used in a more pedestrian sense, to signify devotion to whatever or whomever one might ordinarily be devoted. But the term is most often used in a specifically theological context: love of God. *Bhakti* refers not only to devotion to God but also, in a more general sense, to a relationship with God—to the manner in which we relate ourselves to God.

SJG: Let's now look at the concept of *bhakti* in a broad religious context. *Bhakti* usually is taken to be a subdivision of Hinduism, as a specific, localized aspect of Indian religious tradition. Should *bhakti* be viewed in this way—as a sectarian or cultural-specific phenomenon—or can it be understood in broader, more universal terms?

SG: If I could answer your question in one sentence, I would say that we can translate the term "religion" as *bhakti*. By religion, I mean the human quest for realization of the Divine. That quest presupposes a relation of man to God. And one can be related to God in a number of different ways, depending on one's religious, cultural, or psychological background. In the religious quest one is, in one manner or another, trying to relate himself to God. That relating to God itself is *bhakti*, and the religious experience itself is *bhakti*. You can call it "Hindu *bhakti*," or "Christian *bhakti*," or "Islamic *bhakti*." Any religious quest for God is, in essence, *bhakti*.

To understand *bhakti*, we have to take the clue from the human situation, because it is the human situation that we understand and that we are experiencing. When we say that *bhakti* is a relation, we have to see what kinds of relationships we experience on the human level. So, what are the different modes by which humans relate? On the lowest level, we have the servant-master relationship: one person is serving another. Higher than that, one might be related to another person more intimately as a friend. More intimate still, there is the parental relationship: relating to someone else as his son, daughter, father, or mother. And then finally there is the conjugal or amorous relationship.

Now, if you analyze these basic modes of relationship, you find that of all of them the conjugal or amorous relationship is the most intimate and spontaneous. To satisfy emotional needs, we seek a spontaneous and intimate devotional relation, and that is possible, most fully, in a conjugal relationship. By "conjugal relationship" I don't mean only a husband-wife relationship, but any relationship between a man and a woman—as lovers for instance. This is not to say that any relationship between a man and a woman will be on the highest ethical level—often it is not—but simply that it tends to be the most intense. The most intense man-woman relationship often is one that is illicit. In that relationship, man and woman do not bother about any social strictures or codes. In the husband-wife bond, the relationship is regulated in part by social, familial, and legal constraints; dealings are influenced by motives other than simple love. But two young lovers are not concerned with anything but love. Their love is for the sake of love.

That highest or most intense human model finds its highest and purest expression in our relationship with God. God is the beloved and we are his lovers. But it also goes the other way: God is the lover and we his beloved. When you speak of Krishna-*avatāra,* the descent of Lord Krishna, we see that God has made the journey from the transcendental to the mundane world because He feels unlimited compassion and love for human beings, embodied souls. It is a two-way movement. So that is the highest mode of spiritual life: where no other motive remains except love. In the realm of the quest for *jñāna,* knowledge, one must attain pure knowledge devoid of ignorance. If you attain that state, then you've realized Brahman. But if you attain the sublime state of divine love where there is no other guiding force, no other motive except love for the sake of love, then you have attained the realization of God as Bhagavān—Śrī Krishna. That is the highest religious attainment. If we examine other religious traditions, we will find that many of them fall short of this ideal of a loving, divine relation.

SJG: Generally speaking, a pious person prays to God for the purpose of attaining some tangible advantage from God. That sort of prayer, obviously, is not a spontaneous expression of unconditional love. I once attended an evangelical Christian religious service and listened to a number of worshipers testify that Jesus had answered their prayers by helping them to get promotions at work, cure chronic back pain, and win a television set. *Bhakti* seems to have been lost to many modern Hindus as well. When, recently, I visited the famous Veṅkaṭeśwara Temple at Tirupatī, for instance, I talked with a number of pilgrims who readily admitted to making the difficult pilgrimage for the purpose of securing different boons such as getting a son, curing a relative of a serious disease, and solving economic hardships. So, in practice, it seems that most conventional religiosity—in whatever religious tradition one might look—tends to view God as the appropriate authority to turn to when one is in need of improving one's temporal, worldly existence, rather than the Supreme Beloved who's very existence elicits sublime devotion. And the problem with this kind of motivated religiosity is that if one's self-serving petitions are not indulged by God, one is likely to become a skeptic or an atheist. So we can't really speak of "Christian *bhakti*" or even of "Hindu *bhakti*" unless the individual's approach to God is motivated by selfless, unconditional love. *Bhakti* presupposes a relationship that is not dependent upon fulfillment of any material condition. *Bhakti* is purely spiritual. So then, can we describe *bhakti* (although rarely seen in practice) as the highest development of religion?

SG: Yes, and it is in Vaiṣṇava tradition that the theology of *bhakti* has received the greatest attention and development—

as, for instance, with its analysis of the primary human-divine relationships, the five *rasas*.

SJG: It seems that the concept of *rasa* is a useful model with which to compare Vaiṣṇavism with other spiritual traditions. But it seems that in most traditions, the human-divine relationship is generally confined to the first and least developed of the *rasas*, namely *śānta-rasa*: a passive relationship based upon awe and veneration of God, viewed as the transcendent, majestic, all-powerful Supreme Being. This *rasa* precedes even *dāsya-rasa*, a relationship of greater intimacy in which the devotee enters an active servitor-master bond. *Śānta-rasa* seems to be limited to a kind of passive awe bordering on fear.

SG: It lacks spontaneity and intimacy. And so it will be satisfying only for some people. Vaiṣṇavism is actually the most complete form of *bhakti* tradition in the sense that the full range of possible relationships are present in it. All the possibilities are shown. For most people, *śānta-rasa* will not give the fullest play to their emotional sentiments. Feelings and emotions can be worked out only in a very informal setting. The more informal the relation, the better. God must be totally informal with His devotees for affective spontaneity to exist.

In the Judeo-Christian-Islamic mode of religion, God is a transcendental Being. He is in the transcendental realm, while we human beings are in the phenomenal realm, and these two realms are separate and unrelated. In this two-level concept, it is difficult for the transcendent God to relate to we humans on the phenomenal plane. Also, how can we relate to a fully transcendent God? This is the problem. To remove this problem, various religions have developed some idea of the Divine Descent—in the form of Jesus Christ, Mohammad, and so on. These decents are the links between the transcendental and the phenomenal. But although those links are there, God Himself remains on the transcendental level. Though religious thinkers try to solve the problem, they don't fully succeed. In *bhakti*, God and humans have to be on the same level, so to speak. There must be a one-level relationship. Either you have to rise up to the transcendental realm, or God has to descend to the phenomenal realm. That's why Krishna appears in this world as "nothing more" than a human being, an "ordinary" human child. But Krishna's incarnation is the greatest of incarnations. He is the most complete incarnation, even in the Hindu tradition. All other *devas* or gods, when they came down to earth, appeared with dazzling displays of power and grandeur. But they were not accepted as being complete, as manifesting all the attributes of God. But Krishna is the most complete incarnation. He is the *svayaṁ bhagavān*; He is God Himself. Why? Because He could come completely into a human context, free of godly manifestations. Human beings could immediately relate to Him, without having to think of Him as God. Like Mother Yaśodā, Krishna's foster mother—she was never aware that her son was God. She treats Him like an ordinary son: she instructs Him, she protects Him from danger, she scolds Him, she feeds Him. How intimate a relationship! It is a pure, untainted, intimate relationship in the mode of mother and child.

SJG: So much so that even at times when Krishna manifested His divinity—as when Yaśodā looked within baby Krishna's mouth to see whether he had eaten dirt and she suddenly saw, within His mouth, the entire material creation—she did not want to think of her son as God. So that her maternal sentiment would not be disturbed, Krishna immediately caused her to forget the whole episode.

SG: She immediately thought, "No, I don't want to see this. I just want to see You as my child. I'm not interested in Your divinity. I'm interested only in caring for You as Your mother." In this way, Krishna "deludes" His intimate devotees with the covering veil of His own mystic energy, *yoga-māyā*, so that they might forget His divine grandeur and continue to relate to Him in full intimacy, uninhibited and unchecked by formality.

In Krishna-*bhakti*, a total loving relationship—on one level—is established. In other religions you find mostly grandeur and awe, at best. A feeling of awe remains. But in the Vaiṣṇava religion, that feeling of awe ultimately has to be given up and left behind. In comparing different religious traditions, we should remember that *bhakti* is basic human nature. In any religion, basic human nature is brought into play. But in looking at different traditions, we have to study how and to what extent that basic human nature is expressed, is satisfied, and to what heights it attains. There are many gradations, and in Vaiṣṇavism you will find the highest form of devotional realization and experience.

Bhakti Tradition: Its Origins and Historical Development

SJG: What about *bhakti* as a historical phenomenon? To what point in the religious history of India can we trace *bhakti* religion? As you know, many contemporary historians tend to describe *bhakti* tradition as an almost exclusively medieval phenomenon. Could you comment on that view?

SG: The earliest written documents of Indian religious history are the Vedas, which may be the earliest religious writings in the entire world. It is said, *Veda-mūlaṁ jagat sarvaṁ:* Veda is the root of the whole universe. That means that all concepts are present, at least in seed form, in the Vedas. We don't claim that there is a well-defined Vaiṣṇava system in the Veda; but the root is there. In the Vedas we find gods and people devoted to gods, and that is *bhakti*. We find beautiful passages—right in the *Ṛg Veda*, the earliest of the four Vedas—expressing the various manifestations and nuances of *bhakti:* the servant-master relationship, the filial relationship, and even the amorous sentiment, in connection with this or that deity. So *bhakti* is definitely present in the Vedas, at times in a much refined form.

SJG: In relation to which deities?

SG: Indra, Varuṇa, and other deities. The *bhakti* is directed to any one of a number of *devas*, each viewed, from the perspective of the worshiper, as the highest God. A hymn in the *Ṛg Veda* [X.186.2] addressed to Indra says, "You are our father, our brother, our friend." Even the amorous aspect of *bhakti* is present. Another hymn [*Ṛg* I.62.611] says, "Oh Indra! May my thought touch you even as loving wives love their husband." *Kīrtan*, singing the names of God, is taken as the means *par excellence* for the ultimate spiritual experience in *bhakti* and even *Ṛg Veda* [VI.47.11] accepts that. Also, Indra is identified with Viṣṇu in the Vedas. Indra is *yajña*, sacrifice, and *yajña* is Viṣṇu: *yajño vai viṣṇuḥ*. Viṣṇu in turn is identified—very clearly in the *Bhāgavata Purāṇa*—with Kṛṣṇa, the Supreme Godhead in Vaiṣṇava *bhakti* theology. It's evident, then, that the concept of *bhakti* had taken shape in the Vedas. There are numerous textual evidences for this. This means that even before the time of the Vedas, some form of *bhakti* was present, of which the Vedas are a document. Any scripture is, in an important sense, a document of the prevailing tendencies and practices.

SJG: Are there other examples of the historical antiquity of *bhakti* tradition?

SG: We find much inscriptional and architectural evidence for a widescale popular *bhakti* movement beginning in the centuries before Christ. We also find many literary evidences for *bhakti:* popular dramas and poetry, as well as devotional hymns in the early centuries after Christ.

SJG: Are there other evidences from before the Christian era?

SG: We find reference to Vāsudeva-kṛṣṇa in Megasthene's fourth century B.C. work *Indica*. A little later, we find Heliodorus erecting a monument to Vāsudeva-kṛṣṇa. Paṇini, the great Sanskrit grammarian of the third century B.C., analyzes the terms *bhakti*, Vāsudeva, Kṛṣṇa, Arjuna, and so on. The *Bhagavad-gītā*, accepted as having existed definitely in the pre-Christian era, is one of the most important treatises on *bhakti* and Kṛṣṇa.

SJG: If we take the testimony of the Purāṇas and orthodox Vaiṣṇava historiography, *bhakti* goes back literally millions of years to the beginnings of human civilization in the *Satya-yuga*, the "Golden Age" of Vedic culture. The Purāṇas describe a historically remote but materially and spiritually advanced civilization that was pervaded by theistic devotionalism. So from the orthodox tradition's point of view, this kind of discussion concerning various evidences of *bhakti*'s antiquity is confined to comparatively recent history—the present age, the *Kali-yuga*.

SG: The point is that *bhakti* is an eternal human tendency; it is not merely some kind of historical movement arising out of peculiar social and cultural circumstances. Whenever or wherever there have been human beings, there has been *bhakti*. Perhaps Caitanyaite *bhakti* was not there. Caitanyaite *bhakti* can be viewed as coming out of a particular historical moment. But *bhakti* has always been with us, in some form or other. *Bhakti* is like a river that takes different forms, sometimes widening, sometimes narrowing, and that moves this way and that way at different places and times. Sometimes it is fully manifested, and at other times it is eclipsed or subdued by various historical and cultural forces. It is like language. Sanskrit before Pāṇini is different from Sanskrit after Pāṇini. Words change, grammar and diction change. Fifteenth century English is not the same as twentieth century English, although the language is the same. So even language flows. It is a question of continuity and change.

Bhakti is the same continuing stream, but it appears in different forms and degrees in different periods. Caitanya did not invent something out of the blue. *Bhakti* is an eternal thing which he refined and elevated to its logical limit. So there are any number of scriptural, literary, architectural, and archeological evidences for the antiquity of *bhakti*. But if we view Indian religious history over the past two or three thousand years, it becomes apparent that *bhakti* tradition was strongest and most widespread in the medieval centuries—let's say from the eleventh century onward beginning with the appearance of the great Vaiṣṇava *ācāryas* like Rāmānuja and Madhva. Many ancient *bhakti* strains crystallized into the medieval *bhakti* movement.

SJG: What were the important historical factors which contributed to this upsurge of *bhakti*?

SG: Rather than historical factors as such, I would put more emphasis on philosophical factors. Perhaps I can explain it like this: Look at the life of many intellectuals. What happens during their intellectual training? At first, the student is concerned mostly with logic and other rigid intellectual forms. But later, at some point, that intellectual rigidity ceases to give him satisfaction. There arises a sense of lack. That lacking is in the emotional and religious realm. Many intellectuals will then begin to cultivate the life of the emotions, of the heart. If you study the life of rigorous intellectual thinkers, you will often find that in their mature stage of development, many of them become more religiously or mystically inclined—even scientists like Einstein or Oppenheimer. In the Indian context, look at Madhusūdana Sarasvatī. After Śaṅkara, he was the greatest of Advaitin writers. He was the last great Advaitin philosopher and writer. He wrote a great dialectical work on Advaita called *Advaita-siddhī,* which is considered the last word in Advaita dialectics—highly sophisticated and intellectual. Later in his life, this same Madhusūdana Sarasvatī ended up writing a book called

Bhagavad-bhakti-rasāyana, a devotional treatise on *bhakti*. What need was there for him to write on *bhakti*? He was a Brahman-realized person. What was the need for him to sing the glory of Krishna? In that book he writes beautiful verses such as, *kṛṣṇāt paraṁ kim api tattvam ahaṁ na jāne*: "Beyond the beautiful Lord Krishna, I do not know of any reality." That, Madhusūdana Sarasvatī declares.

SJG: You're saying, then, that the upsurge in *bhakti* at a particular time in Indian history was due, at least in part, to a natural evolution in human temperament?

SG: It was a progressive movement within the collective Indian psychology from the intellectual to the devotional. Prior to the *bhakti* period, the intellectual movement had reached a saturation point with the dialectics of Śaṅkara and the Buddhists, various linguistic philosophies, and *Nyāya*, logic. The natural human tendency towards emotional engagement and satisfaction was being neglected, and due to this lack, the *bhakti* movement caught on very quickly.

SJG: To what extent was the medieval *bhakti* movement a popular reaction against an elitist, brahminical Hinduism?

SG: The *bhakti* movement can be seen in some sense as a revolt against the ritualistic "high" tradition, the brahminical scholastic tradition. We have to bear in mind, however, that this kind of revolt was natural. Religion is a process, a historical process; it is never stagnant. What was good for the Vedic period was not necessarily good for the fifteenth century. The tradition had to be brought into the present. Metaphysical realities, religious concepts, are eternal. But those primeval concepts have to be worked out, from age to age, in the form of practical religious life. You need timely expressions of ancient tradition. In order to accomplish this, you have to constantly review your religious practices.

So, at this time, there was oppression from the brahmanic

ritualistic tradition. It had become overly ritualistic, intellectual and exclusivistic. But with the revival of *bhakti* and the dispensing of ritualistic formality, God became, so to speak, more accessible and immediate. The *bhakti* movement was democratic. It provided, you might say, equal opportunity for all people to work out their salvation. That was not possible in the stagnant brahminical tradition. In this sense the *bhakti* movement was a great revolution.

But it was not that only the oppressed classes were attracted to *bhakti*. All classes participated. Many of the leaders, in fact, were brahmans. Caitanya appeared in a very high brahman family. Tulsīdās was a brahman. Sūrdās was a brahman. Rāmānuja and Madhva were from high brahman families. So it would be a misconception to view the existence of the *bhakti* movement as a model of class conflict. But it did open the gates of salvation to everybody. That was the great and unique contribution of *bhakti*, religiously and sociologically.

Also, we can see that brahminical religion was like a grammar, and the *bhakti* movement is more like poetry. You can view it in terms of a literary journey. First one masters the technique. He learns the rules of grammar and usage and so forth. Then, when he's mastered the technique—when it's become internalized and spontaneous—he can write beautiful poetry. That does not mean that grammar is useless; grammar has its essential role. But when the grammar becomes part of you, you are not so much concerned with the grammar but with literary creativity. So it is natural that from the grammar of brahminical ritual flowed the poetry of *bhakti*.

Brahminical rigidity, however, was not the only catalyst for the *bhakti* movement. This was a historical period, also, in which many alien forces, especially the Muslims, were operating, not only politically but culturally and spiritually as well. There was need for a revival in the Hindu tradition to offset these kinds of alien influences. Muslim domination brought with it various kinds of political and social oppression. With the loss of political power to these outside forces, there was also a loss of intellectual, literary, artistic, and religious freedom. In some times and places it was very difficult for Hindus even to openly practice their religion. You certainly find evidence of this in *Caitanya-caritāmṛta*. At times, to practice one's religion was to risk one's life. Further, in order to defend Hindu social life from Islamic influence, Hindu social codes had become extremely rigid and oppressively conservative. At this point in history, then, there was felt a need for a solution to all these various forms of oppression: religious, political, and social. The *bhakti* movement was the answer.

SJG: Shrivatsa, could you now describe the development of the *bhakti* movement—or conglomeration of *bhakti* movements—from roughly the eleventh to the eighteenth centuries? Who were the major figures and what were the important movements during this devotional renaissance?

SG: To begin with, let me cite a very interesting literary document, dated in the fifteenth century, called the *Bhāgavata Māhātmya* or "The Glories of the *Bhāgavatam*." This glorification of the *Bhāgavata Purāṇa* is found in the *Padma Purāṇa*, and is published in some editions of the *Bhāgavatam*. In it, there's a discourse between the sage Nārada and personified Bhakti, in which the historical development of *bhakti* movement is summarized. Bhakti, appearing in the form of a young woman, says, "Oh sage, I was born in the Drāviḍa land and grew up to maturity in Karṇaṭaka. At some places in Mahārāṣṭra I was respected, but after coming to Gujarat I became old and decrepit. . . . I was subjected to live in that stage for a long time and I became weak and sluggish. . . . But after reaching Vṛndāvana I became rejuvenated, and endowed with enviable beauty. Thus, I appear quite young with a lovely form." Later, in response, Nārada says to Bhakti, "Vṛndāvana really deserves praise, as it is due to its contact that *bhakti* was rejuvenated as a young woman and where she now gleefully dances."

So this gives, beautifully, the historical development of medieval *bhakti* tradition. The *bhakti* movement took birth in South India with the Dravidian saints, the Ālvārs, and so on. Then a little later, Rāmānuja, the first systematic philosopher of *bhakti*, appeared in the Tamil country. He was the first major *ācārya* to declare *bhakti*, aside from *jñāna*, as a legitimate path to realize God. After Rāmānuja, the next great devotional thinker was Madhva, who was born in Karṇāṭaka at the end of the twelfth century. After that, the movement got a big boost from different saints who appeared throughout India, including Mahārāṣṭra, during the fourteenth, fifteenth, and sixteenth centuries. These centuries were very crucial for the growth of the *bhakti* movement. But the *bhakti* movement did not attain its highest development, as the passage implies, until it reached Vṛndāvana. *Bhakti* reached Vṛndāvana, of course, in the form of Caitanya Mahāprabhu because it was Caitanya who, along with His followers the six Gosvāmīs, was the founder of Vṛndāvana in the early part of the sixteenth century. So, the whole history of *bhakti* movement is summarized here quite beautifully.

SJG: When is the latest the *Bhāgavata Māhātmya* could have been written?

SG: According to modern secular scholars, it cannot be any later than a fifteenth century work.

SJG: How is it that a fifteenth century text is describing Vṛndāvana, which was not established as an active pilgrimage center until the sixteenth century? Vṛndāvana was already known, of course, as the sacred place of Krishna's historical descent, but it was nothing more than a remote forest until Caitanya Mahāprabhu and the Gosvāmīs went there and developed it as an active spiritual center in the early sixteenth century. Before that, certainly, no *bhukti* movement flourished there. How do you explain that?

SG: That was my intriguing question to Professor A.L. Basham. He visited the Philosophy Department at Benares Hindu University some years ago and gave a talk on "The Hindu Sense of Time and History." He claimed that except for one or two minor works, Hindus have no historical documents, and they have no sense of time and history. So I quoted these lines from *Bhāgavata Māhātmya* which scholars agree is no later than fifteenth century, and asserted that this description provides a very accurate historical picture of the *bhakti* movement and its development. I said, "How do you explain this? How can you say that the Hindus have no sense of the past? I will say that they have even a sense of the future! Vyāsa has described, in vivid details, *bhakti,* its historical growth, and its establishment in Vṛndāvana."

SJG: What did he say?

SG: What was the point of saying anything? My objection was that, "You are concerned with a maximum of six-thousand years. For you, human history began only six thousand years ago. But for me, it is six *hundred* thousand years, six hundred thousand *million* years! For me it is beginningless. For such a huge span of time, I cannot concern myself with the trivialities of what I ate, where I slept, where I ruled, and whom I killed. I must be interested in something which can sustain me through those millions of years—and that is philosophical and religious ideas and values. So *our* history is concerned with ideas and values. And those ideas and values will sustain you and us both." That was my objection. "You say that Hindus have no sense of time. The classification of time by the Hindus is more elaborate than in any other civilization, particularly with reference to minute mathematical divisions of time." So the western scholars see it all in their own way. They have their own purpose to serve in their academic pursuits. And that's fine; I have no objection.

SJG: You mentioned a few "founding fathers" of *bhakti* tradition—Rāmānuja and Madhva. Now, who were some of the principal *bhakti* saints who appeared later in different parts of India?

SG: First, you have the saints of Mahārāṣṭra: Nāmdev, Tukārām, Ekanāth, and several others. In Bengal, of course, the Lord Himself appeared as Caitanya Mahāprabhu. Then in Assam there was Śaṅkaradev. In the middle country you have Ṣūrdās the great poet-saint, Mīrābāī in Rajasthan, and Tulsīdās the great saint of Benares and Ayodhya, Kabīr, and many others. In the South there were the Ālvārs—Vaiṣṇavite saints who preceded Rāmānuja. One very important *ācārya* of Andhra Pradesh was Nimbārka, who established an important Krishnaite devotional system of philosophy. Another very important *ācārya* was Vallabha of Gujarat who was contemporary with Caitanya.

SJG: Did all of these saints and *ācāryas* found distinct movements, or were some just poets and mystics who did not establish formal religious movements? Also, would it be artificial to make a distinction between those who founded schools of philosophy and those who founded devotional movements?

SG: In some cases you can distinguish between the founding of a philosophical school and the founding of a devotional movement as such. Rāmānuja founded a system of philosophy called Viśiṣṭādvaita Vedānta. Madhva was the founder of Dvaita Vedānta. Nimbārka founded the Dvaitādvaita or Bhedābheda School. Vallabha founded Śuddhādvaita Vedānta. But other saints like Sūrdās didn't found a system of philosophy or establish any line of teachers (*guru-paramparā*), but he commanded a large following which cut across sectarian boundaries.

SJG: Rāmānuja founded a school of philosophy, but he also had a large following, a movement.

SG: By "school of philosophy" we mean a religious movement as well—a well-defined religious movement with a large following.

SJG: So, you're not really making a distinction between founding a philosophical school and founding a religious movement.

SG: I'm making a different kind of distinction. Many saints founded a formal tradition with a well-defined philosophy, a set ritual, set mantra, set *guru-paramparā*. But many other saints, such as Tulsīdās, Kabīr, Surdās, Raidās and Nāmdev were sort of free and floating; they were cutting across all these sectarian bounds. In both cases, movements are involved, but in one case the movement would tend to be rather unstructured and free-floating, and in the other case it would tend to be concerned to some degree with religious formality.

SJG: Such as aligning itself with a long-standing *sampradāya?*

SG: Yes. So one might call one the "popular devotional tradition" and the other the "scholastic devotional tradition." You can make this distinction.

SJG: But aren't there some among these saints whom it might be difficult to neatly categorize in one category or the other? Caitanya Mahāprabhu was the founder of a philosophical school, Acintya-Bhedābheda, yet He led a widespread popular *bhakti* movement that was quite open and liberal.

SG: All these saints had large followings. But some are and some aren't founders of systems. Caitanya led a popular movement, but He actually founded a religious tradition. I would put him in the category of founders of movements. To give an example from the other category, take Tulsīdās. He didn't provide a separate system of thought. Perhaps one could construct a system from his writings, but he himself did not attempt to articulate any distinct system. Caitanya did establish a distinct school of devotional thought.

Also, to establish a religious tradition or philosophical system, one has to provide distinctive commentaries on *Bhagavad-gītā,* Upaniṣads, and *Brahma-sūtra (Vedānta-sūtra).* All founders of new traditions or systems have had to meet this stringent requirement. Although Caitanya Himself did not do this, His followers later did, especially Baladeva Vidyābhūṣaṇa, who wrote the *Govinda-bhāṣya* commentary on the *Brahma-sūtra* and commentaries on the *Gītā* and Upaniṣads. Caitanya Himself did not produce commentaries on these three texts because he considered the *Bhāgavata Purāṇa* to be the natural exegesis on them and therefore didn't see any need to write or commission new commentaries. Caitanya based His movement upon the *Bhāgavata Purāṇa,* viewing it as the final commentary on the three texts.

Inasmuch, then, as Caitanya was strongly concerned with His scriptural heritage, and inasmuch as He taught a distinctive philosophical doctrine, He has to be classed in the category of founder-*ācāryas.* It was only later, in the eighteenth century when there was a challenge against the authenticity of the Caitanya Vaiṣṇavas, that the need arose to present a Caitanya-Vaiṣṇava commentary, and that was provided by Baladeva Vidyābhūṣaṇa. Caitanya Himself viewed the *Bhāgavatam* as the sum total of all scriptures, not only the *Brahma-sūtra, Gītā,* and Upaniṣads, but all scriptures. And this is true. If you really analyze the *Bhāgavatam,* you find that it summarizes the points of view of all scriptures. It's a true compendium of Indian religious and philosophical tradition.

SJG: What were some of the distinctive religious practices and forms of worship within the devotional movements?

SG: In general, the *bhakti* movements attempted to spiritualize, to make sacred, ordinary worldly activities. Take eating, for example. Eating is a common human activity. Everybody eats. But the eating of food was transformed into a religious activity by first offering the food in devotion to the Lord. The food thus became sanctified as *prasāda*, the mercy of God. Aesthetic values were made religious. Poetry, art, dance, song, and drama: all were dedicated to glorifying God by depicting His divine form, attributes, and activities. Artistic pursuits all became saturated with *bhakti*. So the whole of human existence became refined into spiritual existence. The dichotomy between the phenomenal and the spiritual was broken down or, rather, these two realms were brought closer together.

As far as worship is concerned, previously, the stress had been on fire rituals, *yajña*s, the ritual chanting of mantras, all sorts of elaborate sacrifices for material gain. These ritualistic sacrifices gave way to more natural, simple, devotional acts, such as the devotional worship of the form of God in the temple—sacred images of Rādhā and Krishna for example. So there was now more emphasis on simple, natural expressions of religious devotion over mechanical or ritualistic worship performed for temporal gain.

SJG: What about *nāma-saṅkīrtan*, congregational chanting of the names of God? In the Caitanya movement, of course, *nāma-saṅkīrtan* was the principal form of worship. Was this also the case with other *bhakti* movements?

SG: *Nama-saṅkīrtan* was definitely widespread, and music has always definitely been an important part of Vaiṣṇavite traditions. Almost all of these saints wrote and sang songs and hymns and wandered from place to place singing and preaching. I would say that singing was *the* mode of worship. You could say it was a "musical revolution."

SJG: In the movements of which saints did *nāma-saṅkīrtan* play a major role?

SG: In all of them. Take Tulsīdās for example. He is in some ways the most Caitanyaite of saints. He taught that if you even once utter the name of the Lord, you attain the highest revelation, and that there is no easier means of spiritual realization.

SJG: In what form did these various Vaiṣṇava saints sing the names of God?

SG: Some emphasized the name *Rāma*, some *Nṛsiṁha*, and some *Viṭṭhala*. Some chanted the *mahāmantra* as Caitanya did, and others chanted other name formulas. It was Caitanya who first emphasized the *mahāmantra:* Hare Krishna, Hare Krishna, Krishna Krishna, Hare Hare/Hare Rāma, Hare Rāma, Rāma Rāma, Hare Hare. There are many mantras, but this was the *mahā*-mantra, the "Great Mantra" mentioned in the *Kalisantaraṇa Upaniṣad* and in many other places. He, for the first time, really demonstrated the value of the *mahāmantra*. At the present time, the *mahāmantra* is practiced not only by Caitanyaites, but by many different Vaiṣṇava sects all over India. In any case, different mantras that are chanted are always comprised of different names of Krishna or His manifestations. In Paṇḍharpūr (Maharashtra), the Vaiṣṇava followers of Vallabhācārya sing the name *Viṭhobā* or *Viṭṭhala*. Others, in Tirupatī (Andhra Pradesh), worship the name *Veṅkaṭeśwara*. Different names of Krishna are chanted or sung in various combinations by Vaiṣṇavas all over India.

SJG: Do all of these mantras derive from scripture?

SG: All the names come from scripture, but the particular

way in which they are combined and ordered within any particular mantra may or may not specifically derive from scripture.

The Caitanya Movement

SJG: Now with this perspective on the over-all development of *bhakti* tradition, I think we're ready to focus more deeply on Śrī Caitanya and His movement, from which later evolved the contemporary Krishna consciousness movement. Of all the individual *bhakti* movements which appeared during this era, none, perhaps, were as widespread as Caitanya's Krishna-*bhakti* movement and none appear to have so successfully survived into the present. First of all, who *was* Śrī Caitanya?

SG: When we try to understand the personality of Caitanya, we can look at Him from many angles. If we wish to understand Him from a theological perspective, then we have to deal, first, with the concept of *avatāra* in Indian philosophy. This concept is very basic to the religious history and life of India. You're familiar with the theological importance of the concept of *avatāra*, so we don't need to speak about that in detail here, except to say that there are two worlds: the spiritual world and this material world, and for any religious purpose there has to be a point of contact or a meeting ground between the two. That contact or meeting ground is expressed through many concepts in Hinduism such as *avatāra, śāstra* [scripture], mantra, and guru.

Being human, we cannot easily understand anything which is beyond the human category. For the Divinity to be understood by human beings, He has to appear, therefore, in the human category. The highest form of *avatāra*, Śrī Krishna or Śrī Caitanya, comes exactly as an "ordinary" human being. In spite of their tremendous majesty and power, *avatāras* like Matsya, Kūrma, or Nṛsiṁha could not command the same high authority that a simple cowherd boy in

Vṛndāvana could. That is why Krishna appeared in the human context. There was a complete relationship between the devotee and the devoted.

And that same unique situation repeated later in the form of Śrī Caitanya. That is the highest philosophical and religious importance of Caitanya as *avatāra*—that He could appear as one of us. Caitanya is the *Kali-yuga pāvana-avatāra*, the supreme *avatāra* of the age, the dual incarnation of Rādhā and Krishna who came to purify the world.

In Indian theological matters, the *pramāṇa* or proof for anything is scripture. The *Bhāgavata Purāṇa* being the scripture *par excellence*—the culmination of the scriptural tradition—gives proof about the avatarhood of Caitanya. In the fifth chapter of the Eleventh Canto of the *Bhāgavatam* there is a discourse on how the Supreme Lord appears—and how He should be worshiped—in each cosmic age or *yuga*. After describing how He appears and is worshiped in the first three ages—*Satya, Treta,* and *Dvāpara*—the Lord's appearance in the last age, *Kali-yuga*, is described: *kṛṣṇa-varṇaṁ tviṣākṛṣṇaṁ sāṅgopāṅgāstra-pārṣadam, yajñaiḥ saṇkīrtana-prāyair yajanti hi sumedhasaḥ:* "[In the age of *Kali*] intelligent persons mostly perform congregational chanting to worship the incarnation of Godhead who, although His complexion is not blackish, is Krishna Himself, and He is accompanied by His associates, servants, weapons, and confidential companions."

In explaining this verse, all the commentators—Sanātana, Jīva, and others—categorically state that this is the description of Caitanya-*avatāra*. *Kṛṣṇa-varṇaṁ* means "describing or singing the name of Krishna," which was Caitanya's principal activity. *Tviṣākṛṣṇaṁ* means "not blackish [like Krishna] but glowing [like gold]." Because His complexion was very fair, almost golden, Caitanya was known widely as "Gaurahari," "the Golden Lord." Jīva Gosvāmī quotes directly from *Bhāgavatam* (10.8.13), wherein it is indicated that in the *Kali-yuga* Krishna appears in yellow color (*pītaḥ*). The

Sarva-saṁvādinī states, *yo 'kṛṣṇo gauras taṁ kalau sumedhaso yajanti:* the wise worship "Gaura," the fair one, in *Kali-yuga*. *Sāṅgopāṅgāstra-pārṣadum* refers to Caitanya's associates and companions like Nityānanda, Advaita, and so on. And the *yajña* or sacrifice by which this *Kali-yuga-avatāra* is worshiped is *saṅkīrtan*, congregational chanting of the holy names of God. Jīva quotes this Eleventh Canto *Bhāgavatam* verse at the very beginning of his *Ṣaṭ-sandarbha*, and then comments, *antaḥ kṛṣṇaṁ bahir gauraṁ darśitāṅgādi-vaibhavam kalau saṅkīrtanādyaiḥ sma kṛṣṇa-caitanyam āśritāḥ:* "I take shelter of Lord Śrī Krishna Caitanya, who is outwardly of fair complexion but is inwardly Krishna Himself. In this age of Kali He displays His expansions by performing congregational chanting of the holy name of the Lord." Then commenting on this verse in his *Sarva-saṁvādinī*—his own commentary on *Ṣaṭ-sandarbha*—he says, *sva-sampradāya-sahasrādhidaivam:* "Caitanya was the promulgator and presiding deity of His own *sampradāya*;" *śrī-kṛṣṇa-caitanyadeva-nāmānaṁ:* "that deity named Krishna-Caitanya;" *śrī bhagavantaṁ:* "He is Bhagavān [God] Himself;" *kali-yuge 'smin:* "appearing in this *Kali-yuga*;" *vaiṣṇava-janopāsyāvatāratayārtha-viśeṣāliṅgitena śrī bhāgavata-padya-saṁvādena stauti:* "He descended as *avatāra* for the sake of the Vaiṣṇavas."

So there are many direct and indirect references to Caitanya-*avatāra* in scripture—references not only in works by Caitanya's biographers, but in much earlier texts, especially the *Bhāgavatam*.

SJG: A little earlier you mentioned the importance of *nāma-saṅkīrtan*, congregational chanting of the names of God, to the *bhakti* movement in general. Let's go a little deeper into that subject now, especially in relation to Srī Caitanya's movement. First, consider the *mahāmantra* itself, which Śrī Caitanya propagated throughout India, namely Hare Krishna, Hare Krishna, Krishna Krishna, Hare

Hare/Hare Rāma, Hare Rāma, Rāma Rāma, Hare Hare. In your understanding, what actually *is* the mantra? What is it saying?

SG: The meaning of the mantra is, simply, "Rādhe Krishna, Rādhe Krishna, Krishna Krishna, Rādhe Rādhe/Rādhe Krishna, Rādhe Krishna, Krishna Krishna, Rādhe Rādhe." That is the whole meaning.

SJG: Taking "Hare" as Rādha and "Rāma" as Krishna?

SG: This is in the seventh case ending, what you call in English the "vocative case"—when you are addressing or calling someone. In Sanskrit this is called *sambodhana*, "addressing." "Hare" is the vocative form of *Harā. Harati kṛṣṇa-prāṇān iti harā:* "The one who attracts the whole being of Krishna is *Harā*." And that *Harā* is no other than Rādhā. When Rādhā is away from Krishna, Krishna is almost without life. That is the etymological meaning of *Harā*. "Rādhā" becomes "Rādhe" and *Harā* becomes "Hare" in the vocative case. "Krishna" remains as "Krishna." So the *mahāmantra* says, "Oh Rādhe, Oh Krishna." And then, "Krishna Krishna, Rādhe Rādhe." Each word in the mantra has this vocative ending.

In the second line, the new word is "Rāma." *Ramayati rādhikayā sa iti rāmaḥ:* "The one who sports with Rādhā is Rāma." This "Rāma" is Krishna. This is the meaning given by Jīva Gosvāmī.

This mantra is so powerful, because it is all in the form of a prayerful address. In other mantras you do not find this form of direct address. But in this mantra, each word is an address. Being in the form of an address, the force of the mantra is maximized. If I say simply "Śubhānanda," there is not much force. But if I say "Oh Śubhānanda," the potency is much greater and you're more likely to pay attention to me. There cannot be a more forceful way to calling a name than in the direct address form. In the *mahāmantra*, the prayer is focused on Krishna, and because it is focused, He is bound in that prayer. That is how I see the spiritual importance of the *mahāmantra*.

SJG: Kṛṣṇadāsa Kavirāja Gosvāmī writes in *Caitanya-caritāmṛta: Kali-kāle nāma-rūpe kṛṣṇa-avatāra:* "In the *Kali-yuga*, it is in the form of the holy name that Krishna has incarnated."

SG: Actually, this idea derives from the Vedas, where it is said that the Lord Himself is in the form of *śabda-brahma:* the pure Word, the Logos, pure sound. In the *Bhāgavatam* tradition also it is said that the Lord appears in the form of *oṁ-kāra*. The three letters "A" "U" and "M" comprise the sound "AUM," the *praṇava* mantra. That *praṇava* expanded into the *gāyatrī* mantra (om bhūr bhuvaḥ svaḥ . . .), and then *gāyatrī* expanded into *Catuḥślokī*, the four central verses of the *Bhāgavatam*. These four verses then expanded into the form of the full *Bhāgavatam*. So the scriptural tradition itself is produced from pure sound: "AUM." The three letters comprising "AUM" denote the three realities of creation: God, souls, and the material world. Within these three categories exists everything. Everything is found within these three categories, which come from the original sound "AUM" which is Krishna Himself. So, when you speak the word "Krishna," the whole person of Krishna is present in that sound, with all His attributes, qualities, and powers. That's why Caitanya says, *nāmnām akāri bahudhā nija-sarva-śaktis, tatrārpitā niyamitaḥ smaraṇe na kālaḥ:* "My Lord, You have an infinite number of names, and in each of Your names you have invested all of your power."

SJG: How did Śrī Caitanya turn *nāma-saṅkīrtan* into a mass movement?

SG: We're very fortunate that Caitanya's contemporary biographers, like Vṛndāvana dāsa and Kavikarṇapūra, as well as Kṛṣṇadāsa Kavirāja—the greatest of the biographers who, although not quite a contemporary, received the blessings of the Gosvāmīs who were personal associates of Caitanya—provided ample descriptions of Caitanya's spreading of *nāma-saṅkīrtan*.

When Caitanya visited Gayā in His early twenties, His spiritual fire was ignited by the spark which He received from Īśvara Purī, His spiritual master. And when this fire was lit, Caitanya was a different person; He was a changed person altogether. All His rational, intellectual activities dissolved into emotional ecstasy. His movement actually started in the closed courtyard of Śrīvāsa in Navadvīpa. Caitanya, Śrīvāsa, Advaita Ācārya, Nityānanda, and several other Navadvīpa devotees who were all great devotees of Krishna would gather together and dance and chant, day and night, in the closed courtyard of Śrīvāsa. They met secretly so as to avoid any distractions while performing this spiritual practice. People of like mentality and sentiment were gathered together, collectively experiencing profound spiritual states. In a sense, they had to shut out the world. They were afraid that if outsiders were to attend these functions, the intimate experience of this sublime Krishna-*prema*, divine love, might be stifled. But eventually, their spiritual ecstasy could not be confined to the courtyard of Śrīvāsa. It burst out of the courtyard and into the streets of Navadvīpa.

I always think, in a very crude parallel, that Caitanya was like a scientist performing an experiment in his secret laboratory. When a scientist successfully completes an important experiment, he comes out and declares his findings to the press and publishes. So all these devotional scientists were working in the lab of *saṅkīrtan*, this courtyard of Śrīvāsa, and when the experiment was successful, they spread it into the streets.

Within a short amount of time, however, the local Muslim rulers began to suppress the *saṅkīrtan* movement, first by sending soldiers to harass the Vaiṣṇavas by breaking their *khols* [drums] and beating them, and later by enacting a legal ban on this public singing and dancing. *Nāma-saṅkīrtan* has a long history of oppression even up to today, as your movement certainly has experienced. In some cities, officials try to ban your preaching in the airports and even try to stop the public chanting. History repeats itself. Caitanya, although He had no political motives, could not tolerate this oppression. So, one evening, He gathered together thousands of Vaiṣṇavas with drums and cymbals and carrying torches and, circling the home of the Muslim governor of the Navadvīpa region, they all danced and chanted with even greater enthusiasm. The governor, fearing for his life, came out and confronted Caitanya, who spoke with him and convinced him to withdraw the ban. From that time on, the *saṅkīrtan* movement in Navadvīpa flourished unimpeded. So first the chanting was confined to the house of Śrīvāsa, then it pervaded the town of Navadvīpa, then it spread throughout the whole state of Bengal, and then it spread into Orissa and beyond. Wherever Caitanya went, *nāma-saṅkīrtan* spread like wildfire.

SJG: What was a typical *nāma-saṅkīrtan* event like and what was its effect on the participants?

SG: The scene that always comes to my mind is the ecstatic chanting and dancing which Caitanya performed at the Rathayātrā festival in Jagannatha Purī. Annually, devotees from all over Bengal and Orissa would gather together in Purī to have the *darśan* of Lord Jagannātha at His festival, but they would come to Purī also in order to have the *darśan* of this "moving Jagannātha," Śrī Caitanya. So, in the *kīrtan*, Caitanya would be flanked by Nityānanda on His right side, and Gadādhara on His left side. Then Sārvabhauma, Advaita Ācārya, Svarūpa Dāmodara, Rāmānanda Rāya and other of his intimate circle would surround Him, forming a protective circle. Beyond this circle would be the multitude of devotees—some playing cymbals, some drums, some blowing conch shells and various types of horns. All the while, Caitanya would be dancing and singing. While dancing and singing in a frenzy, He would become overwhelmed with varieties of devotional ecstasy, and various extreme physical symptoms of this ecstasy would overpower His body. The description of these transformations are nearly inconceivable to non-devotees. The descriptions of Caitanya's ecstatic chanting and dancing from biographies like *Caitanya-caritāmṛta* and *Caitanya-bhāgavata* are emotionally overwhelming. To get a real idea of the intensity of this *nāma-saṅkīrtan* one should read those texts—with a devotional frame of mind.

SJG: While we're on the subject of Śrī Caitanya's devotional ecstasy, it might be important to point out a rather pervasive view among modern students of Hindu tradition, which is that Śrī Caitanya was always so engrossed in devotional fervor and mystical ecstasy that He didn't get around to, or wasn't able to, formulate a systematic philosophy or articulate it to others.

SG: This is one of the more unfortunate misconceptions about Caitanya, put forward by people who possess a very superficial understanding of Caitanya and His tradition. The main reason that Caitanya's role as philosopher and theologian is doubted is because Caitanya did not personally write out His system. From the traditional Indian point of view, it is not necessary for a system to be written. The Vedas existed for thousands of years before they were compiled in written form. They were presented through oral tradition and transmitted from guru to disciple. In ancient India, people had the mental capacity for memorization and total recall of scripture. Oral transmission was *the* system of religious and philosophical education. You can see an example of this at the time of Caitanya. In *Hari-bhakti-vilāsa*, Gopāla Bhaṭṭa Gosvāmī quotes from 273 different extant works, and there was no library in the entire region which could possibly have had all those works. He obviously had memorized a vast number of religious works in manuscript form. There is no other explanation.

So, although Caitanya did not write philosophical treatises, he did evolve a philosophical and theological system, and did so through lengthy discourses with Sārvabhauma Bhaṭṭācārya, Rāmānanda Rāya, with Sanātana Gosvāmī in Benares, with Rūpa Gosvāmī in Allahabad, and in shorter discussions in South India with Veṅkata Bhaṭṭa, the Tattvavādis [followers of Madhva], some Buddhist monks, and so on. All of these dialogues are recorded in Caitanya's biographies. This was quite enough opportunity for Caitanya to develop a system. And He *had* a system. There is no doubt about it.

There are many other evidences from the biographies that Caitanya was building a system of thought. For instance, when Rūpa Gosvāmī would write a devotional drama, Caitanya would check it very closely for theological and spiritual accuracy. Then, at Jagannātha Purī, Caitanya, Svarūpa Dāmodara, Gadādhara Paṇḍita, Sārvabhauma Bhaṭṭācārya, and others would discuss the drama in a proper scholarly way, scrutinizing minute points of theology. Finally, at the annual meeting of the Vaiṣṇavas with Caitanya in Purī, the literature would be formally presented. There is ample historical evidence, then, that Caitanya did transmit a system of religious thought to His followers and to others.

SJG: Some scholars express doubt, however, about the biographical accounts of Caitanya's theological discourses. The argument put forward is that the philosophical and theological sections of *Caitanya-caritāmṛta* were reconstructed from already existing works by the Gosvāmīs. In other words, Kṛṣṇadāsa Kavirāja—who never actually came into direct contact with Śrī Caitanya and thus couldn't quote Him verbatim—took verses out of the Gosvāmīs' writings and put them into the mouth of Śrī Caitanya so as to fraudulently make Him appear to be the theologian He really wasn't. Now, since it is true that some of the words and instructions attributed to Śrī Caitanya in *Caitanya-caritāmṛta do* derive from earlier works written by the Gosvāmīs, how do we know that these words and instructions originated with Śrī Caitanya, and not the Gosvāmīs?

SG: They are definitely the teachings of Caitanya because the writers of the Gauḍīya Vaiṣṇava works—the Gosvāmīs—themselves acknowledge the fact that they are writing under the direct instruction and inspiration of Caitanya. That is evident, without exception, in the prefaces to their works. The Gosvāmīs heard, gathered, assimilated, systematized, and then wrote Caitanya's teachings in their many philosophical, theological, poetic, dramatic, and instructional writings.

So the whole Gauḍīya Vaiṣṇava system is based upon Caitanya's teachings, which evolved from His own experience. You cannot isolate philosophical thought from personal experience. There can be no "neutral" philosophy, just as there can be no "neutral" religion. Philosophy must have its roots in experience. What we have to understand at this point is that what we translate as "philosophy" is actually *darśan. Darśan* literally means "seeing." According to Sanskrit etymology, we can define *darśan* in two ways: the act, itself, of seeing or that *by which* we see, the process by which we come to the point of seeing. So philosophy is an experience, a "seeing," an immediate realization, or an encounter with something—and that something is ultimate reality, or God. Indian philosophy begins in intuitive vision or experience, or we might say divine, aesthetic experience.

In the western tradition, philosophy is not a matter of direct, experiential "knowing." It is, rather, a kind of armchair game, having little to do directly with life or experience itself. Originally, this was not the fact. But as the philosophical systems evolved, philosophy moved away from its spiritual moorings. In the West, a philosophical system must be a systematic written treatment of a well-defined Weltanschauung with logical treatises and so on. But in Indian tradition, it is the direct, intuitive experience which is primary and crucial. The Buddha did not write a single word. What teachings we have, we get only from His disciples; yet He has a very strong and well developed philosophical system. It is the same with Caitanya. In Indian philosophy, the need is not that you write a big system. It is the claim of spiritual experience which is important. One glimpse of Caitanya's experience ignited a series of explosions, and those explosions were the works of the Gosvāmīs.

Caitanya, of course, was part of the ongoing Vaiṣṇava tradition, but He had some unique experience at one point in Indian history, and that unique experience was first articulated, in literary form, by Sanātana Gosvāmī. Sanātana was the first philosopher to theorize that mystic experience and to bring it into "black and white."

SJG: In which works specifically did he do that?

SG: In *Bṛhad-bhāgavatāmṛta* which presents, in story form, all the important philosophical and theological teachings of the Caitanya movement, and in *Bṛhat-vaiṣṇava-toṣaṇī*, which is a commentary on the Tenth Canto of the *Bhāgavata Purāṇa*. Later Gopāla Bhaṭṭa Gosvāmī wrote *Ṣaṭ-sandarbha* using the prevailing Indian philosophical methodology of *pramāṇa-mīmāṁsā* or epistemology, *tattva-mīmāṁsā* or metaphysics, and *mokṣa-mīmāṁsā* or theory of liberation. This main philosophical treatise was revised and edited by Jīva Gosvāmī, and the work usually appears in his name.

SJG: The Gosvāmīs employed already established philosophical methodologies and categories in order to gain legitimacy for the teachings of Caitanya?

SG: Not legitimacy. They were not after proving their legitimacy. They wanted to show, logically and rationally, what their religious experience was. There was need to distinguish the unique features of Caitanya's experience and teachings. People could say that *bhakti* was already prevalent—Rāmānuja preached *bhakti*, Madhva preached *bhakti*. But what was unique about Caitanya? So the Gosvāmīs used the methodology of comparison to show what was unique about Caitanya's experience and His system. Their task was the rationalization of their religious, mystical experience.

SJG: Now, what does that really mean: "rationalization of their mystic experience"? What is the need for doing that? If the essence of Caitanya's teaching was ecstatic, devotional experience, why did the Gosvāmīs feel the need to create a formal philosophical system at all? Why was systematic philosophy needed?

SG: It was very much needed. As I explained before, first you have the intuition. In this case, the intuition was the experience of Caitanya. Then that spark, that fire, ignited thousands of fires in the hearts of those who came into contact with Him. But to keep that fire burning, fuel was needed and proper fanning was required. To provide that fuel and that fanning—to keep that intuition alive and to make it accessible to others—was the great task of the Gosvāmīs.

SJG: But to keep that fire alive, why wouldn't it have been enough to simply propagate *nāma-saṅkīrtan*? Wouldn't it have been sufficient simply to encourage adherence to those spiritual practices which lead to *bhakti*?

SG: Yes, *saṅkīrtan* is the highest thing; it is complete in itself. But man is a rational animal. He needs to properly understand things in terms of the categories of reason. We do not always operate in a spontaneous intuitive mode. That which we may experience in a mystical state of consciousness has to be in some way translated into the language of ordinary rationality. Even for a predominantly emotional person, reason is not dead. It is a question of proportions. A *bhakta*, a devotee, must have rational and intellectual faculties. He must not only be emotionally satisfied, but must be rationally or intellectually satisfied as well. A person who is fundamentally a rationalist isn't necessarily emotionally arid. He has emotions, but those emotions are subordinate to his intellect. So the Gosvāmīs wanted to show that this special intuition or vision of the reality of Bhagavān, of Śrī Krishna, could be arrived at rationally, philosophically. One could arrive at this vision, this realization, most quickly if one simply followed Caitanya's teachings and example. But most people have difficulty accepting something uncritically or unquestioningly. A man will question something told to him according to his own mental and intellectual proclivities. He will put that intuition or experience to the test, applying the prevailing intellectual methodologies. You cannot really make a clear-cut division between those with emotional needs and those with intellectual needs. The important matter, really, is whether you reach the final destination. Whether you approach the goal predominantly through the use of emotion or through the use of intellect, it is the final goal which is important. The Gosvāmīs presented texts which provided set guidelines for attaining the goal of realization of Krishna. Their object was not to "reduce" transcendental experience to intellectual formulas, but to make spiritual life attractive to the rational mind, and that was done by adopting the current logical and linguistic conventions and so forth.

So, the beginning is mystical, the end is mystical, and inbetween is reason. The reason leads you to mystical experience—wherein reason itself falls short. No amount of reason can fully explain or reveal any experience. No kind of logic can explain how red pepper is so hot and sugar so sweet. No amount of reason is sufficient; it has to be experienced. So in Indian tradition, then, philosophy is not an end in itself. It is simply a tool by which one can better understand the nature of, and to revive or provide access to, mystical experience. To put it another way, the task of Indian philosophy is to provide textbooks for mystical experience. Caitanya and the six Gosvāmīs had the experience, but how would others reach that experience? They had to provide some guidelines for others to follow.

SJG: Besides the claim, which you've amply discredited, that Śrī Caitanya was too much the mystic to create a systematic theology, some scholars also claim that He was also too much the mystic to organize His own movement, and so the task of organization and administration was left to close followers like Nityānanda and Advaita. Is there any truth to that claim?

SG: Some scholars like S.K. De, who's written a history of the movement, writes that in His ecstasies, Caitanya had no time for philosophical thinking or organizational activities. This is not an accurate claim. Nityānanda and Advaita were great organizers no doubt, and they played a key role in spreading the movement throughout Bengal. But it was Caitanya Himself who directed and oversaw all these activities. There are many evidences that Caitanya was very much alive to the current political, historical, and cultural situation, and that He was deeply concerned with establishing His movement on firm footing. We know from *Caitanya-caritāmṛta* and *Bhakti-ratnākara*, for instance, that after hearing about the unique qualities and capabilities of Rūpa and Sanātana—who were at that time high-ranking officials in the Muslim government of Bengal—Caitanya purposefully visited Ramakeli to meet them. It was not a chance encounter. He wanted to bring them into His movement. Caitanya's meeting with Rāmānanda Rāya—who, in addition to having a political post in Orissa, was an exalted Vaiṣṇava and Kṛṣṇaite theologian—was also intentional. Caitanya personally organized the preaching activities of Nityānanda, Advaita, and Haridāsa Ṭhākura in Bengal. He sent the six Gosvāmīs to Vṛndāvana to revive it as a Vaiṣṇava pilgrimage center and as a headquarters for the movement, to build temples for the worship of Rādhā and Krishna, and to establish a scholastic and literary community there for the production of a systematic theology. While living in Jagannātha Purī, every year Caitanya would make sure that Śivānanda Sena brought as many Vaiṣṇavas from Bengal as possible to Purī for the Rathayātrā festival, and He would make sure that Śivānanda properly hosted them. He would allocate duties and maintain long-term correspondence. He was like a general directing an army from one place.

These are all sheer organizational skills which Caitanya demonstrated up until the last moment of His life. He was a miraculous personality. He was always in high *mahābhava*, totally lost in the other world, yet at the same time He was attentive to any minute worldly detail. Both sides were complete in His personality. So there are many things now coming to light about Caitanya. But because this kind of information remains largely in Bengali and Sanskrit, and not many scholars are proficient in these languages, these things are not very widely known.

SJG: I am sometimes a little surprised by the shallowness of modern writings on Śrī Caitanya and His movement. Most scholars seem to have a very one-sided view of His personality.

SG: Modern scholars do not want to go into all these details of Caitanya's life and personality. They find interest only in *saṅkīrtan* and in Caitanya's ecstasies, neither of which do they understand very well. They claim to be authorities on Caitanya and His movement but they don't care to read the important texts of the tradition. How many modern scholars have read the works of the Gosvāmīs? Very, very few. They don't care to! And then from a position of ignorance, they make so many misleading statements, such as the claim that Caitanya's followers split into two opposing camps: the community in Vṛndāvana and the community in Bengal—the so-called brahmanization and ritualization of the Vṛndāvana community by the Vṛndāvana high priests as opposed to the purer devotion and worship in Bengal. All these are nonsense ideas proposed by scholars who don't read anything and are perpetrated by other scholars who don't bother to check the facts for themselves.

SJG: After Śrī Caitanya passed from the scene, under whose leadership did the movement continue? How did the movement fare in the centuries that followed?

SG: While Caitanya was on the earth, He was the central figure of the movement. He personally supervised not only the activities in Bengal and Orissa, but the activities in Vṛndāvana as well. When he passed away, a lacuna was created, but that lacuna was not too deep because He had groomed able successors. The intellectual leadership was in the hands of the six Gosvāmīs residing in Vṛndāvana who wrote texts to give a philosophical foundation to the movement. They commanded tremendous respect throughout the entire movement. The burden of administration fell mainly upon Jīva Gosvāmī. He was responsible for seeking donations, purchasing land for temples, building temples, creating libraries, and so forth.

SJG: All this in addition to his prolific scholarly and literary output?

SG: Yes, he accomplished both. Jīva was a remarkable person. He was a great intellectual and scholar as well as a great organizer.

In Bengal, the main figure was Nityānanda, along with Advaita Ācārya, Rāmānanda Rāya, Svarūpa Dāmodara, and others. So up to the end of the sixteenth century there was no lack of qualified leadership and the movement was quite cohesive. After this first generation consisting of those who had had direct association with Caitanya, leadership of the movement fell mainly upon three persons: Śyāmānanda Prabhu of Orissa, and Narottama dāsa Ṭhākura and Śrīnivāsa Ācārya from Bengal. They were active in the early seventeenth century. Śrīnivāsa Ācārya was a disciple of Gopāla

Bhaṭṭa Gosvāmī, Narottama was a disciple of Lokanātha, and Śyāmānanda was a disciple of Hṛdaya Caitanya. These three missionaries took responsibility for carrying the message of Śrī Caitanya from Vṛndāvana to the eastern part of the country. They carried manuscripts from Vṛndāvana to Bengal, Orissa, and other places, and propagated the teachings.

One important event in the history of Caitanya Vaiṣṇavism was the Kheturi Mahotsava, a great historic convention of Caitanyaites organized by Narottama dāsa Ṭhākura and held in the village of Kheturi in Bengal at the beginning of the seventeenth century. During this festival, many matters of philosophy and ritual were discussed and decided, such as what the proper system of Caitanya worship should be. Organizational matters were also discussed. In addition, Narottama had images of Rādhā and Krishna prepared, and sent to different places to be installed for worship. This meeting, which played an important role in the history of the sect, was presided over by Mā Jāhnava, the wife of Nityānanda.

After Śrīnivāsa, Śyāmānanda, and Narottama, Hemalatā Ṭhākurānī, the daughter of Śrīnivāsa, like Mā Jahnavā before her, became a great spiritual leader of the movement in Bengal. Soon afterwards, the leadership of the movement passed into the hands of hereditary lineages—blood lineages—both in Bengal and Vṛndāvana. In Bengal, the lineages from Advaita Acārya and Nityānanda—beginning with Nityānanda's son, Vīracandra—came into prominence. In Vṛṇdāvana, the Gosvāmīs in the hereditary succession from Dāmodara dāsa Gosvāmī, an immediate disciple of Gopāla Bhaṭṭa Gosvāmī, established their authority. The immediate and subsequent successors of Rūpa, Sanātana and the other Gosvāmīs had been disciples rather than hereditary descendents, and these disciplic successions maintained the various temples established by the Gosvāmīs. Early in the eighteenth century, however, the king of Jaipur advised these custodians of the Gosvāmī temples to start family lineages in order to maintain the worship of the Rādhā-Krishna images in those temples. So, all these hereditary lineages assumed leadership positions.

Two very important figures in the late seventeenth and early eighteenth centuries were Viśvanātha Cakravartī and his disciple Baladeva Vidyābhūṣaṇa. Both were great scholars who wrote many important commentaries and philosophical works on *bhakti*. It was Baladeva's commentary on *Vedānta-sūtra,* called *Govinda-bhāṣya,* which played an important role in Caitanya's movement becoming accepted as an authentic and distinctive Vaiṣṇava *sampradāya* or sect. Traditionally, for a sect to be considered legitimate theologically, it must produce its own distinctive commentary on *Vedānta-sūtra*. Caitanya Himself had not commissioned a *Vedānta-sūtra* commentary because He considered the *Bhāgavatam* to be its natural commentary. Later on in the eighteenth century, however, Baladeva wrote his *Govinda-bhāṣya* in response to a formal challenge against the legitimacy of the Caitanya sect. The traditional account is that he composed the entire commentary in one night under the direct inspiration of the Krishna image established and worshiped by Rūpa Gosvāmī—the Govinda deity. Hence his title for his commentary: *Govinda-bhāṣya* or "The Commentary of Govinda." It is a very important and highly regarded work.

SJG: Śrīla Prabhupāda dedicates his *Bhagavad-gītā* commentary to Baladeva Vidyābhūṣaṇa in appreciation for his having composed *Govinda-bhāṣya.*

Now, what about the subsequent history of Caitanya Vaiṣṇavism, from the eighteenth century onwards?

SG: Although it did not continue, perhaps, with quite the same vitality as it did in the sixteenth and seventeenth centuries, the movement continued to be a very important religious force. From the time of Caitanya to the very present, Caitanya Vaiṣṇavism has been the single most powerful and widespread Vaiṣṇava sect in the northeastern part of the Subcontinent.

SJG: Isn't it true, however, that beginning probably in the eighteenth century, the movement was eclipsed to some degree by the Sahajiyā movement, or at least that the orthodox Caitanya Vaiṣṇava sect began to be confused with the Sahajiyās, who claimed to be followers of Caitanya?

SG: Yes, that is somewhat true.

SJG: Who, exactly, were the Sahajiyās? Did the Sahajiyā movement arise out of orthodox Caitanya Vaiṣṇavism, or was it a separate movement?

SG: The Sahajiyās were actually a separate phenomenon that had already existed for centuries but which later began to identify itself with Caitanya Vaiṣṇavism in order to improve their religious credentials and gain popularity. They originally came from the ranks of decadent tantric Buddhists. There were many such Buddhists in Bengal, and many of them were taken into the Vaiṣṇava fold and purified. But many other tantric Buddhists, as well as tantric Hindus, remained free and floating. But they were influenced by Caitanya Vaiṣṇavism which was, of course, very prominent in Bengal, and they adapted the Gauḍīya Vaiṣṇava system to their own tantric sexual practices.

SJG: How was that accomplished?

SG: In Tantrism, the absolute truth is conceptualized as the union of the ultimate male-female principle, which is symbolized or embodied in all male-female relationships. In Hindu Śaivite Tantra, for instance, all men and women are viewed as incarnations of Śiva and Śākti. In Buddhist Tantra, they are embodiments of Upāya and Prajñā. That supreme divine union is effected through a certain kind of esoteric ritual sex performed between a man and a woman. This tantric system was grafted onto Caitanya's theology, to the great detriment of Caitanya's system. In the Vaiṣṇava Sahajiyā sects, all males and females are viewed as physical manifestations of the principles of Rādhā and Krishna. Ritual sensualism thus brings about in men and women pure love between their inner selves as Rādhā and Krishna. Rādhā and Krishna are therefore not deities to be worshiped—they merely represent principles to be realized in humanity. The Sahajiyās gradually appropriated the whole Caitanya Vaiṣṇava theology and reconditioned it in terms of decadent tantric philosophy and practice.

SJG: From the orthodox Vaiṣṇava point of view, then, what is the Sahajiyā "heresy"?

SG: Their heresy is their self-identification as Rādhā and Krishna and their sacrilization of sex. They try to imitate Rādhā and Krishna, not understanding that the intimate loving pastimes between Rādhā and Krishna have nothing to do with mundane sensuality. They turn something that is lofty and sublime into something immoral and perverted. That is their heresy. So, because the Sahajiyā phenomenon became widespread, and because they identified Caitanya as their founder and *Caitanya-caritāmṛta* as their scripture, naturally they began to become confused with the orthodox Caitanyaites. Gradually, Caitanya Vaiṣṇavism came to be viewed, at some times and places, as a sex religion—especially in Bengal where the Sahajiyās were very strong. Late in the nineteenth century, the Caitanyaite saint Bhaktivinoda Ṭhākura was one of those who sought to correct the Sahajiyās and to clear the good name of Caitanya Vaiṣṇavism, and his work was carried on by his son, Bhaktisiddhānta Sarasvatī, your guru's spiritual master, who founded the Gauḍīya Maṭha early in this century.

SJG: I find that even now many people have a tendency to confuse orthodox Caitanya Vaiṣṇavism with the Sahajiyās and to view the whole tradition as a kind of esoteric eroticism.

SG: Such people miss the basic import of the Caitanya tradition. The Caitanya movement is against sexualism. This esoteric eroticism is not found in the Caitanya movement but in the Sahajiyās. People make this mistake because they don't focus on the doctrinal and behavioral aspect of the Caitanyaites.

SJG: It seems to me that some of the interest on the part of many contemporary scholars in the devotional mysticism of Rādhā and Krishna is at least partly motivated by a kind of prurient interest in what appears to them as esoteric eroticism.

SG: Yes, that's quite true. In fact, the whole modern world is obsessed with eroticism and sexuality.

SJG: Everyone likes to read about some other person's sex life, especially if it's out of the ordinary. In one early, mass-market paperback on ISKCON—one, thankfully, that wasn't very successful—a teaser on the back of the book promised that the book "reveals candid details about the Hare Krishna people's strange sexual habits." Those "strange sexual habits" turn out—I suppose disappointingly to some people—to be celibacy.

SG: Of course. In the modern world, celibacy is a strange sexual habit!

This fascination with esoteric eroticism, by the way, is related to the general tendency among many students of Vaiṣṇavism to focus exclusively on the esoteric aspects of Vaiṣṇava tradition. This fault is found not only in the western scholars, but even in Indian scholars and devotees. They are not interested in *vaidhi-bhakti,* the preliminary spiritual practices; they are far more interested in *rāgānuga-bhakti,* the esoteric principles and traditions of Caitanyaism. *Rāgānuga-bhakti,* advanced, spontaneous love of Krishna, comes about through a gradual, progressive process of *vaidhi-bhakti,* regulated purificatory and spiritual practices. By emphasizing *rāgānuga* to the neglect of *vaidhi*, they lose sight of the fact that *rāgānuga* rests on a foundation of *vaidhi*. Without *vaidhi*, *rāgānuga* is not possible.

SJG: Some even deprecate *vaidhi* as regimental and restrictive because it involves strict adherence to ascetical and ritual practices—as if simply by will or by contrived emotionalism they can instantaneously raise themselves to an advanced stage of ecstatic devotional mysticism.

SG: All these ideas are artificial and misleading and they tend to cheapen the whole process of Krishna-*bhakti*. This imbalance of interest in the esoteric principles is the call of the time, you might say. It's the current fashion, a fad. They want to go right away into the intimate things without going through the necessary preparation. But that is a big mistake. The foundation must be there. That is why Caitanya commissioned the writing of *Hari-bhakti-vilāsa*, a tremendous compendium on Gauḍīya Vaiṣṇava practice and ritual.

SJG: Now, to get back to the main line of our discussion—the historical development of the Caitanya movement into recent times—you mentioned that the movement has been a major religious force, especially in Bengal, up to the present. What about the nineteenth century? You mentioned the missionary activities of Bhaktivinoda Ṭhākura. Are there any other important evidences of the movement's vitality or influence at that time?

SG: Yes, it was definitely a force to reckon with. When Rāmakrishna wanted to prove his credentials, he claimed to be the reincarnation of Caitanya! And when the Brāhmo Samāj, a reformist movement, came up, their main attack was on the Caitanyaites (they attacked it as idol-worship and sentimentalism). These two examples give very strong indication of the strength and influence of the Caitanya movement in the nineteenth century. Of these two very powerful nineteenth century Hindu movements—the Rāmakrishna Mission and the Brāhmo Samāj—one takes support from it and the other decries it!

SJG: And what about the twentieth century?

SG: Yes, Caitanya Vaiṣṇavism is still an important force. There are millions of Caitanyaites all over Bengal, Orissa, Assam, Tripura, Manipur, and here in Uttar Pradesh. There were even thousands of Caitanyaites in the northwestern regions, up to Afghanistan, who migrated to the Delhi area after the partition of India and Pakistan. The establishment of the Gauḍīya Mission by Bhaktisiddhānta Sarasvatī and its successful spread throughout India did a lot to strengthen the movement and it brought Caitanya's teachings to the attention of many educated Indians. And out of that Gauḍīya Mission emerged your guru, Śrīla Prabhupāda, who has brought Caitanya Vaiṣṇavism to the whole world.

Bhakti Abroad: Caitanya's Children In America

SJG: So, Shrivatsa, as a Caitanyaite and an observer of the Krishna consciousness movement, how do you view the significance, historically and culturally, of the spread of the Caitanya tradition to the West?

SG: When I reflect on Śrīla Prabhupāda's achievement, I become a sort of Hindu chauvinist. I am not ashamed of it. The process initiated, rather imperfectly, by Rāmakrishna, Vivekānanda, and others was brought to its logical and ultimate end by spreading and making "Rāma" and "Krishna" household words throughout the world. That is the greatest achievement, and it is a great political achievement.

SJG: How is it a great political achievement?

SG: In that Indian spiritual culture has been spread throughout the world. What the Muslims could do only by the tremendous sword, and the Christians could do only with great financial resources and state power, has been done by one solitary man, without any ill effects.

SJG: It's often taken for granted that Hinduism, in contradistinction to Christianity, Islam, and Buddhism, is not a missionary religion. Yet isn't it a fact that Caitanya Vaiṣṇavism has always been a missionary tradition? Didn't Caitanya Mahāprabhu directly instruct his followers to spread Krishna consciousness?

SG: Yes! Any truth is for spreading. Not only Caitanya, but look at Śaṅkarācārya. What did he do? All his life he traveled throughout India and spread his message. The Buddha did the same. Rāmānuja, Madhva, all the Vaiṣṇava theologians and saints—they were all missionaries like Caitanya. In addition to preaching himself, Caitanya instructed all his followers to preach the message of Krishna-*bhakti* from door to door and from village to village. *Yāre dekha, tāre kaha 'kṛṣṇa'-upadeśa, āmāra ājñāya guru hañā tāra' ei deśa.* Caitanya said, "Whomever you meet, teach him about Krishna. Become a guru and liberate everyone in this land." Caitanya Himself, the six Gosvāmīs, and later the trio of Śrīnivāsa, Narottama, and Śyāmānanda were all missionaries in the real sense. Jīva Gosvāmī and other gosvāmīs ordered this trio to leave Vṛndāvana and to preach in the eastern part of the country. Special copies of Gauḍīya Vaiṣṇava manuscripts were prepared to be sent with them. During their long journey, these manuscripts were stolen by a king who thought that the chests carrying the manuscripts might have contained a treasure. The loss of the manuscripts caused a great crisis, but in time Śrīnivāsa recovered the manuscripts and that king became his disciple. It's a very interesting story. Anyway, this trio definitely had a great missionary spirit.

SJG: Is there anything unique about ISKCON's missionary activities in the West in light of this Caitanyaite preaching tradition?

SG: One significant difference between historical Caitanyaism and ISKCON is that you have to deal with people who are not even in the broad category of Hinduism. Historically, the Caitanyaites were preaching to people who were already Hindus, even Vaiṣṇavas. Most of those to whom they preached were already worshiping Krishna or Viṣṇu, and they even studied the same scriptures as the Caitanyaites. Their preaching was mostly a matter of "polishing." But you ISKCON devotees have to deal with people who are completely "raw." That is a big difference. Śrīla Prabhupāda's going to the West to preach Krishna-*bhakti* was a very bold move. He was very courageous.

Śrīla Prabhupāda also faced a unique twentieth century situation in which materialism has become so predominant. In America, what does it say on the currency notes and the coins?

SJG: "In God We Trust."

SG: Yes. They say "In God We Trust" on their money. What they really mean to say is "In Money We Trust." Money is their god. In such a materialistic culture, what Prabhupāda achieved was remarkable. He had remarkable results: he spread the spiritual message of Caitanya even in a culture which had no grounding in Hindu culture and which was so steeped in materialism.

SJG: Why do you think he was so successful?

SG: If you study the situation in detail, you have to take into account the American social and political situation which might have created a favorable climate for his teachings. But these were auxiliary factors. They were not the primary factors. The primary factor which brought about this kind of revolution was the strong personal convictions and personality of Śrīla Prabhupāda, and the great spiritual philosophy he preached. This was unique.

SJG: Can you make a general assessment of Śrīla Prabhupāda's role in Vaiṣṇava history, viewing that history as one of expanding and broadening its scope? Classical brahminical Hinduism was an elitist and exclusivistic approach in which religious wisdom was the property only of the brahmans. Later, with the *bhakti* renaissance, spiritual life was opened up to all levels of Hindu society. Then, in the nineteenth century so-called "Hindu renaissance," the spreading of Hindu *dharma* took on a more catholic and ecumenical face with the founding of many different types of Hindu missionary societies which were responding, in part, to western religious and cultural influences. Most of that missionary activity, however, was still confined to India. But then later, with Śrīla Prabhupāda's journey to the West, Hinduism actually moved into a foreign country, the United States, and then into all parts of the world. Could you comment on or refine this historical picture?

SG: Śrīla Prabhupāda was actually a part of the large historical prophesy. In the same *Bhāgavata Māhātmya* which I was discussing earlier, in which the historical development of *bhakti* tradition is discussed, personified Bhakti says, *idaṁ sthānaṁ parityajya videśaṁ gamyate mayā:* "I will leave this country and go abroad." So *bhakti* has been traveling abroad through Prabhupāda! *Videśam* means "not this country," "another country." *Deśa* means "country" and *vi* means "another." *Deśa* may also mean "place," so *videśam* can mean "another place."

SJG: But in the context of that account in *Bhāgavata Māhātmya,* in which personified Bhakti is detailing her movement from one region of India to another, can't *videśam* refer simply to "another place" within India? Why should it specifically denote a place beyond the Subcontinent?

SG: No, when Bhakti is talking about different places in India, she names them. She refers specifically to South India (Drāviḍa), to Karnāṭaka, to Gujarat, Vṛndāvana, and so forth. If she was saying that she will go to another place within the Indian context, then she would have named the place, as she did in each previous case. But when she says *videśaṁ gamyate mayā*, it is clear that it means another place entirely outside of the Indian context. This is how I read this intriguing statement. Krishna-*bhakti* is a universal phenomenon and so it is only natural that it should travel throughout the entire world. And this long-awaited journey was made possible by Śrīla Prabhupāda.

SJG: One way in which *bhakti* has travelled to the West with Śrīla Prabhupāda is in the form of *bhakti-śāstras*, the scriptures of *bhakti*, some of which Śrīla Prabhupāda translated into English. Can you comment, Shrivatsa, on his choice of texts to translate and make available in the West?

SG: There is no doubt that he made a wise selection of texts to translate and comment upon. As for the *Bhāgavata Purāṇa*, we've already discussed its importance to some degree. The *Bhāgavatam* is of central importance not only for the Caitanya *Sampradāya*, but for all Vaiṣṇava and Hindu tradition. There is no exaggeration in saying that the *Bhāgavatam* is the most popular religious book in India.

SJG: More popular even than *Mahābhārata* or *Rāmāyaṇa*?

SG: Yes, *Mahābhārata*, *Rāmāyaṇa*, *Viṣṇu Purāṇa*, anything. In Hindi-speaking areas there is one rival: the *Rāmacaritamānasa* of Tulsidās. But *Rāmacaritamānasa* follows the *Bhāgavatam* almost literally on the doctrinal side. There are verbatim verse translations from the *Bhāgavatam* in the *Rāmacaritamānasa.* Indirectly, the *Bhāgavatam* itself is spoken.

SJG: The importance of *Bhagavad-gītā,* of course, is understood.

SG: Yes, the importance of the *Gītā* is already widely known.

Of the *Caitanya-caritāmṛta,* I remember a saying of the greatest scholar in our family, Śrī Damodara Gosvāmī, who lived in Benares and expired thirty years ago. He was one of the greatest scholars in the history of Benares and all of India. Any great scholar will bow down to his name. He used to tell my father when he was a student, "If you want to read one single work which gives the total perspective of Caitanya's thought, read *Caitanya-caritāmṛta.*" As a student of Gauḍīya Vaiṣṇavism, when I consider the *Caitanya-caritāmṛta,* I bow down to the genius of Kṛṣṇadāsa Kavirāja because he shows his mastery not only in presenting the life of Caitanya, but in presenting a beautiful, consummate philosophical summary of all the works of the Gosvāmīs. In *Caitanya-caritāmṛta* one can find brilliant crystallizations of philosophical treatises, theological treatises, aesthetics, and poetry from the works of the Gosvāmīs. He provides hundreds of quotes from the works of the Gosvāmīs. So through the nectar of Caitanya's life, Kṛṣṇadāsa Kavirāja presents a full compendium of Gauḍīya Vaiṣṇava tradition. So Śrīla Prabhupāda has done a great service for all Vaiṣṇavas, as well as for scholars, by translating and commenting on *Caitanya-caritāmṛta.*

SJG: What is the importance of Rūpa Gosvāmī's *Bhakti-rasāmṛta-sindhu,* upon which Śrīla Prabhupāda wrote a summary-study titled *The Nectar of Devotion*?

SG: *Bhakti-rasāmṛta-sindhu* is a textbook of devotional practice, an exposition on the philosophy of devotion, and a study of devotional psychology. It is one of the most important of the Gosvāmīs' works, so we are fortunate that Prabhupāda made this work available in English.

SJG: What about the *Īśopaniṣad*? Śrīla Prabhupāda chose it from among all the Upaniṣads to translate and comment on.

SG: *Īśopaniṣad*, or *Īśa Upaniṣad*, is very important because Baladeva Vidyābhūṣaṇa wrote a commentary on it. Of all the Upaniṣads the *Īśa Upaniṣad* has the most pronounced theistic tendency. It is a must for Vaiṣṇavas. Even the Advaitins say that Śaṅkarācārya softened his hard-core monism when he commented on the *Īśa Upaniṣad*.

I myself have read most of the seventeen volumes of Śrīla Prabhupāda's translation and commentary on *Caitanya-caritāmṛta*, as well as *The Nectar of Devotion*, some of his *Bhāgavatam* commentary, and parts of the *Kṛṣṇa* trilogy. I appreciate his intensity of devotion and his deep focus on the subject. He is a great devotee presenting and explaining devotional texts in a way only a great devotee can.

What is significant is that for the first time, these devotional texts are being made so widely available. If these texts are not available, what effect will they have? If you keep your big *śāstra* in your own cupboard, nobody will know about it. Making these Vaiṣṇava texts available is one of Śrīla Prabhupāda's greatest contributions. Apart from the masses, his books have also reached well into academic circles and have spurred academic interest in the Caitanya tradition. There's no escaping that. That is another positive effect of his writings.

The significance of making these texts available is not merely academic or cultural; it is spiritual. *Jñāna*, knowledge, is spread, proper doctrines are made known, people come closer to reality. All problems arise from ignorance. If ignorance is destroyed, all problems are solved. That's why it is stated in so many philosophies, like that of Jīva Gosvāmī, that ignorance, *ajñāna*, is the greatest enemy. *Ajñāna-timirāndhasya.* And that is the sole purpose of Lord and guru:

to destroy ignorance. I don't mean *jñāna* and *ajñāna* in the technical Śaṅkarite sense, but in the broadest metaphysical sense. That *ajñāna,* most fundamentally, is ignorance of the Lord, of Krishna. That is the greatest *ajñāna.* If you don't know Krishna, then how will you know anything? Krishna is everything; everything is related to Him. And by knowing Him, you come to love Him. If you don't love Him, you will love this material world which is *duḥkhālayam,* a place of misery, and *aśāśvatam,* temporary. So, to spread knowledge, as Śrīla Prabhupāda has, is to make a definite contribution towards human happiness.

SJG: Unlike most interpreters of Indian tradition, who in their writings have highlighted the theoretical, philosophical component of the tradition, Śrīla Prabhupāda draws the reader into the experiential dimension of Vaiṣṇava spirituality. He generated not only intellectual interest, but he actually transformed lives.

SG: That is true. In Indian tradition there is no clear dichotomy, as there generally is in the West, between the intellectual/religious sphere and the practical sphere of life. So what Śrīla Prabhupāda did was more reflective of Indian tradition. His approach was more natural. Religion is not a "subject;" it is not an academic discipline like Physics or Chemistry. When I was in America, I used to tell university people that in India there are no academic departments of religion, except those very recently begun by Christian missionaries. In America, there are divinity schools everywhere, but in a religious country like India there is no "Department of Religion." Why is that? Because in traditional Indian culture, everything is religion. Even linguistically, in Indian languages, there is no separate word for "religion." Religion is not a separable category. The mode of being itself is religious. Religious conceptions dominate and pervade all dimensions of human life: family, business, statecraft—

everything. The human being is intrinsically religious: *homoreligiosus.* Śrīla Prabhupāda did not try to turn Vaiṣṇava tradition into an intellectual curiosity. He presented the tradition as it is—a spiritual mode of existence. His practical, experiential approach to the Vaiṣṇava texts was the proper approach.

SJG: I'd like to raise one question, Shrivatsa, that has been a matter of controversy in India from time to time, concerning non-Indian members of ISKCON. Simply put, the issue is: can they become brahmans through a traditional *dīksā,* initiation by a guru, or is brahminical status simply a matter of birthright? On the one hand, many caste Hindus seem to feel that brahmanhood is determined by birth in a brahman family, and therefore one not born into a brahman family—let alone one born not even into a Hindu/Indian family—can never actually become a brahman. Such people resent the western devotees being awarded brahminical status. On the other hand, many other Hindus in India respect the western Vaiṣṇavas as bona fide brahmans and find support for their position in Vaiṣṇava texts which indicate that brahmanhood is a matter not of birth but of personal quality. We know, for instance, that Śrī Caitanya de-emphasized caste and taught that anyone, regardless of birth, can become a Vaiṣṇava and attain spiritual perfection by entering the path of *bhakti,* chanting the Lord's holy names, and so on. He also taught that a Vaiṣṇava by nature is possessed of all brahminical qualities. On that basis, can't a non-Hindu who enters the Vaiṣṇava fold become recognized as a brahman? Śrī Caitanya's movement was egalitarian and anti-caste, was it not?

SG: Yes, that is an often cited characteristic of the Caitanya movement. And in substance this is correct. But we have to talk about this with a little caution. In dealing with Indian religious history, you must always keep in mind the principle of "continuity and change." This is one category through which the whole Indian religious phenomenon will become clear. In religious history there is neither only change—because everything is rooted in ancient tradition—nor is there stagnation—because there is always historical change and flow. So on the sociological side of the Caitanya movement, some things were continued from tradition. This fact applies, in part, to the idea of caste system. Caste system is very much bound together with Indian religious and sociological thinking. It is an all-pervasive concept. You cannot think of Indian life without caste system. Even today, after so much talk of eradicating the caste system, it is still very powerful. Of course, Caitanya did sort of protest against the caste system, and He even transgressed it. There was one incident in which someone was converted to Islam and wanted to again become a Hindu, and the brahmans told him that the only way he could again become a Hindu was to "eat fire." In other words, that he should commit suicide, and then take birth again as a Hindu. That was the obvious implication. But Caitanya said, "There's no need for eating fire. You simply chant the name of Krishna and you'll become Hindu." There is also the case of Rūpa and Sanātana Gosvāmī. They had had some connections with the Muslims. Sanātana is even quoted in *Caitanya-caritāmṛta* as writing, "I am so low of status and thus how can I write on these *smṛtis* which are the work of a brahman?" But Caitanya saw no need to perform any purificatory ritual on Rūpa and Sanātana. He accepted their purity of heart, which is what really matters in spiritual and religious matters.

SJG: And there's also the example of Haridāsa Ṭhākura who was born a Muslim but who Śrī Caitanya named the *Nāmācārya*—the Great Teacher of the Holy Name.

SG: I would say that Caitanya actually gave his highest respect and love to Haridāsa, because for Haridāsa He broke His great penance of not begging. When Haridāsa expired,

Caitanya went to the gate of the Jagannātha Temple and He sat there chanting and weeping, and He begged food from all the people in order to celebrate the passing of Haridāsa by feeding the Vaiṣṇavas. And he personally carried the dead body of Haridāsa to the shore of the sea. Caitanya never did this for anyone else. But for Haridāsa, all his rules and regulations and vows and penances broke away. So, for spiritual matters, Caitanya vehemently deplored any emphasis on the caste system. But insofar as ordinary social codes were concerned, he did not openly defy it. He said that if the feelings of others are hurt, why transgress the social principles?

The caste system has importance only within the realm of worldly existence—family and social affairs. The moment you transcend the social system, the system becomes meaningless. In this respect, the other characteristic of Hindu thought is the duality of involvement and transcendence. There is always the possibility for involvement in the world, and there is always the possibility for transcending it. Take, for instance, the role of *sannyāsī*. In the order of *sannyāsa*, there is no caste. The street sweeper and the high-class priest are both together in the realm of *sannyāsa*. *Sannyāsa* is a spiritual status that transcends the social structure. So there is certainly opportunity for any human being to transcend this system, if he wishes to.

I'll give you another example. There may be some minister in New Delhi, like Jagjivan Ram, who comes from a low caste. Then there may be people like Indira Gandhi, Charan Singh, and Atalbihari Bajpeyi, who are all brahmans and *kṣatriyas*. They may well eat with Jagjivan Ram and even have social intercourse with him. But other members of those different caste communities, on the village level, cannot mix. This is an example of a kind of political transcendence of the social level. So, in a higher realm, one can transcend lower, social realities and forget about those realities, whether the medium of transcendence is political, economic, or spiritual. But the transcendence must be there.

In the western context, ISKCON can be viewed as a model

of social transcendence. In this spiritual order, people transcend their identities in the American cultural and social milieu, and form a transcendental community. They may be German, French, British, or American, Catholic, Protestant, or Jewish, rich or poor, educated or uneducated—in one stroke, all transcend their past social identities, wash away their differences, and form a transcendental egalitarian community.

SJG: Now, take that Hare Krishna devotee who has achieved social transcendence in the American context and put him in India. Take me for example. I took birth in a family of prosperous, carnivorous, liberal-Jewish professionals with genealogical roots somewhere in Eastern Europe—definitely not one of your standard Hindu castes. Can I become a brahman? Is that possible?

SG: Again, I will say that by becoming a Hare Krishna devotee you become a brahman, no doubt. Caitanya said that any *cāṇḍāla* [outcaste] who has Krishna-*bhakti* is better than a brahman that doesn't. So that is the rule for spiritual life, for the higher level. But, my question is, will a brahman in Vṛndāvana marry his daughter to you?

SJG: Most likely he wouldn't.

SG: Yes, that is my answer.

SJG: You mean that brahminical status is determined by social consensus?

SG: Yes, it is a social institution. On the worldly level, you have to acknowledge the social reality. Suppose there is a small temple in Vṛndāvana, and they are looking for a brahman priest. They will prefer an ignorant Indian brahman over a knowledgeable, pure western brahman. These things are a little hard to understand, but that is the way it is. On the religious side, they will accept you. We have accepted you on an equal plane. There is no problem. But on the social plane, it will be difficult. It will take time.

SJG: But is that due merely to social rigidity, or due to some lack of brahminical attributes on our part?

SG: No, it is just a problem of cultural alienation. You come from a distant culture, a distant place with different habits, different language. So that distance has to be overcome. And time will be the only factor which will correct this. What is ultimately important, of course, is the spiritual level. *Bhakti* is the important thing. The test of your value as a Vaiṣṇava is your *bhakti*, your love for Krishna.

SJG: What about the question of ISKCON's authenticity as a Caitanya Vaiṣṇava movement? What would you suggest, Shrivatsa, as suitable criteria for determining ISKCON's fidelity to the Caitanya tradition?

SG: I think that perhaps there is no real occasion for this question arising, for this reason: Take the Caitanya tradition in India. It may look like a homogeneous, monolithic tradition. But it is not. Even here in Vṛndāvana, you might find ten different types of Caitanyaites. Their behavior will differ, even their *tilaka* marks will differ. That is the basic nature of any Hindu tradition: it seeks pleasure in difference rather than in sameness. The difference is very much welcome in any Hindu tradition. So, I might say that the Hare Krishna movement is one more school within the Caitanya tradition. It is certainly not something alien. The members of ISKCON fall directly under the Caitanya *Sampradāya*. But there is no need for it to seek any sort of formal legitimacy. It is already legitimate. But in some ways, the ISKCON people will be a distinct group within the Caitanyaite tradition.

SJG: In what sense distinct?

SG: In India, there are Bengali Vaiṣṇavas, Oriya Vaiṣṇavas, Assamese Vaiṣṇavas, the Vaiṣṇavas of Vraj, and so on. Caitanya Vaiṣṇavism is not a monolithic entity. There are different identities within that broad category. In the same way, the Indian Caitanyaites and the western Caitanyaites are different. I don't take American Caitanyaism, if you want to call it that, as something which is distinct from my own religious being. I'm not directly involved in ISKCON administratively or organizationally. But as a student of the Caitanya tradition, I take it as a part of the whole being or unit of Caitanya Vaiṣṇavism. But still there is a difference in cultural background—what we call "ethos." You cannot say that the western Caitanyaites are one-hundred-percent like the Indian Caitanyaites, as the Indian Caitanyaites cannot be one-hundred-percent like the western Caitanyaites. So that separate cultural identity will be there. But the western devotees are definitely Caitanyaites. There is no doubt about it.

SJG: Isn't a Caitanyaite simply anyone who is following the precepts of Caitanya?

SG: Of course, that is the meaning of "Caitanyaite."

SJG: But doesn't that designation transcend relative cultural orientation? To some degree, of course, one is conditioned by the culture of one's birth. But when we speak of "Caitanyaism" or "Krishna consciousness" are we not speaking of something which ultimately transcends relative culturation and that is on a purely spiritual level?

SG: Yes, it does transcend all social considerations—on the spiritual level. But we are also social beings: we come within a particular cultural matrix, and we can't escape that. Only in that do you differ. Not on the spiritual side. On the spiritual side, even the caste system becomes meaningless. Any social or cultural distinction is meaningless on the spiritual side. That is the transcendental realm. But so long as you are on the human level, the social level, the differences are bound to be there. You cannot escape that difference, on the material side.

SJG: I suppose from our point of view, we could speak of cultural differences between American ISKCON devotees, and French, Japanese, Mexican, or African ISKCON devotees.

SG: When I speak of differences, I do not mean that their spiritual beliefs or their spiritual experiences are different or that their ultimate spiritual attainment will be different. But in some ways their personal styles might be a little different.

SJG: Could you elaborate a bit on what those differences of style might be?

SG: I think it would simply be a matter of pointing out the difference between an Indian lifestyle and the western life style, or the differing psychological bearings of people of different cultures. For instance, for an American Vaiṣṇava it is more difficult, perhaps, to cope in India. From his western vision, he will experience that things seem to go very slowly and are inefficient due to the less hurried atmosphere and a lack of technological sophistication. It takes a long time to make a phone call, or to conduct any sort of official business, and so on. Faced with these problems, the American Vaiṣṇava might become impatient or angry. But for an Indian Vaiṣṇava it is perfectly normal and he is not upset. You come to visit me and I say, "Alright, I will be with you in two minutes," and I still do not turn up after two hours. And you think, "He said he is coming in two minutes and he has not come in two hours." For me, that might be all right, but for you, it appears completely immoral, not keeping my word. So much depends upon culturation. An Indian Vaiṣṇava is ready to pick up the *prasāda* from the street and eat it, whereas a western Vaiṣṇava will think twice about doing that, fearing that he might get cholera or dysentery. So there are so many differing cultural habits and individual habits which go into your religious person. But as far as doctrines are concerned, they are one and the same. There might be minor nuances of interpretation and application on some points, of course, but there will be no dispute on fundamental doctrine. So, on the higher level, identity is supreme, and on the lower level, difference is supreme. That is how change and continuity work.

SJG: Do you think that there is anything in the western culturation or mentality which can significantly hinder the western devotees from attaining the highest spiritual goals?

SG: I do not feel that the western Vaiṣṇavas are handicapped by their own cultural or ethnic backgrounds. There is nothing to prevent them from following on the path of Caitanya and achieving the highest goals. They are fully entitled to that through having adopted the Caitanya Vaiṣṇava path and through having come under the guidance of Śrīla Prabhupāda and the present gurus as well, if they are teaching truly according to the *Bhāgavata Purāṇa*. There is nothing to stop them from attaining the highest spiritual goals. The emphasis should always be on the purity of the philosophical and spiritual side of the tradition. The externalities ultimately are not so important. The emphasis should be on the spiritual side of the movement. This is the crucial thing.

SJG: Ultimately, then, the real test of the authenticity of ISKCON is the spiritual authenticity of its members.

SG: Yes, the criteria should be spiritual. The evidence of the legitimacy of the Hare Krishna movement is that it has established the Caitanya tradition in the West, in a part of the world where formerly it had not existed. The criterion of fidelity is how well it will be able to establish its authority in the West. The question of authenticity or fidelity doesn't concern the Caitanyaites in India. The question doesn't arise for us. It arises only in that place where the tradition has not yet been established.

Any new movement which arises—even if it arises within a familiar cultural background—will face opposition, as you see at the beginnings of the Caitanya movement in India. It faced very stiff opposition: intellectual, social, and political. You know the famous discourse between Caitanya and Prakāśānanda Sarasvatī, the great Śaṅkarite scholar and leader, at Benares. That was a turning point for the public view of the authenticity of the Caitanya movement in India. Before that, people would say, "This Caitanya is a strange *sannyāsī*. He's a mystical and emotional person who sings and dances like a fool." He was ridiculed like that. Then, after the famous discourse at the Bindu-Mādhava Temple in Benares, Prakāśānanda himself became a follower of Caitanya. And there was also the persecution I mentioned earlier of the Vaiṣṇavas of Navadvīpa by the local Muslim rulers. So these kinds of obstacles were faced by Caitanya Himself.

So the real criteria of the fidelity, or authenticity, of the Hare Krishna movement will be the faith, steadfastness, and total commitment of its members. Its religious and spiritual authenticity will be proved only by its strength. You may write a hundred books on the legitimacy and authoritativeness of the Hare Krishna movement, but that may not prove very much. But if there are ten devout Caitanyaites in the West, the movement is legitimate and authoritative. The number is insignificant. But the integrity, the sincerity, and the faithfulness of the devotees is the only proof, and sufficient proof, of its authenticity.

When, in the West, someone comes to know that I am

a Caitanyaite, they immediately ask me what I think of ISKCON. It is a question that I have to deal with any number of times. I consistently answer with one remark: the strength of the movement is not that they've published and sold nearly 100,000,000 copies of the Hindu scriptures, nor that they have magnificent temples throughout the world, or that they have attracted 10,000 or 100,000 devotees to the movement worldwide. But even if there is one sincere devotee in the movement, the movement is very significant and important. And I sincerely believe that in this movement, there *are* many sincere *bhaktas*, some *very* sincere *bhaktas*. And because of *their* force the movement is existing. It is not surviving due to money or power. It is the spiritual power and the spiritual existence of those sincere devotees which is sustaining the movement. That is my strong belief.

GLOSSARY

FURTHER READING

INDEX

GLOSSARY

ācārya—spiritual master or teacher

acintya-bhedābheda-tattva—doctrine of inconceivable oneness and difference between God and His creation and creatures

advaita—nondual/nondualistic

Advaita Ācārya—intimate follower of Caitanya

Advaita Vedānta—Pantheistic and monistic school of Indian philosophy

Advaitin—a follower of Advaita Vedānta

Ālvārs—twelve Vaiṣṇava poet-saints of South India (ca. A.D. 65–940)

āratī—temple ceremony of worshiping consecrated images

artha—economic development; pursuit of prosperity

āśramas—the four traditional Hindu stages of life: student, householder, retired, and renounced life

ātma(n)—self or soul

avatāra—a descent or incarnation of God

Baladeva Vidyābhūṣaṇa—eighteenth century Caitanya Vaiṣṇava saint and scholar who wrote *Govinda-bhāṣya*, a Caitanyaite commentary on *Vedānta-sūtra*

Bhagavad-gītā—one of the chief sacred works of Vaiṣṇavism consisting of Krishna's teachings to the warrior Arjuna; forms part of the *Mahābhārata*

Bhāgavat—the *Bhāgavata Purāṇa*

Bhāgavatam—the *Bhāgavata Purāṇa*

Bhāgavata Purāṇa—the most popular of the Purāṇas and a central text of Vaiṣṇavism which advocates devotion to Krishna

bhajan—a song of praise or devotional hymn

bhakti—devotion; worship; service

Bhakti-rasāmṛta-sindhu—an important sixteenth century treatise on Krishna-*bhakti* by Rūpa Gosvāmī, one of Caitanya's intimate followers

Bhaktisiddhānta Sarasvatī—son of Bhaktivinoda Ṭhākura; founder of the Gauḍīya Maṭha institution and preceptor of A. C. Bhaktivedanta Swami Prabhupāda

Bhaktivedanta Swami—see Śrīla Prabhupāda

Bhaktivinoda Ṭhākura—nineteenth century saint who effected a revival of Caitanya Vaiṣṇavism; father of Bhaktisiddhānta Sarasvatī

Bhakti-yoga—the spiritual path of devotion to God

bhedābheda—see *acintya-bhedābheda-tạttva*

brahmacārī—one in the *brahmacarya* order

brahmacarya—the stage of life in which one lives with a teacher as a celibate student of the Vedas

Brahman—the impersonal Absolute

brahman—the highest *varṇa* or caste; a teacher or priest

Brahma-sūtra—see *Vedānta-sūtra*

Brāhmo Samāj—a Hindu reform movement founded in the late nineteenth century by Ram Mohan Roy

Caitanya—medieval Vaiṣṇava saint (1486–1534) worshiped as a full *avatāra* of Rādhā and Krishna; founder of Gauḍīya Vaiṣṇava tradition, source of Krishna consciousness movement

Caitanya-bhāgavata—important sixteenth century biography of Caitanya written by Vṛndāvana dāsa Ṭhākura

Caitanya-caritamṛta—the most authoritative and canonical of the biographies of Caitanya; composed in the late sixteenth century by Kṛṣṇadāsa Kavirāja Gosvāmī

darśan—"seeing"; direct apprehension of reality; philosophy

deva—a god or demigod

dharma—duty; essential nature; religion

dīkṣā—initiation by a guru

dvaita—dual/dualistic

Dvaita Vedānta—dualistic school of Indian philosophy

Gauḍīya Maṭha—the religious institution founded in early twentieth century India by Bhaktisiddhānta Sarasvatī dedicated to the precepts of Caitanya

Gauḍīya Vaiṣṇavism—the religious tradition founded by Caitanya which advocates the devotional worship of Lord Krishna and His eternal consort Rādhā as the Supreme Godhead

Gopāla Bhaṭṭa Gosvāmī—one of the "six Gosvāmīs" of Vṛndāvana

Gosvāmīs—six intimate followers of Caitanya who settled in Vṛndāvana to establish it as a pilgrimage center and to write a systematic philosophy for Caitanya's sect

Govinda-bhāṣya—a Caitanyaite commentary on the *Vedānta-sūtra* by Baladeva Vidyābhūṣaṇa
gṛhastha—householder; married person
guru-paramparā—succession or lineage of teachers
guru-pūjā—ceremonial worship of the spiritual master

Hare Krishna mantra—see *mahāmantra*
Haridāsa Ṭhākura—a saintly follower of Caitanya, born Muslim, upon whom Caitanya conferred the title "Nāmācārya," "Teacher of the Holy Name"

Jagannātha—"Lord of the Universe"; a famous image of Krishna worshiped at Jagannātha Purī, Orissa
japa—individual meditation on divine names of God
Jīva Gosvāmī—the chief philosopher and administrative organizer among the "six Gosvāmīs" of Vṛndāvana
jñāna—spiritual knowledge, wisdom

Kali-yuga—according to traditional Hindu calculation, the current cosmic age (beginning around 3000 B.C. and lasting a total of 432,000 years) characterized by a decline in spiritual values and the rise of materialism
karma—action or work
Karma-yoga—actions performed unselfishly, renouncing the fruits to God

kīrtan—see *bhajan*
Krishna—the Supreme Personality of Godhead whose incarnation on earth is recounted in the Tenth Canto of the *Bhāgavata Purāṇa*
Krishna-*avatāra*—Krishna as divine descent
Krishna-*bhakti*—devotion directed to Krishna
Kṛṣṇadāsa Kavirāja Gosvāmī—the author of *Caitanya-caritāmṛta*
Krishna-*līlā*—divine sports or pastimes of Krishna
kṣatriya—the second *varṇa* or caste; a political administrator or soldier

mādhurya-rasa—the amorous or conjugal type of devotion for Krishna
Madhva (Madhvācārya)—thirteenth century founder of the Dvaita school of Vaiṣṇava philosophy

Mahābhārata—the great Hindu epic recounting the struggle between the Kauravas and the Pandavas and embodying ancient Indian history, religion, and culture
mahābhava—the highest form of ecstatic devotion for Krishna
mahāmantra—the "Great Chant" propagated by Caitanya consisting of names of God: *Hare Krishna, Hare Krishna, Krishna Krishna, Hare Hare/Hare Rāma, Hare Rāma, Rāma Rāma, Hare Hare*
Mahāprabhu—"The Great Master", an epithet of Caitanya
mantra—a sacred word formula or prayer addressed to a deity
māyā—illusion
mokṣa—liberation; release from the cycle of rebirth

nāma-saṅkīrtan—the religious practice, propagated by Caitanya, of congregational singing of the divine names of God
Narottama dāsa Ṭhākura—important early seventeenth century Gauḍīya Vaiṣṇava poet-saint who was active in propagating the sect
Nimbarka (Nimbārkācārya)—eleventh century founder of the Dvaitādvaita (Dualistic Nonduality) school of Vaiṣṇava philosophy
nirvāṇa—freedom from the phenomenal world
Nityānanda—Caitanya's intimate companion, viewed as an incarnation of Krishna's brother Balarāma, who propagated Caitanya's sect in Bengal

Pāṇini—ancient Sanskrit grammarian
paramparā—see *guru-paramparā*
Prabhupāda—see Śrīla Prabhupāda
prasāda—food sanctified through devotional offering to God
pūjā—worship
Purāṇas—ancient Sanskrit epic texts which form the scriptural basis for popular, devotional Hinduism

Rādhā—the cowherd maiden who is Krishna's internal energy, greatest devotee, and eternal consort
rāgānuga-bhakti—the ecstatic, spontaneous devotion of a spiritually advanced devotee
Rāmacaritamānasa—the Hindi version of the *Rāmāyaṇa* composed by the North Indian medieval saint Tulsīdās
Rāmānanda Rāya—close companion of Caitanya whose discussions

with Him, as recorded in *Caitanya-caritāmṛta,* help form the basis of Caitanya's school of devotional philosophy

Rāmānuja (Rāmānujācārya)—eleventh-twelfth century founder of the Viśiṣṭādvaita school of Vaiṣṇava philosophy

rāsa-līlā—Krishna's divine circle-dance with the gopis, cowherd maidens

rasas—the principle denoting a soul's intrinsic relationship to Krishna of which there are five: *śānta-rasa* (neutrality), *dāsya-rasa* (servitude), *sākhya-rasa* (friendship), *vātsalya-rasa* (filial), and *mādhurya-rasa* (amorous or conjugal)

Rathayātrā—the famous chariot festival of Jagannātha Purī in which the forms of Jagannātha, Subhadrā, and Baladeva are taken in public procession

Ṛg Veda —the oldest of the four Vedas, India's oldest religious texts

Rūpa Gosvāmī—intimate follower of Caitanya and one of the "six Gosvāmīs" of Vṛndāvana

sādhana—regulative spiritual practices

sādhu—holy man, saint

Sahajiyā—generic term for various pseudo-Vaiṣṇava sects heavily influenced by Tantrism

Śaivism—the worship of Lord Śiva as Supreme Deity

Śaivite—a worshiper of Lord Śiva

Śakta—a follower of Śaktism

Śaktism—Tantric school that worships the female energy of a deity

sampradāya—sect or denomination

Sanātana Gosvāmī—one of the "six Gosvāmīs" of Vṛndāvana, and a great devotional scholar

Śaṅkara (Śaṅkarācārya)—eighth-ninth century founder of Advaita Vedānta school of philosophy

Śaṅkarite—a follower of Śaṅkara; an Advaitin

saṅkīrtan—see *nāma-saṅkīrtan*

sannyāsa—the renounced order

sannyāsī—a renunciate, monk

śānta-rasa—the state of relating to God in the mood of passive awe

Sārvabhauma Bhaṭṭācārya—the great Advaitin scholar who was converted to Vaiṣṇavism by Caitanya and became the latter's disciple

śāstra—scripture

Ṣaṭ-sandarbha—Jīva and Gopāla Bhaṭṭa Gosvāmīs' magnum opus, a systematic philosophy of Krishna-*bhakti*

śiṣya—disciple
smṛtis—sacred scriptures supplementary to the Vedas, including the Purāṇas, *Mahābharata,* and *Bhagavad-gītā*
śraddhā—faith
Śrī Caitanya—see Caitanya
Śrīla Prabhupāda—honorific title for A. C. Bhaktivedanta Swami, the founder and spiritual master of the Krishna consciousness movement
Śrīmad-Bhāgavatam—see *Bhāgavata Purāṇa*
Śrīnivāsa Ācārya—important early seventeenth century Gauḍīya Vaiṣṇava saint active in propagating the Caitanya sect in the eastern part of India
Śrīvāsa—intimate, early follower of Caitanya in the courtyard of whose home Caitanya initiated the practice of *nāma-saṅkīrtan*
Suddhādvaita—"Purified Non-dualism" school of Vaiṣṇava philosophy founded by Viṣṇusvāmī in ancient times and revived by Vallabha in the sixteenth century

tantrism—a generic term for religious sects which conceptualize the Supreme as the union of the male and female principles
tilaka—religious markings of clay displayed on the body for the purpose of purification and of sect-identification
Tulsīdās—medieval poet-saint of North India who wrote *Rāmacaritamānasa*

Upaniṣads—a division of the Vedas (*śruti*) consisting of 108 separate philosophical treatises, stressing mostly the impersonal aspect of the Absolute

vaidhi-bhakti—the preliminary, regulative stage of Bhakti-yoga; precedes *rāgānuga-bhakti*, spontaneous devotion
Vaiṣṇavism—the religious tradition centered on the worship of Viṣṇu/Kṛṣṇa and Their various manifestations
Vallabha (Vallabhācārya)—sixteenth century reviver of the Suddhādvaita school of Vaiṣṇava philosophy
varṇa—social/occupational division; caste
Vāsudeva—a name of Krishna
Vedānta—the end or ultimate philosophy of the Vedas; a term applied to any of a number of interpretations of the *Vedānta-sūtra*, especially that of Śaṅkara
Vedas—a body of ancient revealed scripture forming one important

basis of classical Hindu tradition
Viśiṣṭādvaita Vedānta—"Qualified Non-dualism" school of Vaiṣṇava philosophy founded by Rāmānuja
Viṣṇu—the four-armed plenary expansion of Krishna
Viśvanātha Cakravartī Ṭhākura—late seventeenth and early eighteenth century Caitanya Vaiṣṇava saint and scholar; guru of Baladeva Vidyābhūṣaṇa
Vṛndāvana—the abode of Lord Krishna with its earthly manifestation in the district of Mathura (in Uttar Pradesh, India) and its spiritual manifestation in the highest of the spiritual planets, Kṛṣṇaloka or Goloka-Vṛndāvana
Vṛndāvana dāsa Ṭhākura—the author of *Caitanya-bhāgavata*

yajña—sacrifice
yoga—"union" or a path towards union with the Supreme
yoga-māyā—Krishna's "internal" energy by which He preserves the intimate devotion felt by His eternal devotees by obscuring His divinity
yuga—"age," of which there are four, which cycle perpetually through cosmic time: *Satya-yuga, Treta-yuga, Dvāpara-yuga,* and *Kali-yuga*

FURTHER READING

The following lists of recommended reading cover primary and secondary source materials on the Krishna consciousness movement (writings by the movement's founder, disciples, and academic observers of the movement), recent books and articles on issues concerning new and alternative religious movements in general, primary and secondary materials on Caitanya Vaiṣṇavism, and studies on devotional Hinduism in general. These lists are by no means exhaustive, but simply indicate some of the standard and important works in these fields. As with any bibliography, some of these materials do not necessarily reflect the views and orientations of the editor. This is especially true in the case of works of modern academic scholarship, insofar as the perspectives of adherents of religious traditions and those of outsiders who study them may sometimes differ.

Major Works By A. C. Bhaktivedanta Swami Prabhupāda

(Except where otherwise noted, all works are published by the Bhaktivedanta Book Trust, Los Angeles.)

Bhagavad-gītā As It Is. Complete Edition. New York: Macmillan Publishing Co., 1972.

Bhagavad-gītā As It Is. Abridged Edition. (BBT) 1975.

Kṛṣṇa: The Supreme Personality of Godhead (A Summary Study of Śrīla Vyāsadeva's *Śrīmad-Bhāgavatam*, Tenth Canto). 3 vols. 1970.

The Nectar of Devotion: The Complete Science of Bhakti-yoga (A Summary Study of Śrīla Rūpa Gosvāmī's *Bhakti-rasāmṛta-sindhu*). 2nd ed. 1982.

The Nectar of Instruction (An Authorized English Presentation of Śrīla Rūpa Gosvāmī's *Śrī Upadeśāmṛta*). 1975.

Śrī Caitanya-caritāmṛta of Kṛṣṇadāsa Kavirāja Gosvāmī. 17 vols. 1974–1975.

Śrī Īśopaniṣad. 1969.

Śrīmad-Bhāgavatam of Kṛṣṇa-Dvaipāyana Vyāsa, Cantos 1-10. 30 vols. 1972–1980.

Teachings of Lord Caitanya. 1974.

The Krishna Consciousness Movement (ISKCON)

Back to Godhead ("The Magazine of the Hare Krishna Movement"). Satsvarūpa dāsa Goswami, Editor-in-Chief. Editorial offices: 51 West Allens Lane, Philadelphia, Pa. 19119.

Brahmānanda Swami. "How the Teachings of Lord Caitanya Came to the Western World." (3 parts) *Back to Godhead* 66:7–10, 1974; 68:6–11, 1974; 10(1):9–15, 1975.

Daner, Francine. *The American Children of Kṛṣṇa*. New York: Holt, Rinehart & Winston, 1976.

Eck, Diana. "Krishna Consciousness in Historical Perspective." *Back to Godhead* 14(10):26–29, 1979.

Ellwood, Robert S. "The International Society for Krishna Consciousness." In *Religious and Spiritual Groups in Modern America*. Englewood Cliffs: Prentice-Hall, Inc., 1973.

Goswami, Satsvarūpa dāsa. *Śrīla Prabhupāda-līlāmṛta* (A biography) Vol. 1: *A Lifetime in Preparation: India 1896–1965;* Vol. 2: *Planting the Seed: New York City 1965–1966;* Vol. 3: *Only He Could Lead Them: San Francisco/India 1967;* Vol. 4: *In Every Town and Village: Around the World 1968–1971*. Los Angeles: Bhaktivedanta Book Trust, 1980–1982. Additional volumes forthcoming.

.*He Lives Forever: On Separation from Śrīla Prabhupāda*. New York: The ISKCON Press, 1979.

.*Letters from Śrīla Prabhupāda*. Port Royal, Pa: Gitanagari Press, n.d.

Johnson, Gregory. *An Alternative Community in Microcosm: The Evolution of Commitment to a Vedic Sect*, Ph.D. thesis, Harvard University, 1973.

."The Hare Krishna in San Francisco." In *The New Religious Consciousness*, edited by Charles Y. Glock and Robert N. Bellah, pp. 31–51. Berkeley and Los Angeles: University of California Press, 1976.

Judah, J. Stillson. *Hare Krishna and the Counterculture*. New York: John Wiley and Sons, 1974.

."The Hare Krishna Movement." In *Religious Movements in Contemporary America*, edited by Irving I.

Zaretsky and Mark P. Leone, pp. 463–478. Princeton: Princeton University Press, 1974.

."My Impressions of Śrīla Prabhupāda." (An Interview) *Back to Godhead* 14(8):29–33, 1979.

Moody, Jonathan Fredric. *Ethics and Counter Culture: An Analysis of the Ethics of Hare Krishna*, Ph.D. thesis, Claremont Graduate School, 1978.

Ries, John Patrick. *"God is Not Dead, He Has Simply Changed Clothes . . ." A Study of the International Society for Krishna Consciousness*, Ph.D. thesis, University of Wisconsin, 1975.

Sharma, Arvind. "The Hare Krishna Movement: A Study." *Visvabharati Quarterly* 40(2):154–178, 1974.

Śubhānanda dāsa (Steven J. Gelberg). *Preaching is the Essence.* (ed.) Los Angeles: BBT, 1977.

.*The Spiritual Master and the Disciple.* (ed.) Los Angeles: BBT, 1978.

."Is the Krishna Consciousness Movement 'Hindu'?" Paper presented at the 1980 annual meeting of the Australian Association for the Study of Religions, Canberra, A.C.T.

.*Śrī Nāmāmṛta: The Nectar of the Holy Name.* (ed.) Los Angeles: BBT, 1982.

."ISKCON After Prabhupāda: An Update on the Hare Krishna Movement." Paper presented at the 1982 annual meeting of the American Academy of Religion, New York City.

New And Alternative Religious Movements: Issues, Perspectives, And Controversies

Anthony, Dick; Needleman, Jacob; and Robbins, Thomas, eds. *Conversion, Coercion and Commitment in New Religious Movements*. New York: Crossroads Books, forthcoming.

Barker, Eileen, ed. *New Religious Movements: A Perspective for Understanding Society*. New York and Toronto: The Edwin Mellon Press, 1982.

Bromley, David G., and Richardson, James T., eds. *The Brainwashing/Deprogramming Controversy: Sociological, Psychological, Legal, and Historical Perspectives.* New York and Toronto: The Edwin Mellon Press, forthcoming.

,and Shupe, Anson D. *Strange Gods: The Great American Cult Scare.* Boston: Beacon Press, 1982.

Cox, Harvey. *Turning East: The Promise and Peril of the New Orientalism*. New York: Simon and Schuster, 1977.

Ellwood, Robert S. *Religious and Spiritual Groups in Modern America*. Englewood Cliffs: Prentice-Hall, 1973.

Glock, Charles Y., and Bellah, Robert N., eds. *The New Religious Consciousness*. Berkeley and Los Angeles: University of California Press, 1976.

Melton, J. Gordon, and Moore, Robert L. *The Cult Experience: Responding to the New Religious Pluralism*. New York: The Pilgrim Press, 1982.

Needleman, Jacob, and Baker, George, eds. *Understanding the New Religions*. New York: The Seabury Press, 1978.

New York University Review of Law and Social Change. Special Issue on "Alternative Religions: Government Control and the First Amendment." 9(1), 1979–1980.

Richardson, Herbert, ed. *New Religions and Mental Health*. New York and Toronto: The Edwin Mellon Press, 1980.

Robbins, Thomas, and Anthony, Dick, eds. *In Gods We Trust: New Patterns of Religious Pluralism in America*. New Brunswick and London: Transaction Books, 1981.

."Deprogramming, Brainwashing, and the Medicalization of Deviant Religious Groups." *Social Problems* 29(3):283–297, 1982.

Shapiro, Robert. "Mind Control or Intensity of Faith: The Constitutional Protection of Religious Beliefs." *Harvard Civil Rights—Civil Liberties Law Review* 13(3):751–797, 1978.

Shupe, Anson D. *Six Perspectives on New Religions: A Case Study Approach*. New York and Toronto: The Edwin Mellon Press, 1981.

, and Bromley, David G. *The New Vigilantes: Deprogrammers, Anti-Cultists, and the New Religions*. Beverly Hills: Sage, 1980.

Wilson, Brian, ed. *The Social Impact of New Religious Movements*. New York: The Rose of Sharon Press, 1981.

Caitanya Vaiṣṇavism

Bhaktisiddhānta Sarasvatī. *Shri Chaitanya's Teachings*. Part 1: Madras: Sree Gaudiya Math, 1967; Part II: Sree Mayapur: Sree Chaitanya Math, 1974.

Bhaktivedanta Swami Prabhupāda, A. C. see p.267

Bhaktivinoda Ṭhākura. *Jaiva Dharma*. (Translated by Bhakti Sadak Nishkinchana) Madras: Sri Gaudiya Math, 1975.

.*Sri Chaitanya Mahaprabhu: His Life and Precepts*. 7th ed. Calcutta: Gaudiya Mission, 1946.

.*Tattva Viveka, Tattva-Sutra, and Amnaya-Sutra*. (Translated by Narasimha Brahmachari) Madras: Sree Gaudiya Math, 1979.

Chakravarti, Janardan. *Bengal Vaiṣṇavism and Sri Chaitanya*. Calcutta: The Asia Society, 1975.

Chakravarti, Sudhindra Chandra. *Philosophical Foundations of Bengal Vaiṣṇavism*. Calcutta: Academic Publishers, 1969.

De, S. K. *Early History of the Vaiṣṇava Faith and Movement in Bengal*. 2nd. ed. Calcutta: K. L. Mukhopadhyay, 1961.

Ghose, Shishir Kumar. *Lord Gauranga*. Bombay: Bharatiya Vidya Bhavan, 1961.

Kapoor, O. B. L. *The Philosophy and Religion of Sri Caitanya*. Delhi: Munshiram Manoharlal, 1977.

Kennedy, Melville T. *The Chaitanya Movement: A Study of the Vaishnavism of Bengal*. New York: Oxford University Press, 1925.

Law, Narendra Nath. *Śrī Kṛṣṇa and Śrī Caitanya*. London: Luzac and Co., 1949.

Majumdar, A. K. *Caitanya: His Life and Doctrine*. Bombay: Bharatiya Vidya Bhavan, 1969.

Mukherji, S. C. *A Study of Vaishnavism in Ancient and Medieval Bengal (Up to the Advent of Chaitanya)*. Calcutta: Punthi Pustak, 1966.

Sanātana Gosvāmī. *Śrī Brihat Bhāgavatāmritam*. (Translated by Bhakti Prajnan Yati) Madras: Sree Gaudiya Math, 1975.

Sanyal, Nisikanta. *Sree Krishna Chaitanya*. Madras. Sree Gaudiya Math, 1933.

Sen, Rai Sahib Dineschandra. *The Vaisnava Literature of Mediaeval Bengal*. Calcutta: University of Calcutta, 1917.

Sinha, Jadunath. *The Philosophy and Religion of Chaitanya and His Followers*. Calcutta: Sinha Publishing House, 1976.

Tirtha, Bhakti Pradip. *Sri Chaitanya Mahaprabhu*. Calcutta: Gaudiya Mission, 1947.

Vaiṣṇavism And Bhakti

Bhandarkar, R. G. *Vaiṣṇavism, Saivism, and Minor Religious*

Systems. Varanasi: Indological Book House, 1965. (First published in 1913 in the Encyclopedia of Indo-Aryan Research.)

Bhattacarya, Siddhesvara. *The Philosophy of Śrīmad-Bhāgavata.* 2 vols. Santiniketan: Visvabharati, 1960.

Chatterjee, Chinmayi. *Studies in the Evolution of Bhakti Cult.* 2 vols. Calcutta: Jadavpur University, 1976, 1981.

Dasgupta, Surendranath. *A History of Indian Philosophy.* Vols. 3 and 4. First Indian Edition. Delhi: Motilal Banarsidass, 1975.

Goswami, Bhagbat Kumar. *The Bhakti Cult in Ancient India.* Varanasi: Chowkhamba Sanskrit Series Office, 1965. (First published in 1924 by the author.)

Jaiswal, Suvira. *The Origin and Development of Vaiṣṇavism.* Delhi: Munshiram Manoharlal, 1967.

Macnicol, Nicol. *Indian Theism: From the Vedic to the Muhammadan Period.* 2nd ed. Delhi: Munshiram Manoharlal, 1968.

Majumdar, A. K. *Bhakti Renaissance.* Bombay: Bharatiya Vidya Bhavan, 1965.

Raychaudhuri, Hemchandra. *Materials for the Study of the Early History of the Vaishnava Sect.* Delhi: Oriental Books Reprint Corporation, 1975. (First published in 1920 by the University of Calcutta.)

Singer, Milton, ed. *Krishna: Myths, Rites and Attitudes.* Chicago: University of Chicago Press, 1966.

Sircar, D. C., ed. *The Bhakti Cult and Ancient Indian Geography.* Calcutta: University of Calcutta, 1970.

INDEX